Com:

This is a family saga of extraordinary importance. The book in your hand is a door to healing; your healing. Take the time to dive into this story. Don't be in a hurry. You are entering a world of larger than life, sometimes fascinatingly eccentric characters, all of whom have something to gift you.

There is plenty of drama but the treasure is in the details. Are you anxious for your own future? Do you need to be lifted from a condition of despair, apathy or confusion? Keep reading. I know the road is long but people like Peter and Linda have journeyed before you and endured and overcome. I found solace and inspiration in their story. You will too.

John Dawson
President Emeritus Youth With A Mission International

It is a joy to commend this inspiring autobiography of Peter and Linda's life. We have so many special memories of their remarkable ministry in Bristol. These include the earliest days at Blackhorse and Patchway with Hugh Thompson, and Pip'n'Jay, Tell Bristol, Days of Prayer and Fasting at WEC and BCF and Olveston. We especially remember such close fellowship with the amazing BCF team. Many of these are still our very dear friends. *Having Nothing, Yet Possessing Everything* reflects the wonderful Bristol legacy of George Muller's life of prayer and faith in God. We also pray 'that everyone who reads these words of faith can also receive the abundance of grace, freely offered through Jesus'.

Rob Scott-Cook, so grateful for God's faithfulness in the planting and growth of the Woodlands Church Family and helping to build Bristol as a City of Sanctuary and a City of Hope, remembering the poorest of the world over fifty-two years of ministry, 1970–2022

I, together with my dear wife, Christine, who recently passed away, have known Peter and Linda as close friends for pretty well all of the years covered in these pages. We have laughed and cried together, ministered together, here in the UK and overseas, more times than I care to remember. We have spent extended days in ministry and leadership forums and discussions as well as conferences beyond number and yet, neither Christine nor I knew of half the miracles recorded here. Like many of us, Peter mentioned that he loved to read the great missionary stories of the past. Well, here is one such story which has taken place in the very world in which we live and, as such, can be a great inspiration for us to believe that what Jesus is doing for them, he can do for us.

John Noble
Chairman of the UK National Charismatic and Pentecostal Leaders' Conference 1984–2006

As I read Pete and Linda's book I could almost imagine myself sitting opposite them in a pleasant restaurant or a comfortable lounge with a wood fire burning. I hear their voices recalling sixty years of ministry but also of life with all its ups and downs. It's a book with extraordinary detail, at times painfully honest and vulnerable, yet packed with significant steps of obedience and faith. This is not a 'how-to' book, but it provides refreshing insights on relationships and lessons learnt in the nitty-gritty of church life.

Steve Clifford
Former General Director of the Evangelical Alliance UK 2009–2019, Chair of the Pioneer Trust Board and Advisor to Churches

It has been a privilege – and in turn, fascinating, moving, and inspiring – to read *Having Nothing, Yet Possessing Everything.*

Iain McDonald
Old friend and retired medical doctor, Former Regional Medical Officer at British Embassy Moscow

Having Nothing *yet* Possessing Everything

Sixty Years of Miracles

Peter & Linda Lyne

malcolm down

PUBLISHING

Cover design by Angela Selfe
Art direction by Sarah Grace

Printed in the UK

In Memoriam

Sunday, 29th January, 2023, David Disney was, in the words of his wife, Hillary, and his daughter, Ruth, 'Promoted to Glory!'

In the chapter of this book entitled 'Linda's Story' there is a picture of David with his sister Karen and step sister Linda. Having battled a terminal illness for several months, Dave remained strong in his faith in Jesus and his love for all his family. He died just as this autobiography was being published.

Dedication

To our children and our children's children

Peter & Linda Lyne
Waipu, Northland, New Zealand, September 21st, 2022

Acknowledgements

Special thanks are due to Hilary Green who typed our manuscript during the Covid years.

Cora McDonald has been another great support with editing and proofreading. She and husband Iain are some of our oldest friends from the Olveston Community. Cora, you have been stretched to the limit on our behalf and we are truly grateful!

Mike and Corrine Hoare provided us with a home in the cabin on the side of their boat shed where much of the writing was completed. We came for six weeks and stayed more than two years!

Our indefatigable son-in-law, Pete, and daughter, Amanda, have developed such a lovely apartment for us on the side of their property above Waipu, Northland. When I had the joy of marrying them more than three years ago, Pete little knew what he was getting into. He was hoping for a boat but got in-laws instead!

George, your constant encouragement and help know no bounds. What a neighbour!

And as always, my long-suffering wife, Linda, who has been with me every step of the way and contributed her remarkable story to this book, as well as carefully correcting all my mistakes. It's helpful that we still love each other after fifty-three years.

The Abraham call on our lives is all very well, but what about our children? To say that it has not always been easy for them would be an understatement. The constant dislocation, upheavals, new schools, having to leave old friends and make new ones – the list goes on and on. Yet, they have done amazingly well and are a credit to us.

Amanda was born in Southmead Hospital, Bristol, eleven months into our marriage. In those days, mother and baby were not turfed out as soon as possible. In fact, Linda and Amanda were moved to a cottage hospital for fourteen days. On the day Linda was to come home to our rooms in an elderly friend's house, I failed to mention something that had happened the night before. I had picked up a dishevelled young man who was hitchhiking. He was obviously in great need, so I sought to share the gospel with him en route to Bristol, but I realised he needed more than words. I took him home, fed him, then let him sleep in our bed, while I took the sofa in the lounge. When he left the following morning, he left something behind. When Linda and Amanda arrived, to great excitement, we eventually put Amanda in the swing cot right next to our bed. It wasn't long before some red blotches appeared, and we discovered that we had fleas! Out came my story, and to say that Linda wasn't well pleased would be putting it mildly!

Richard and Simon both had home births: Richard at Kingston Drive, close to Blackhorse, and Simon in the Old Meeting House, Olveston. Bossy Cotton oversaw this, and it was a good job she was there because I was the only help. The oxygen ran out when Linda was in labour, and Bossy detected that the cord was wrapped round Simon's neck.

When we took our first flight to New Zealand, British Airways gave the children Junior Jet Club books. These had to be given to the pilot on each flight, and they recorded details of the journey which they then signed. Many years later, a pilot came back to us and said, 'I can't believe it! Your children have flown more than I have.'

What I must say is that all the airline staff were very complimentary of the way our children behaved on all these flights. Linda reminded me of a night in Honolulu Airport with our children standing in line, backpacks on their backs at midnight, boarding a flight to New Zealand. It never seemed to be a problem. It's such a joy that we are still together in New Zealand after all these years. We have ten precious grandchildren and we're typical grandparents, so proud of them all, and our special daughters-in-law, Richard's Anna, and Simon's Bella Jane. Not forgetting our other family, Linda's very special twins, Tanya and David, who you will meet later in the story, and the much loved clutch of children and great grandchildren who are all in the UK.

Further thanks and appreciation:

Special thanks to all our friends, those who made it into the story and those who did not. Inevitably, some will have been missed out. However, for the sanity of our friend and editor, Cora, we had to stop somewhere. There are just so many who have enriched our lives over the years – too many to mention. To the many churches who have embraced our ministry and taken us to your hearts, we thank you. To all the individuals who have blessed us beyond measure, we are indebted to you. We couldn't have done it without you!

Contents

Chapter 1

We Know We Have What
We Asked of Him[1]

In 1973, when I was thirty years of age, a series of miracles happened to Linda and myself that has shaped our lives and established in our thinking the principle embodied in the title of this book, *Having Nothing, Yet Possessing Everything.*

It began, as so often is the case, through intensive prayer. From 1966 when I left my job as a teacher, I gave myself to helping a fledgling church-plant at Blackhorse – a housing estate in the north-east of Bristol. I owned a car and was graciously allowed to live at home with my parents as I had very little income, and consequently, had closed my bank account! I sought to visit every home personally with a *Gospel of John* and taught in our house meetings and prayer meetings. We hired a local school for our church meetings and Sunday school and, increasingly, I took a lot of responsibility for teaching and preaching. It was amid all this activity that a specific prayer was born, 'Lord, we need a substantial house for our activity. The church needs a fireside! We need to give hospitality and have a life-centred base to all that we do.'

---

1. 1 John 5:15 NIV

For someone with no personal resources, this was a challenge, and the prayer became more specific as I focused on a unique house in our area that I could see meeting the criteria that the Lord had laid on my heart.

Stockwell House was a large detached property in substantial grounds, situated halfway up the hill from our council housing estate towards the more affluent suburb of Downend. I can honestly say that before I met Linda in 1970, I had been praying for this particular house for several years. I used to stop at the top of the hill where there was a five-barred gate overlooking the fields and I would lean over this gate, asking the Lord to release this home to me.

I used to rise around 6am and spend at least the first hour in prayer and meditation. One particular morning the Lord drew my attention to a huge promise in 1 John 5:14-15

This is the confidence we have in approaching God: that if we ask anything according to his will, he hears us. And if we know that he hears us – whatever we ask – we know that we have what we asked of him.[2]

I was so overwhelmed by the presence of God and the assurance that my prayer of faith for Stockwell House had been honoured, that I recorded in the margin of my Bible, 'God gave me Stockwell House this morning!' When my dad brought me a cup of tea before he left for work, I told him immediately, 'Dad, God has given me Stockwell House this morning.' He looked gobsmacked, but he was used to my faith statements and assured me I was on the right track.

---

2. 1 John 5:14-15 NIV

Later I was driving past the house when I saw an older couple from our congregation walking up the steep hill. I stopped to offer them a lift and as Mr Bushell got into the car, he said, 'You know this place is up for sale.' I was stunned, especially as there was no *For Sale* sign on display. With suppressed excitement, I drove the Bushells home, then turned round to return to the property.

I parked outside, walked straight in and rang the bell. A young man came to the door and I said to him, 'I understand this house is for sale?'

He replied, 'Yes, it is.'

At that moment, a voice from inside the house called him back to the kitchen and a few moments later he returned and told me, apologetically, 'I'm sorry. It's been withdrawn from the market.'

I felt like the bottom had dropped out of my world. How could I have got it so wrong? The prayer of faith and the subsequent events seemed to confirm all that I had felt for so long, even though at that time I had no resources to buy the house.

In the two years that followed, a lot of wonderful things happened for me. I met Linda three days after I had prayed a prayer of faith similar to the one asking for Stockwell House. In a sacred spot, overlooking Polzeath Beach in Cornwall, I prayed for and received a wife according to God's promise,

We know that we have what we asked of him.[3]

---

3. 1 John 5:15b NIV

I left Cornwall the following Saturday to take my first wedding, in Exeter, Devon. After the wedding, I drove to a hotel in Exmouth to lead a holiday conference for the next week with a diverse group of people I had never met before. At dinner in the restaurant that evening, I saw Linda with a group of young people from her church in Derby. I can say that we were instantly attracted to each other, so much so that I proposed to her within three days. My ministry programme was so full that I couldn't include our own wedding until the following May, some nine months away. We have often said we should have married immediately, so sure were we that the Lord had destined us for each other. This was a decision neither of us has ever regretted, and we celebrated our fiftieth anniversary in 2021.

That prayer of faith was remarkably fulfilled but my previous one, for Stockwell House, had disappeared into the ether! But had it? Some may feel that I am stretching this a little bit, but I am sure there were aspects of my genuine prayer that God intended to bring to pass.

In the second year of our marriage, we were renting a home from a missionary couple serving in Bangladesh. Their house was in Kingston Drive, a road just below the grounds of Stockwell House. I came to feel that this was significant. One day, we received a letter from Gwyn and Joyce Lewis to say that they were returning from the mission field and needed their house back. We scarcely had time to pray about this when I had a phone call from my fellow evangelist, Hugh Thompson, with a special request. He and I had been working together on another housing estate, in Patchway, north Bristol. Hugh asked me if I would go with him to view a house that he felt would make an excellent base for their growing house-church. I was happy to join him the following morning. When I climbed into his car to drive to the location of the house, Hugh said to me, 'You know that the Old Meeting House in Olveston is up for sale?'

My response was that I had never been to the village of Olveston and knew nothing about this property. Undeterred, Hugh pressed on, 'I think I should take you to see it. I have met the couple who are selling it – Nigel and Kirstie de Rivaz. They are Christians, planning to move to Cheltenham.'

With that, I succumbed. We visited Hugh's potential property, surrounding it with prayer, then headed out on one of the most important journeys of my life.

We drove up the A38 towards Thornbury but turned off into the valley of the River Severn to the picturesque villages of Tockington and Olveston. The first turn brought us to an ancient triangle in the heart of the old village and on a narrow country lane stood the Old Meeting House, a historic gem. It dated back 400 years to the origins of the Quaker Movement led by the remarkable George Fox. Just beyond the house was the village duck pond and across the road, behind high walls and huge trees that had come from all over the world, there was a quintessential English manor house with a village water pump outside the gate. The whole scene took my breath away. When you have worked for many years on British council housing estates, you can forget how glorious the English countryside is!

Hugh and I walked up the small flagstone path to the heavily studded front door. Standing smiling in the doorway were Nigel and Kirstie.

The 400-year-old Quaker Meeting House

I thought I had never met them, but then discovered I had prayed with them at the end of a crowded event in St Philip and St Jacob Church[4] near Bristol city centre. Hugh cracked one of his jokes. 'I've brought a buyer for you. He has three books of Green Shield stamps to offer!'

Embarrassingly, this was fairly accurate. If we collected stamps at our local petrol station, we might save up for a free frying pan! We all laughed and walked into this amazing building. It was the kind of house I had been praying for over the last few years.

Downstairs, the lounge and dining room had heavy oak shutters that could be taken down to link with the historic Quaker meeting room that occupied the back section of the house. The high vaulted meeting room was entirely

---

4. Often called Pip'n'Jay

suitable for our purpose. Running along the end of the room was the original elders' bench where George Fox, a hero in British Christian history, had stood to preach.

Two of the upstairs bedrooms had windows looking down into the meeting room. There were two bathrooms upstairs and a further large bedroom over the garage. The whole house had central heating throughout and new carpets. Part of the floor in the kitchen consisted of the old cobble stones of the original road out of the village. Everywhere, there were amazing wooden beams rescued from shipwrecks in the River Severn.

I was so overwhelmed by it all, I scarcely knew what to say. I emerged from the Old Meeting House like a man who has seen a vision that he has prayed for a very long time but had seemed unattainable. I couldn't wait to tell Linda what I had just seen. As soon as I had shared the news, I promised to take her down to the village in the next couple of days so she could see for herself this amazing house in its unique location.

This time, I didn't have the temerity to go in without an invitation, so we parked up and wandered down to the duck pond. All Linda could say to me when we drove away from the village was, 'It must be wonderful to live there.'

At the end of the week, our phone rang. It was Nigel de Rivaz with a mind-blowing suggestion. 'Peter, Kirstie and I have been praying ever since your visit with Hugh, and we believe you are meant to come into our house!'

I was dumbfounded and simply said, 'But Nigel, we have no money at all and couldn't possibly purchase your house.'

'Don't worry about that,' Nigel said. 'If you can arrange to come, we'll set up a simple rental agreement so that you are able to move in here. We feel that it's meant to be, that God wants you to be here!'

With that, I promised we would make it a matter of urgent prayer and seek the counsel of our spiritual advisors. This included my father and the elders of the Blackhorse Church, Hugh Thompson and some of our national leaders. I said to Hugh, 'You have a bigger family than us, so perhaps you should go there.'

He wasn't having this, and all the people we took counsel with felt it had the mark of the Holy Spirit on it. We subsequently discovered a pile of brochures with an auction date and learned that Nigel and Kirstie had received a pre-auction cash offer for the house.

It was on a warm summer's day in 1973 that we delivered our frugal belongings to the house, along with our daughter Amanda and our new baby, Richard. As I walked over the flagstone path in the front garden to the doorway of the Old Meeting House the Lord spoke to me so clearly:

Having nothing, and yet possessing everything.[5]

Paul's incredible statement from 2 Corinthians chapter 6 would explain so much of what has happened to us on this incredible faith journey, which we are still experiencing. When Nigel and Kirstie ironed out the details with us, we paid a very modest rent, which included all the oil that

---

5. 2 Corinthians 6:10b NIV

fired the new central heating system, and after the first six months they returned all we had paid to buy more furniture!

Our move to Olveston proved decisive for the future course of our ministry. Sceptics will say, 'Ah, you just struck lucky with a very generous Christian couple', and they'll put it all down to coincidence. But the whole of our lives has been accompanied by extraordinary signs right up to today, and one thing that Linda and I know is that the Lord hears and answers prayer. Coincidence? I prefer to believe that Jesus is the co-ordinator of incidents!

However, I will say this: my prayer of faith for Stockwell House didn't come to pass in the way I planned. We pray according to the knowledge that we have at the time. It's not that the prayer is necessarily misguided but there are elements beyond our comprehension that only the great clearing house in heaven can sort out! Had we stayed on at Blackhorse at this time we would not have had the freedom to develop the Olveston community that so helped shape the future Bristol Christian Fellowship and many other churches in which we had a significant role.

Chapter 2

The Paradox!

The Concise Oxford Dictionary describes a paradox as:

- a statement contrary to received opinion
- a seemingly absurd though perhaps well-founded statement
- self-contradictory
- conflicting with pre-conceived notions of what is reasonable or possible.

The Gospel of the Kingdom is shrouded in mystery! When Jesus began to teach the remarkable parables of the Kingdom in Matthew chapter 13, he warned his disciples

The knowledge of the secrets of the kingdom of heaven has been given to you, but not to them.[6]

At the heart of this extraordinary life-changing Kingdom is a strange paradox that runs through the whole of the gospel. Failure to understand this will lead to confusion and result in extremes of emphasis that will sadly undermine important truths that the Lord wants to impart to us. *Having Nothing, Yet Possessing Everything*, the title of this book, is an example that the Apostle Paul includes in a list

---

6. Matthew 13:11 NIV

of such paradoxes, that he declares to have been his life experience:

Through glory and dishonour, bad report and good report; genuine, yet regarded as imposters; known, yet regarded as unknown; dying, and yet we live on; beaten, and yet not killed; sorrowful, yet always rejoicing; poor, yet making many rich; having nothing, and yet possessing everything.[7]

It is this last statement that was given to us prophetically in extraordinary circumstances and that has been engraved on the whole of our faith journey for fifty years. But more than our experiences, and even far beyond the extremities of Paul's life that he has described so graphically, is the example of our Lord Jesus Christ, who we are privileged to serve. His brief human life, from his incarnation until its climax through death, resurrection and ascension, is the ultimate paradox! He is *The Son of God* but the title he repeatedly used during his time here on earth is *The Son of Man*.

On the one hand, the remarkable catechism in Philippians chapter 2 tells us

Who, being in very nature God, did not consider equality with God something to be grasped, but made himself nothing, taking the very nature of a servant, being made in human likeness and being found in appearance as a man, he humbled himself and became obedient to death – even death on a cross!

---

7. 2 Corinthians 6:8-10 NIV

And then Paul declares that

> *God exalted him to the highest place and gave him the name that is above every name, that at the name of Jesus every knee should bow, in heaven and on earth and under the earth, and every tongue confess that Jesus Christ is Lord, to the glory of God the Father.[8]*

In Hebrews chapter 1, even more remarkable information is given to us concerning the pre-existence of Christ and his involvement in the creation of the universe! God spoke in many ways in the past, but now he has granted to us the supreme revelation of his Son

> *Whom he appointed heir of all things, and through whom also he made the universe. The Son is the radiance of God's glory and the exact representation of his being, sustaining all things by his powerful word.[9]*

Not only did Jesus begin all this with his Father, but he also upholds it by his powerful word, and will be the central figure in the transition of this decaying universe into the glorious liberty of the children of God[10] and the establishing of the new heavens and earth as foreseen by John in Revelation chapters 21 and 22, and foretold by the Old Testament prophets, especially Isaiah. This is succinctly described by Paul in Ephesians chapter 1,

> *He made known to us the mystery of his will according to his good pleasure, which he purposed in Christ, to*

---

8. Philippians 2:6-11 NIV
9. Hebrews 1:2-3 NIV
10. Romans 8:21

be put into effect when the times reach their fulfilment – to bring unity to all things in heaven and on earth under Christ.[11]

---

11. Ephesians 1:9-10 NIV

Chapter 3

Beginnings

Nell and Ern

I was born towards the end of the Second World War – January 30th, 1943. My parents had moved down to Bristol from London with my older brother, Alan, as Dad was not called up in the early stages of the war. Eventually, he was conscripted to go to Egypt right at the end of the conflict to help clear up Hitler's mess in the Middle East. So I lost my father for a good eighteen months as a young child. To help with this difficult circumstance, Mum moved back to London where my grandparents had a shop in Sydenham High Street.

My only connection with Dad during this time was through packs of American chewing gum that frequently arrived with his letters. This gum was not available in the UK, and our meagre supply of sweets was rationed anyway. My auntie Ivy, Mum's sister, and Uncle Will, my dad's brother to whom she was married, plus their son John, also lived with us, so we were quite a community. Yes, in our family, two brothers had married two sisters, in case you're wondering.

It was a happy home, and certainly quite prosperous in spite of the devastation all around us. My grandmother had been the wardrobe mistress at Drury Lane theatre in Covent Garden and Grandad worked the lights. That's where they met. Elizabeth got a taste of a different life as the stars of Music Hall, like the famous Lillie Langtry, took a liking to her and used to give her fancy clothes, fur coats and other baubles. She became quite an entrepreneur, using her exceptional cooking skills to provide dinner parties for the posh people up in the big houses by the Crystal Palace.

Spurred on by her success, she set up her own drapery business at 289 Sydenham Road, in south-east London, something that always fascinated me as a young boy. Gran used to take me to her wholesale supplier, Cooks of St Paul's. I can still remember walking across the bomb sites around the great cathedral to the warehouse that housed Cooks. They had an internal moving escalator that always delighted me, and Gran used to buy me nice clothes from the store, even long trousers when I wasn't supposed to have them. As I grew older, I couldn't fail to notice how the German bombs had devastated all the area around St Paul's, but Christopher Wren's masterpiece was left intact!

Dad came home from the war with lots of exciting stories and photographs. He had even managed to go to the Holy Land, and we had New Testaments with wooden covers from the Mount of Olives. Although Mum and Dad moved back to Bristol, we regularly went up to 289 for the main festivals, Christmas and Easter, and I used to go up by myself on the train during the holidays, being met at Paddington Station by Grandad Jackson.

All my family seemed to be Christians and the London folks were initially very involved with the London City Mission (LCM). Later, my grandparents were greatly impacted by the Pentecostal healing evangelist, George Jeffries. One day, at a meeting in the old Kensington Temple, George preached and called people forward for baptism as was his custom, so Grandad went forward in his best suit and went home to Sydenham dripping wet on the train!

When George began to develop his Bible Pattern Churches, Elizabeth turned the main lounge above the shop into one of the first house-churches, which they called The Upper Room, and there was a huge tapestry of Leonardo De Vinci's *Last Supper* over a wall at the end of the room. I can still remember being taken to prayer meetings at George Jefferies' Bible College on Clapham Common. George used to walk up and down among the people, praying in tongues and laying hands on people – scary stuff for a small boy.

Back in Bristol we became part of Foster Baptist Church, Downend, a strange move on the part of my parents, who were very evangelical in their beliefs. This was a social liberal church and our minister was in fact a Freemason. However, I think my parents saw it as part of their mission field, as Dad ran a huge Sunday school for 300 children and Mum helped organise Campaigners – a Christian version of Scouts.

Although Dad was in full-time senior roles in an office equipment business, particularly supplying schools, at the same time he was a zealous lay preacher, especially out in the villages around Bristol. It wasn't long before I got roped into all this. Dad used to take me along to all his country churches to pump the organs. Often there was a discreet curtain that I could sit behind for this task, with my supply of chewing gum and comics. Our whole social life centred on the church with lots of clubs, societies and events. There was no TV in the early days, but we did listen to fifteen minutes of *The Archers* every night.

I didn't begin primary school until I was five years old, but I owe an enormous debt to my dad's father who came to live with us. I never knew my paternal grandmother, but Grandad Lyne, who was a semi-invalid, walking with special sticks, was an enormous factor in my early life. He taught me to read, sitting on his knee with a big old family Bible. One of the reasons I can read so confidently today, especially Old Testament passages with difficult names, is because of my grandad. He also taught me to play cards – look out! – and billiards on a table that we could lay out in our lounge. He loved to watch the football in the park and always had time for me in my formative years.

When I was a little older, Dad confided in me that as a young man his great ambition was to work full-time for the London City Mission. Even while he pursued his job with the Lion Company, he did a two-year correspondence course with the LCM. He passed with flying colours and in every way he would have been their ideal candidate. Then, they called him to London for two days of intensive interviews. At the end of this, they said he had acquitted himself well and the rest would be a formality.

The final morning was a medical and it was a huge surprise for such an able sportsman to be told he had a threatening heart condition. The leaders of the Mission were so distressed by this that they sent him to a specialist in Harley Street. This eminent doctor simply confirmed their fears and said Dad would struggle with the physical demands of a missioner's life.

For Dad, it was like the bottom had dropped out of his world. He crossed London in a daze of disappointment, finally slumping into a carriage on Paddington's platform 1 for the return journey to Bristol. Then a miracle happened! Dad said the train compartment was filled with the presence of the Holy Spirit and the Lord assured him that all would be well.

For fifty years he toiled without let-up, working as Area Manager for his office equipment company. I think he may have had no more than three sick-days in his entire working life. At the same time, he was a tireless lay pastor and church worker as well as running his huge Sunday school. He was chairman of the Cleevewood Football Club and rarely missed a Saturday afternoon on the touchline. In spite of his disappointment, he told us that his constant prayer was that his three sons would know the Bible better than he did. I'm sure this prayer was answered.

My father had been a great sportsman in his youth. I still have the newspaper cuttings of when he played centre forward for London Boys against Scotland at Stamford Bridge, Chelsea's famous stadium. He scored the winning goal. Incredibly, they wanted him to stay on and play for England, but this was the time of the Depression. He simply had to go out and get work. Footballers didn't get to buy Ferraris in those days. Dad was equally good at cricket and there has always been a tradition of sporting excellence in our family.

Perusing these initial comments, people who know me well, will see certain familiar threads that shaped my future. My ability to read and speak in public, something that many people shy away from, is just second nature to me. At primary school, there was not an annual prize-giving when I was not asked to recite, usually standing on a school bench in the early days. I was always asked to perform in the Christmas nativity in the parish church.

When I moved up to grammar school, the same thing happened. I won two prizes every year: the Headmaster's Prize for Public Speaking and The Newman Prize for Physical Education. Regarding the first prize awarded by C.N. Ridley, our somewhat aloof headmaster, he wrote on my report, 'A well-mannered little boy who knows how to speak well and is not afraid of doing so.'

I was twelve years old at the time and I have to say it's the last time he wrote anything positive about me. This was not necessarily his fault. I loved Kingswood Grammar School, but not for any academic reason. I never did my homework! In the first year, I set up a desk in the boys' toilets and would borrow books of anyone who turned up so I could copy their homework. Having subsequently spent years as a teacher, I must confess I misbehaved in class; I had a quick tongue and was always full of pranks.

I was mad about sport and great at socialising. It was a co-ed school and they didn't nickname me 'Lips Lyne' for nothing. In sport I ended up as captain of rugby, cricket and gymnastics, but C.N. Ridley refused to make me a prefect, partly because I was a heavy smoker and could be quite disruptive. I was popular at school but didn't quite fit the grammar mould and was not expected to do well at examinations. In spite of this, I scraped through and managed to secure a place at Britain's top sporting establishment, Loughborough College, where I was to study Physical and Religious Education. My time there was to change the whole course of my life.

Looking back, I can see that my grandmother Elizabeth was a Victorian matriarch and a gifted leader. I inherited her love of cooking and hospitality, and my mother, also a very good cook, taught me a great deal. I remember at the school fete in my first years at grammar, winning a prize for my Victoria sandwich sponge. Fishy Salmon, the chemistry teacher, was furious that I pipped him at the post. Even though I loved cooking, boys had to do woodwork and I spent several years sharpening pencils.

Having had a strong spiritual foundation, through my parents and grandparents, I began to rebel against the expected norms by the time I was nine years old. While becoming a very good liar, I still had to live the sort of life my parents expected of me. Our chapel, Foster Baptist, was a couple of hundred yards from an old cider pub called The Foresters Arms. I was out every night of the week at clubs and societies, and from my early teens, my mates and I adopted a back room in the pub. There was a small corridor with a hatch that opened into the Public Bar. We would knock on the hatch and order cheese and onion rolls and glasses of cider, then sit in the back room puffing on our Woodbines and setting the world to rights. I realise culture has shifted dramatically, but even as a small boy, I could go to Roy Watkins, who ran our local sweetshop, and purchase individual cigarettes. Later we would splash out and buy a five-pack of Woodbines that Wills produced in those days.

Somehow, I managed to live a double life. My parents were members of the Lord's Day Observance Society, so we weren't allowed to listen to the radio and could only read certain books on the Sabbath. We had to attend three services on a Sunday, wearing posh clothes, but no swimming or football were allowed. As strong supporters of the Temperance Society, they would have been devastated to know that I had a regular place in the pub.

I remember once, my mum suspected, quite rightly, that I had been masturbating. In a kind of embarrassed way, she told me not to touch that! I think that was the full extent of my sex education. Don't get me wrong, my parents were lovely people and really cared for us boys. It was just that, like school, I didn't really fit the mould. Despite this, when I went out early in the mornings to do my paper round, I used to ride my bike down Badminton Road, look up into the heavens and say, 'God, I really believe in you.'

Something must have stuck. I never did take to the idea of evolution, always sensing that there was a divine purpose and order about things. Looking at my haphazard approach to structure and study, it's a miracle that I survived sixth form and got into Loughborough College. I really wanted to join the circus and work with animals!

Somehow, God had other plans for me.

Chapter 4

Eleven Plus

An important threshold is reached in the British system of education at eleven years of age. Dreaded by many pupils, it could make or break the future course of their life. For me, this was confronted in 1954, the year after the Coronation of Queen Elizabeth II.

There were three potential levels of education beyond primary school: grammar, technical and secondary modern. How you performed in the eleven-plus examination would determine which school you went to.

Grammar was the elite, providing excellent academic preparation, with all the trimmings of good sports teams, choirs, orchestra, dramatic productions and all the kudos of a grammar tie.

Technical was a step down but provided good preparation for taking up apprenticeships in building and plumbing, cooking and dressmaking. However, the secondary modern school, which was in a street close to where I lived in Staple Hill on the outskirts of Bristol, was regarded as 'the pits'. It was considered, probably unjustifiably, as an academic death sentence. Usually you left a school like this by the time you were 16 and there was little hope of going on to further education.

In later years, socialist governments pioneered the concept of comprehensive schools, with mixed success, seeking to house everyone in one catch-all situation. When Tony Blair was leading the government that had pushed for this, he chose to send his children to a private school! Outside of this were the elite 'Public Schools' – a complete misnomer, as they are anything but public, usually requiring a huge financial commitment as well as privileged connections. Eton and Harrow would be typical of this, often providing a career path to Oxbridge (Oxford or Cambridge), if you can make the grade.

The eleven-plus examination loomed over our final year of primary school and our teachers coached us intensively so that we didn't stumble at this all-important hurdle. My class was the top class, and our desks were arranged in rows with the first row for the top students, excelling at reading, writing and arithmetic – the three Rs. I was invariably in this top row. I passed the eleven-plus, and soon afterward was interviewed for a place at Kingswood Grammar School on the Bath side of Bristol, very close to where the great John Wesley began his open-air ministry.

I now began a downhill slide, pretty much entirely of my own doing. I was adopting certain habits, which were not helping my academic development. How can I describe this? The fact that I started in the A stream and ended up in D is a clue. There was no stream lower for me to be placed in. The trouble is, I didn't think I was there to work. I was a social animal and very mouthy with it. I had a quick tongue and was opinionated.

Some of the staff didn't help either. Mr Trott, our maths teacher, was a big slob of a man. I can still remember what he said to me in our first maths lesson, 'Lyne, I didn't like your brother and I shan't like you.'

My reaction to this was, 'Well, stuff you!'

From that day on, although I had excelled in arithmetic at primary school. I just opted out. I recall achieving 7% in my GCSE maths paper when I was 16. No surprises there, as I conceived various strategies for doing no work.

Don't get me wrong. I loved school but my focus in those years was not on academic success. I enjoyed all sports and as my time at Kingswood went on, an interesting development took place. Our physical education master was a man called Jimmy Wilde. I remember his slight figure in an old navy-blue tracksuit, who must have been pushing sixty. He didn't seem to have a lot of energy left and gradually he put more and more responsibility into my hands. I was a natural leader and used to organise team games, athletics and gymnastics. I loved sorting out the gym, getting classes into groups and teaching them new skills. As time went on, I became captain of rugby, cricket and gymnastics and Jimmy entrusted me with more and more leadership.

Although Headmaster C.N. Ridley had a down on me, he couldn't deny that I was the best public speaker and debater in the school. So why did I not flourish in other spheres in my time there? I was a social animal and every night of the week, I was involved in clubs and societies, many of which were spawned by our church. I was in Campaigners and Christian Endeavour, an excellent organisation that taught us to run our own programme, including a monthly social night which was very popular. We produced our own plays and concert nights. I just loved acting and performing.

My mother insisted that I learn to play the piano, something I didn't want to do at the time as I was in a lot of sports teams. I had to play rugby for the school on Saturday mornings and I usually turned out for a soccer team on Saturday afternoons. Mum sent me to Mrs Punter for piano lessons. She was a top teacher in Bristol and had several star pupils but I was not one of them! The reason for this was simple. I did not practise! I devised a scheme where I kept watch for my mother coming home from shopping or visitation or leading women's meetings – she was like an unpaid deaconess. As she came up the road, I would plonk myself on the piano stool, feigning a good half hour's practice.

Things came to a sticky end at Mrs Punter's. She always kept me waiting while her pet students performed, then got me on the stool at the end of the session in stark contrast to all the others. One afternoon she wasn't happy with my pathetic attempt at a piece I was supposed to have practised. She swept me off the piano stool to show me how to play, then foolishly declared, 'That was better, wasn't it?'

I shouted 'NO', and with that, she hit me over the head with the music books and threw me out!

Strange as this may seem, it became like a reverse psychology. From that time on, I determined to teach myself and did quite well. I first learned an old hymn, 'Tell Me the Old, Old Story', which was relatively easy in C major.

Over the years I developed to the point where I often led worship, from a piano. However, I knew my limitations and have always regretted not pursuing basic scale and chord structures so that I could be more accomplished. I also developed as a singer, becoming the soloist with our school jazz band.

Jazz captivated me through my teens. We had a great concert venue in Bristol, the Colston Hall, and the cheapest seats were on the stage. I went to see all the jazz greats, live, from the New Orleans Trad bands, like George Lewis, and Kid Ory, and the big bands of Count Basie and Duke Ellington, and Ella Fitzgerald's phenomenal singing. I saw them all and even spoke to my hero Louis Armstrong on one occasion. I would have nothing to do with the emerging pop music, which I thought was trivial, but developed a liking for opera and ballet.

Our system of education at grammar school was totally rigid. Because I was a boy, I wasn't allowed to do domestic science where I almost certainly would have excelled but was made to do woodwork which I hated. Similarly, we lived in a soccer-crazy country, but grammar insisted that instead of our national sport we had to play rugby, the elitist alternative. In spite of this, I tried to attend every home game of Bristol Rovers, who never came to much and still haven't!

You will have noticed from my comments on domestic science that we were a co-educational school. This was a happy situation for me as I was popular with the fairer sex, and this provided another distraction. I had lots of girlfriends.

One thing that happened during my school years was that I became addicted to smoking. I started when I was nine years old and by twelve was quite a heavy smoker. It must be said that there was more of a cultural acceptance of smoking at that time than there is today. Bristol was the city of W.D. & H.O. Wills tobacco, and by the age of eleven I would regularly buy a five-pack of Wills Woodbines. It progressed from there, so that I couldn't imagine life without cigarettes. I had to smoke before school and during the morning and lunchtime breaks. Bunny Stone and I developed a nice little cave in the bushes down the lane from the school, where we would sit and puff through our breaks.

As with my music lessons, this all required a certain duplicity as far as my parents were concerned. They had made me sign a Temperance Society pledge when I was young and they hated drinking, smoking, pubs and everything that went with them. I had a cache for my cigarettes in a gap in the park wall at the end of the street and would head straight up to the bathroom on arriving home for much teeth-brushing and swilling of the mouth to try and remove the smells attached to me. I never became much of a heavy drinker, but tobacco had me well and truly hooked. I began to do early morning paper rounds, which helped fund my habits and gave me freedom to smoke early in the morning as well.

At the end of our road where we lived was Page Park, which was a very important part of my development from early on. We spent a lot of time there. We played football and cricket, we built dens in the trees and bushes, we did putting and tennis. Games were devised that encompassed the swings and slide in the centre of the park. Then, two or three times a year, the travelling Fun Fair arrived. I became a regular with Charles Heal's team, helping to set up and break down the rides and side shows, earning lots of free tickets. We loved it! The noises and the smells, with so many flashing lights! One year, a boxing booth was set up. Another, a striptease show that intrigued all us adolescent boys. Then we had Tommy Toes Jacobsen who did everything with his feet as he had no arms.

One night at the boxing booth was memorable. The local bully was a boy called Alan Whiting. We were all afraid of him as he was mouthy and violent. At the start of the show, there were fanfares and music, and the travelling boxers came out onto a raised platform, offering to take on all comers. One of the boxers was a fairly slight boy in his late teens. With much bravado, Alan Whiting volunteered to take him on. We absolutely jammed into the tent for this event. It was only three rounds and in the first, Alan Whiting came from his corner, arms flailing like an express train. I thought he was going to kill the slender boxer. However, with agile footwork he managed to avoid most of Alan's wild swings. Come the second round, Whiting was so puffed out, he could scarcely get out of his corner. The young boxer moved in with a fantastic hook that left Alan cold on the canvas. We were jubilant! He never recovered his aura of fear after that salutary lesson.

Along with the fairs, my biggest passion was the circus, and in Bristol we had the biggest and the best come to Durdham Downs. Billy Smart's, Chipperfield's, I saw them all several times and was convinced my future lay with them. In the early days I wanted to be an aerialist and I set up my own little shows in the park trees. My stage name was Marius, and I was never happier than when I was hanging from a slender branch.

Subsequently, I was desperate to become a wild animal trainer and I wrote to Billy Smart's to get a placement to train under their great star, Alex Kerr. Alas, my parents really put their foot down on this, but my love for the big cats has never left me. Alex Kerr's book *No Bars Between!* was my favourite. On the front cover is a picture of his four-year-old daughter kissing their pet tiger on the nose. At winter quarters in Windsor, he used to take the tiger on a lead to the pub. On a visit to our local seaside resort of Weston Super Mare, he was pictured romping in the sea with Nizam. I followed him closely and have never forgotten his performances in the Big Top with a huge array of dangerous animals. In later life, I am still fascinated by John Aspinall's story and the creation of the biggest breeding ground for gorillas and tigers at Howletts stately home near Canterbury.

The reason I'm telling you all this is to paint a picture. I had so many interests and activities. I was in the school choir and played double bass in the orchestra – not very well, I hasten to say. I was in plays and musicals. I was the Devil's Disciple in the stage play by George Bernard Shaw. I loved singing in the Gilbert and Sullivan musicals. I loved going on camps and even arranging them.

Words that I hear so often today, 'I'm bored!' never crossed my lips. I hear so many young people say that, despite all their electronic wizardry. Regularly, we raided people's orchards for apples and pears. We didn't get ferried everywhere by car. We went on the buses to our football games and biked everywhere. We thought nothing of cycling ten miles to Severn Beach so that we could swim in the Blue Lagoon swimming pools. If we were hungry and couldn't afford the fish and chips, we loved having a 'penneth of scrumps', those lovely fatty scraps from the fish fryer.

Chapter 5

Loughborough

At eighteen years of age, I finally left home for my three-year course at the Loughborough Teacher-Training College, situated in the Midlands triangle of Derby, Leicester and Nottingham. Loughborough was the premiere college for P.E. students, and I was encouraged to go there by my cousin John, who had been the British Army Cross Country Champion.

My first year in college was not to be in a Hall of Residence but the alternative was a very attractive option. I was based in the delightful village of Cossington, midway between Loughborough and Leicester. Our most famous resident, who lived in the manor house, was Lady Isobel Barnet, a popular figure on BBC Radio. I joined seven other students in an idyllic thatched cottage with whitewashed walls. George and Irene Sidwell had no children, so we became their family for a year, and they really spoiled us.

We shared, two to a room, and after an excellent dinner would stroll up to the village pub. Then, after our return, the big square table in the kitchen was set up with fresh crusty bread and cheese. Here, for the first time, I got into the delightful cheese, Red Leicester. We would light our cigarettes and put the world to rights! I don't recall doing a lot of work there.

We lads got on well together. A bus would pick us up in the morning to take us into college. Our curriculum was training in every sport, with a subsidiary subject (mine was Religious Education) and classes in English, Anatomy and Physiology. On Sundays, I would stroll along to the local Baptist church in Sileby. I think I was the only practising Christian student in my group, and not a very good one at that, but it made for some animated discussions. I was even asked to preach at the Baptist church one Sunday morning.

I freaked out my roommate on my first night in Cossington, by kneeling down to pray, but then he got his own back. I came in late one night and he wasn't there. When I got into bed and was drifting off to sleep, a pair of hands came up from under the bed and tried to strangle me! Tony was like that. He told us that he once jumped out on his grandmother in the dark and nearly gave her a heart attack.

Life was good. Being sportsmen, we loved our course, although our Religious Education lecturer, Canon Thompson, was deadly boring! Trevor, a mature student, kept us amused as he would always fall asleep, but tilting sideways, so we watched in anticipation as he reached tipping point and fell on the floor! It made no difference to the Canon as he simply droned on.

There were three main holidays and I always hitch-hiked home. The focus of every year was a month's teaching practice. My first was at the Taylor Street Junior School in a depressed inner-city area of Leicester. It was an old three-storey building with the flat roof being used as a playground. The staff liked me because when they went off to the staffroom for lunch, I organised team games on the roof. I became very popular with the pupils, as well as the staff, and received an outstanding report at the end of my practice. I hadn't realised how important this was, but my college tutor, the young Jeffrey Archer, gave me an excellent grading at the end of this first year.

Teaching the secondary students in years two and three was more challenging, but even there I had some success. I hated the Secondary Modern school on a rough Nottingham housing estate, especially as the headmaster used to yell four-letter words at the pupils in the corridor. Imagine that today! However, my day started, not at the school, but at a swimming pool near the city centre, and during that term we succeeded in getting every child swimming.

I don't remember a lot of involvement in the church the first year, but two incidents stand out in my mind. Every so often, the Christian Union, or CU as it was called, had a big open lecture for the students. I was dragged along by one of my friends on the Religious Education course. I remember the lecture hall being packed and the unfortunate incident that occurred. The speaker really annoyed me for some reason, and not being a shrinking violet, I took him on from the floor. In the end, an older guy in my row took me out as I was disrupting the whole meeting. It turned out he was the vice president of the university that our college was linked to!

Another, older student, took me under his wing. We called them 'mature students' as they had completed a two-year course and then returned for an extra year when that became mandatory. This guy's name was famous in the UK – Tom Farrell – an Olympic athlete who had been the captain of the British team at the Commonwealth Games in Australia. He was an amazing Christian, unashamed of his faith, and he drove me home during that first year, which was eight miles out of his way. When we got to Cossington, he would spend ages talking to me about the gospel. Later on, I heard him speak at Melbourne Hall in Leicester to a huge congregation of students, but he always had time for me – one on one.

Years later, when I was leading the Sidcup Church on the edge of London, Tom would ask me to go in and speak at some of his lunchtime meetings in the business heart of the city. He had been ordained as an Anglican vicar and his ancient church was right in the city wall, behind the Bank of England.

I had a special girlfriend when I was at Loughborough. I had met Heather Bensley when I was on holiday in Paignton, Devon, some two years earlier and we had continued to correspond and get together when it was possible, as she lived on the Essex side of London. I remember, during this first year at Loughborough, that I went home for two special events. I was going to be baptised at Foster Baptist in Bristol where I had been brought up. Also, I had been asked to speak at the Christian Endeavour Convention that same weekend. I'm not at all sure that I had been 'born again' at that time but I was certainly seeking.

Heather came down on the train to be with me and to meet my parents. I remember my dad, on shoe-cleaning duty, said that he had never known anyone with so many shoes! I really liked Heather. She was a very beautiful girl with a warm personality. Her parents liked me as well.

I hitch-hiked down to London for her firm's annual dance. Waiting outside Loughborough for a long time to get a ride, I thought I was never going to make it in time. Heather worked for British Petroleum (BP) in the heart of the city. However, something special happened. A guy pulled over, and said yes, he was going to London. Amazingly, the new M1 Motorway had just opened, and we made it in record time.

Over the next two years, we continued to meet, and I know Heather would have wished for engagement and marriage. Somehow, I just couldn't commit, not because there was anything wrong with her. She was a very special girl. Looking back, I can see the Lord was putting a restraint on my life and that he had some unique plans for me.

For the second and third year I moved into Morris Hall, just a short walk from the college refectory. I can see now that as students in those days we had a very privileged existence. Morris Hall was brand new, and we had our own beautifully furnished rooms and a shared common room. We had three cooked meals a day in the refectory, the evening dinner being served by waitresses. Later in the evening, a large urn of hot drinks with sandwiches and cakes would arrive in the common room. All our tuition was paid for, and we received an extra weekly allowance for expenses. Today, I see our students struggling with huge loans and I feel sorry for them.

In that second year at college, I got more involved with the Christian Union, which was quite big in Loughborough, and eventually I was voted on to the committee as Prayer Secretary. I was yet to meet my Waterloo! Sunday nights, we met at a lovely Christian lady's house for supper and fellowship. I would get on the piano, and we sang a lot of hymns and choruses. We didn't have the plethora of worship bands that we have today.

Teams of us would go out to take Sunday meetings in various village chapels and that's where I cut my teeth as a preacher. We got connected with the Woodhouse Eaves Baptist Church, on the edge of Charnwood Forest. The lay pastor Stan Hollins and his wife were very hospitable, and he took the risk of putting me on one Sunday evening. I especially remember it as I preached for an hour on the book of Job, and one dear old lady spoke to me on the way out saying, 'I'll know next time. I'll bring my sandwiches!'

Would there be a next time? Well, there would be, but a lot of changes would happen to me first.

Chapter 6

Break-up and Break-through

I came to realise that I couldn't continue my relationship with Heather as I wasn't prepared for the commitment she needed. After her last visit, I wrote and said I should stop seeing her. I'm fairly ashamed that I did this by mail and not in person. It must have hurt her deeply. Her father spoke to me later and enquired if there was no possibility of my seeing her again. By then, I had determined to lay down any thought of such a relationship.

Sometime later, after I had graduated and I was living at home and teaching in Bristol, I had a lovely letter from Heather suggesting we meet again as she wanted to talk to me. I was thrilled at the prospect as I felt particularly lonely and began to plan a weekend in Essex. As I walked out to my car and was about to turn on the engine and drive to school, the Holy Spirit spoke to me! It was almost an audible voice: You must write to Heather and tell her honestly that you don't feel you should see her again.

With this, peace settled upon me, and I knew, for whatever reason, I had made the right choice. If I have any explanation at all, it was something that had happened to me just before my last meeting with Heather. I had travelled with a Bristol friend up to the National Christian Endeavour Convention in Liverpool. One night, at a meeting in the Methodist Central Hall with some 2,000 people present, the great Keswick speaker, Reverend George Duncan from St George's Tron in Glasgow, delivered a message I will never forget!

In all that huge crowd, it was as if God had singled me out. He preached on the life of Samson in the book of Judges. He called him 'the child of destiny' and yet, Samson never fully realised his destiny because his passions were uncontrolled. His downfall was through a Philistine woman named Delilah who beguiled him to share the secret of his strength: not a massive, muscle-bound body but a Nazirite vow that had separated him to God. When the Philistines had gouged out his eyes and bound him, they imprisoned him until a great feast for their god, Dagon. Samson's hair and his strength had begun to grow again but sadly, he was the equivalent of a suicide bomber! As he brought down the temple of Dagon, Scripture says,

Thus he killed many more when he died than while he lived.[12]

What a sad epitaph!

When George finished preaching, I was so convicted by the Holy Spirit, I could scarcely move out of my seat. I pushed through the people to speak to George Duncan but crowds surrounded him, so I went back to the room where we were staying. For some reason, I knew that God had set me apart as a 'child of destiny' and that last bastion of my emotions and desires had to be surrendered to him.

---

12. Judges 16:30 NIV

Since I made the monumental decision to break up with Heather and turn away from casual relationships, it was as though the pace quickened for me. I had been longing to know God, and developed the spiritual disciplines of study and prayer, all of which I must confess was fairly hard work.

A freshman had come up to Loughborough that year, David Leeper, and a real bond was forged between us. He invited me to go to an unusual retreat, immediately after Christmas (1963). So it was that we travelled to the Sussex town of Worthing for the very first Prayer and Bible Week organised by South African evangelist and Bible teacher, Dennis Clark. Little did I know what we were in for! Dennis and his delightful wife, Beth, had a home that looked out over Broadwater Green. They had settled in the UK and Dennis became European Director of Youth for Christ.

On arrival we discovered that the next eight days were to be devoted to worship, prayer and serious Bible study – in fact, three sessions a day, with most sessions lasting at least two-and-a-half hours. Wow! I thought I was in for a spiritual marathon. Actually, they proved to be days of heaven on earth. We would sing a little, then Dennis taught us with his unique sense of humour and vast Bible knowledge, followed by a time of reflection and intercession. More than anything, Dennis taught us to pray. He constantly reminded us that head knowledge would get us nowhere; it all had to be translated into our hearts and daily living. I was a thirsty man, desperate to know God. I am sure I had come to the right well by divine appointment.

I was staying with Ron and Margaret Jenkins who were hugely supportive of my quest and we became firm friends. Several days found me broken in confession and repentance. One day, I remember going back to the house in Balcombe Avenue in a state of what the old Revivalists would have called 'conviction of sin'.

Once, earlier in my life, I had stolen a lot of money from my father. I had forgotten about this as time had gone on, but this was the sin that broke me up. I had committed many sins, but this, more than any other, seemed to require immediate attention. I wrote to my father, confessing what I had done and asking his forgiveness. Out of my meagre resources I sought to make some restitution.

Within two days, I received a wonderful reply completely forgiving me and releasing me from the debt. During these amazing days it was like I had a bath on the inside. The burden of my sins, which I wasn't aware that I was carrying, rolled off me.

In the latter part of the week, Dennis began to teach us about the baptism of the Holy Spirit. This was fairly new territory for me, and I am sure, for most Christians at that time, but Dennis was so helpful, even though he had been raised among the Brethren in South Africa who were staunchly opposed to this teaching and the expectation of spiritual gifts.

I don't believe I was baptised in the Holy Spirit during those days but what did happen was that I was truly born again of the Spirit. I understood why John Wesley spent the whole of his fifty years in itinerant ministry riding on horseback all over the British Isles, declaring again and again, 'You must be born again.'

As I became more and more involved with the Christian Union in Loughborough, and by now I was the chairman, in my final year, something continued to perplex me. It was summed up by the Apostle Paul's words in 2 Corinthians 5:17:

> *If anyone is in Christ, he is a new creation.*
> *The old has passed away; behold, the new has come.*[13]

For me, this just wasn't true. Neither did it seem to be true for most of my contemporaries. We were not this new creation; the old had not gone – it was very much in evidence! When I left Dennis Clark's home at the end of that first week in January 1964, I felt like a new creation. I can honestly say, I have never gone back from this. Perhaps, the most remarkable thing of all was that the Bible, a book that I had really struggled with, came alive. God began to speak to me through Scripture.

In addition to Dennis and Beth Clark, two other couples were about to come into my life who would have a profound influence on me and the Charismatic Movement worldwide: Arthur and Eileen Wallis and Campbell and Shelagh McAlpine. During that first Prayer and Bible Week Arthur had sent Dennis a poem from New Zealand where he had been involved in ground-breaking ministry. The poem was called *The Laws of the Kingdom* and amazingly dovetailed with the themes that Dennis had been sharing with us. Arthur and Eileen were to become good friends, and when Linda and I married, Arthur was the preacher. In fact, on the first day of our honeymoon in Devon, Linda

---

13. 2 Corinthians 5:17 ESV

and I spoke at a meeting in their house-church in the tiny village of Talaton near Exeter.

It was through Dennis that I came to meet both these couples. When I returned to Loughborough, I was keen to get the benefit of Dennis's charismatic ministry into our Christian Union. I wrote to him, asking if he could come for a particular weekend of teaching in the near future, but his calendar was very full. However, he mentioned that his friends Campbell and Shelagh McAlpine had just come from New Zealand, and I should contact them as an alternative. I received a very positive letter in response from Campbell that included an unexpected bonus.

Ever since the Prayer and Bible week, I had begun to read the Bible consecutively. My aim was to read the Old Testament once, and the New Testament twice in my first year. I soon began to realise that this was not simply academic study, but that I would meet the Lord through this Living Word.

Being in my last two terms at college, I had to look for a job. All my fellow students were studying the *Times Educational Supplement* each week, and many were securing interviews at different schools with a considerable degree of success. For some reason I had no peace about this and found it difficult to respond when friends in my Hall of Residence asked me what I was going to do.

One morning as I was praying and meditating in Scripture before going to breakfast, the Lord spoke to me through the words of King David in Psalm 27:

Wait for the LORD; be strong and let your heart take
courage,
and wait for the LORD![14]

Had this been emblazoned in neon lights on the wall of my room, it could not have been more clear! I went to my lectures that day with a spring in my step, knowing that I had to wait for God's direction.

The next day, my response from Campbell McAlpine arrived. He agreed to come to our weekend event, but what shook me was the postscript to his letter. You've guessed it! Psalm 27:14. I can't tell you what this did for me. It was so encouraging and endorsing. I had never met Campbell McAlpine and he had no idea of what I was facing in terms of a job application. This small incident established a great truth within me:

Your word is a lamp to my feet and a light to my path.[15]

A sceptic will say, 'That was just coincidence.' Since it has happened over and over again in my life, hundreds of times, I have another explanation! God is the co-ordinator of incidents – supernatural incidents. No wonder Jesus said,

My sheep hear my voice.[16]

For weeks after this, I refused to panic or become stressed into some futile action. One day, in our common room, I picked up the *Times Educational Supplement* and there

14. Psalm 27:14 ESV
15. Psalm 119:105 ESV
16. John 10:27 ESV

was a job advertised at a new comprehensive school in my home city of Bristol. Immediately, I felt a quickening of response within me. Within days of making an initial enquiry I was granted an interview.

On the day I presented myself to the school in Bristol, there were at least half a dozen applicants, including another guy from my Hall of Residence in Loughborough. We were invited to take a guided tour of the school before being interviewed in the principal's office. The first room I walked into was that of one of the housemasters, John Forster, brother of renowned British Bible teacher, Roger Forster. On the wall of his study was a plaque with the words of Jesus embossed on it:

I am the way, and the truth, and the life.
No one comes to the Father except through me.[17]

Immediately, I felt the Holy Spirit say to me, 'This is your job.' The subsequent interview seemed almost a formality. I secured my place at Hartcliffe School, which, in turn, positioned me back in Bristol. I was to work at one of the newest comprehensive schools in the country, on one of the neediest housing estates in the city.

During the last two terms in Loughborough, certain important things happened. Being chairman of the large Christian Union carried quite a lot of responsibility, and it was also time for finals! A very important set of examinations lay ahead. My prayer was very specific: Lord, I will do all that you require of me but please help me in my finals!

---

17. John 14:6 ESV

He did, and I am now the proud owner of a diploma from Loughborough College and a certificate for education from Nottingham University. Subsequently, I was awarded a BA degree as we were pioneers of the three-year course.

During these months, I began to preach more in the chapels scattered across the countryside. I think my time in Loughborough had been a training ground for so much that was to come. My future was being shaped!

Chapter 7

Blackhorse

After graduating from Loughborough in 1964, I returned to live at my parents' home in Staple Hill, Bristol. In the summer vacation before I started my teaching job, my friend Dave Leeper and I joined a Scripture Union beach mission at Port St Mary on the Isle of Man – an excellent training ground for a young evangelist.

Then I took some time to engage in door-to-door visitation in the large blocks of flats opposite the school where I was to begin teaching in September. I was seeking to talk with anyone I could about Jesus. This was much more challenging than the beach mission at Port St Mary, but a great preparation for my future work.

I made a good friend in Mrs Webber. She was an elderly widow, very much alone and uprooted from her home in the seaside town of Burnham. When I knocked on her door, she invited me in for a cup of tea, something she told me she would never normally have done. So began our friendship, which involved me regularly explaining the Bible to her and praying with her. She remained stalwart in faith, and I continued to visit her long after I had left Hartcliffe, until she passed away.

Another council estate, at Blackhorse on the north-east edge of the city, was to become my mission field. Little did we know that in coming days it would be joined to the edge of the largest housing development in Europe. I discovered a small group of Christians, mostly Baptists and Methodists, who had joined together to set up a Sunday school in the Blackhorse primary school.

To prepare for this, they had begun meeting in one another's homes to pray and plan for their weekly work among the children. Having been exposed to a house-church in my grandmother's Upper Room in London, now I encountered the all-important relational dynamic that would influence my thinking so much in the future.

My move to join these good folks in Blackhorse proved to be a crucial 'placing' for me. So much happened as a consequence! Years later, the Lord spoke these words in my heart with great clarity: Of equal importance with a man or woman's gifting by God and their calling is where they are placed.

Throughout my life, I was going to see just how important this placing would be. The Scriptures that came to my mind back in 1964 were in 1 Corinthians 12:18 and 1 Corinthians 12:28, where Paul is talking about the function of the Body of Christ. The Greek word used here is *tithemi*, literally, to set, place or put.

> *God set ('has placed' NIV) the members every one of them in the body, as it hath pleased him.* [18]

Likewise with the ministry gifts of the Holy Spirit: apostles, prophets, teachers, miracle workers, etc., it says in verse 28,

---

18. 1 Corinthians 12:18 KJV

66

God hath set ('placed' NIV) in the church, first apostles . . .

So many times, people have said to me, 'I went there for my studies, or my job, or my relationship but it was when I went there that everything came together.'

A bonus of my being placed with the small group of Christians in Blackhorse was that they asked my father to be their pastor, so Mum and Dad became a crucial part of this unfolding story. Dad remained in his job as a sales manager, but he and Mum gave themselves tirelessly to the work of this emerging church.

My late grandmother, Elizabeth Jackson, left me a legacy, which enabled me to sort out some transport, so very necessary as my parents' home was in north-east Bristol and I had to travel across the city. Hartcliffe is situated on a large council estate bordering the Mendip Hills, south-west of the city.

I used Grandmother's legacy in three ways. First, I set apart a generous gift to Eric Hutchings' evangelistic mission in the Colston Hall, Bristol. Giving generously was always going to be an important part of my Christian life. Secondly, I paid for a series of driving lessons in Loughborough. My third investment of the legacy was to purchase a new car. Reading this today, it seems absurd in the light of current transport costs, but I bought a brand-new Minivan for £390, and my first tank of petrol for less than £1!

That Mini was to serve me well for the next four years until I required a more suitable vehicle for my travels to Eastern Europe, smuggling Bibles and all sorts of important things to the churches suffering under communism. I managed to pass the test at my second attempt. My days of hitch-hiking all over the country were soon to come to an end, and instead, I would be able to pick up many hitch-hikers and help them with a lift and my life story! I was zealous to share the gospel with everyone I could. It's a mark of how society has so dramatically changed that to be a lift-giver or a lift-taker is now so much more hazardous than it was in my youth.

During my lunchtimes at the school, I used to drive my Minivan up a very steep hill on the edge of the Mendips to a spot where I could see the whole city before me, with the famous Clifton Suspension Bridge in the distance. Much time was spent in intercession for Bristol and a growing burden was established for the needs of our many council housing estates where the social problems were often acute.

I tried to return to my old, liberal Baptist church but found that I was singing from a different song sheet. To stay on, I would have been increasingly in conflict with the pastor and deacons, so I looked for a new sphere in which I could grow spiritually.

A series of incidents occurred in my life that served to equip me for an unknown future. The first had to do with my relationship to the third person of the Trinity, the Holy Spirit. Since sitting under the teaching of Dennis Clark at the first Prayer and Bible Week, a great thirst for the Holy Spirit had awakened in me. I read, I prayed, I asked people to 'lay hands' on me. Nothing happened until early on Good Friday morning 1965.

On this memorable day, I awoke very early in the morning, about 2am. I got down on my knees and opened my Bible to the point where I had arrived in my daily consecutive reading. It was Psalm 2, the great prophetic psalm about the ascension of Jesus. For the next two hours, I was enthralled by its significance, especially the phrase in verse 6,

I have installed my king on Zion, my holy hill.[19]

When interpreting Biblical prophecy, it is so important to see how the New Testament interprets the Old Testament. Psalm 2 led me on to a remarkable incident in Acts chapter 4 where the Apostles Peter and John led the Early Church in a powerful prayer centred on an evident fulfilment of Psalm 2. Peter and John had been arrested by the temple guard shortly after the miraculous healing of a beggar at the Gate Beautiful. Such was their popularity because of this extraordinary miracle that the Jewish leaders could not simply keep them in prison. Instead, they threatened them not to teach or preach in the name of Jesus. Remember, these were the same men who had instigated the crucifixion of Jesus. As Peter and John reported these events, the whole company joined in a prayer focused on Psalm 2, declaring Jesus to be God's Anointed Servant who the rulers of both Jews and Gentiles were guilty of silencing. Their prayer was so specific,

Now, Lord, look upon their threats and grant to your servants to continue to speak your word with all boldness, while you stretch out your hand to heal, and signs and wonders are performed through the name of your holy servant Jesus.[20]

---

19. Psalm 2:6 NIV
20. Acts 4:29-30 ESV

The amazing postscript to this prayer was that the place in which they were praying was shaken, and they were all filled with the Holy Spirit and spoke the Word of God boldly! That Good Friday morning, it was as though I entered the fulfilment of this psalm.

When I was still at Loughborough, I went one night to hear the Revd Duncan Campbell speak. He had been a leader during the revival in the Hebrides Islands off the coast of Scotland. He had witnessed the same phenomenon one night when a young man stood to pray in a cottage meeting. The house in which they were praying was shaken and they went out into the village in the middle of the night to find the whole community alive to the presence of God.

No doubt this eye-witness account stirred me, but the fulfilment of Psalm 2 for the Early Church excited me even more. I prayed my own very specific prayer. It went something like this: 'Lord, you fulfilled your Word so dramatically in the lives of your servants, I want you to do the same for me. I can't live on second-hand experience. I need to know for myself that this is true. If I can do the work to which you are calling me, please, Lord, shake me!'

With that, the power of God fell upon me, wave after wave, like massive volts of electricity. I was left prostrate on my bedroom floor, overwhelmed by God's presence. More than that, I saw the King in Zion! Just as Peter had preached on the day of Pentecost, I saw that . . .

God has raised this Jesus to life, and we are all witnesses of it. Exalted to the right hand of God, he has received from the Father the promised Holy Spirit and has poured out what you now see and hear.[21]

---

21. Acts 2:32-33 NIV

I saw and heard! I was shaken from head to foot. I remained lost in the presence of God, so much so that I have never doubted again!

Some have asked me, 'Did you speak in tongues or prophesy?'

My answer, 'At that moment, no.'

I was so consumed with the exaltation of Jesus and the fulfilment of his promise, that nothing else seemed to matter. The whole development of spiritual gifts and the outworking of this would come later.

Two other events happened around this time that involved further visits to Worthing. One night, my friend David Leeper and I went round to Campbell McAlpine's home. Campbell was away on a ministry trip, but we enjoyed rich fellowship with his wife Shelagh, who was herself extremely gifted spiritually. During a time of prayer, she suddenly stopped and spoke directly to me. She gave me a Scripture from a special Hebrew translation of Proverbs 4:12,

As you go, step by step, I will open the way before you.

Shelagh used the analogy of the Children of Israel under Joshua's leadership crossing the River Jordan to enter the Promised Land. The Jordan was in full flood, but the Lord told Joshua to get the priests who were carrying the Ark of the Covenant to step into the swollen river. As the soles of their feet touched the waters, they parted so that all Israel could enter the land of promise. Shelagh said to me, 'Peter, God is going to require you to take many steps of faith, but you must be prepared to step out on the promise of God, even though it seems impossible!'

This became perhaps the most important guideline for the rest of my life. I knew that my time in Loughborough College and my teaching job were simply stepping-stones to a whole new direction for my future.

On another visit to Worthing, I called at the McAlpines' house when Campbell was there. I needed his counsel about spiritual gifts, having received such a dramatic baptism by the Spirit. As always, he was extraordinarily wise. I had two 'sticking points' regarding speaking with tongues – one practical and one theological. Addressing the theological issue first, my summary ran something like this, 'I know I have been baptised in the Holy Spirit. I know that the gifts of the Spirit, all of them, are for today; they haven't vanished down some dispensational drain! I'm glad that people are speaking in tongues, and I wish I was as well. The reason I'm not is because of Paul's teaching in 1 Corinthians 12:27-30. This passage included the question, *Do all speak in tongues?* The answer to this question is obviously, no. And this had been my own excuse for some time.'

Campbell directed me to Paul's further teaching in 1 Corinthians chapter 14. We are to *eagerly desire spiritual gifts, especially prophecy* (verse 1). Paul said he spoke in tongues more than all of the Corinthian church (verse 18). The purpose of this being that he who speaks in tongues edifies himself (verse 4), that is, he is 'built up' spiritually. Campbell's summary was that in saying this, Paul made it clear that we were under the umbrella of God's will in our expectation.

The passage that I was struggling with in 1 Corinthians 12 had to do with God's appointment of special gifts in the context of the church (verses 28-29), not the issue of prayer for personal edification. Hearing this, a major stumbling block for me was removed and faith was quickened in my heart.

However, Campbell's advice on my other issue was even more helpful. Countless times I had asked for this gift in prayer, both privately and publicly, then I remained stoically in place, expecting God to wobble my tongue and speak through me! But, as Campbell pointed out, in that memorable beginning of all things on the day of Pentecost . . .

all of them were filled with the Holy Spirit and BEGAN TO SPEAK in other tongues as the Spirit enabled them.[22]

Strange as it may seem, I had not realised this before! I had to speak if I was going to speak in tongues. I saw it immediately and said to Campbell, 'Please pray for me now!' I knew this was mine and hesitantly began to speak a few syllables I had never uttered before. He would have had me stay longer but I had to drive back to Bristol some 150 miles for another engagement.

I drove home rejoicing and the very next day something special happened. I had been to Sainsbury's supermarket with my mother, and I unloaded her shopping when we returned. While Mum was preparing lunch, I went up to my room and knelt in prayer. Suddenly the flood gates opened, and a torrent of language poured forth.

22. Acts 2:4 NIV

As the days continued it increased, deepened and gave me a tremendous sense of being built up in the Spirit so that I could fulfil my work of ministry. I learned a great lesson. In many ways, the function of this most reviled of spiritual gifts was a key to the successful function of all the other spiritual gifts! Mark 16:20 says,

Then the disciples went out and preached everywhere, and the Lord worked with them and confirmed his word by the signs that accompanied it.[23]

God works with us, not independently of us. Spiritualist mediums often go into trance and are 'taken over', but Paul says of New Testament prophets,

The spirits of prophets are subject to the control of prophets.[24]

The great healing evangelist, Smith Wigglesworth, used to say, 'Many Christians are waiting to be moved by the Holy Spirit. I move the Holy Spirit!' This statement would upset many people, but I think I understand exactly what he meant. The impact of all this Holy Spirit activity on me personally was dramatic: absolute brokenness.

I was eager to see this imparted to our infant church. In addition to our Sunday school, where I took responsibility for a handful of teenagers, we started to meet publicly as a church on Sunday evenings. I was keen to get Campbell McAlpine up to Blackhorse to meet with the church and

---

23. NIV
24. 1 Corinthians 14:32 NIV

a weekend was arranged in which he was able to share in some depth his experience of the riches of our inheritance in Christ.

At the time we hadn't fully realised we were coming into a global movement of the Holy Spirit. The Charismatic Movement, as it was called, was being birthed simultaneously all over the world. Christians from across the whole denominational spectrum were encountering the power of the Holy Spirit and spiritual gifts in a new way. Until then, it had been the Pentecostal churches who had embraced these truths, often being kept at arm's-length by mainstream Christians. That was all about to change.

I will never forget Campbell's opening address at our weekend in my old Baptist church which we had hired for the occasion. He preached on the raising of Lazarus in John chapter 11, bringing a sense of conviction and deep repentance. When he spoke about the baptism of the Spirit on the Saturday evening, many responded to a simple invitation to receive the Holy Spirit and things began to happen immediately.

One of our leaders, Tony Hares, was unable to be at the meeting. He was at home in the bath when the Holy Spirit fell on him and he began to speak in tongues, something not common to Congregationalists at that time. He and his wife Margaret became a powerful influence through their home on the estate.

I decided we needed an additional meeting on Friday nights at my parents' home. Initially, we arranged one a month, but quickly moved to every two weeks, meeting from 8pm until midnight. We called this the half-night of prayer, and it quickly became an important focal point in the life of our young church.

A significant thing happened to me in all this. I felt we needed good Biblical teaching at these gatherings, so I wrote to Dennis Clarke requesting tapes of his teaching on various themes. His response was unexpected, but life-changing! He basically said, no, he would not send me the tapes. In his words, we needed someone full of the Holy Spirit to bring messages from the Lord appropriate to that meeting. Selflessly but wisely, he put me on the spot. How many would say 'Great – they want my teaching!' But he didn't, and I knew I had to respond.

I was often late home from work, feeling especially knackered at the end of the week, but I made a decision to grasp this opportunity. I thought: 'I'll do a series on the Gifts of the Spirit!' A bold step as I knew very little, so I mugged up a good book on the subject by a great Pentecostal teacher, Harold Horton, and I gave myself to preparation and prayer, meditating in the Word of God.

The first night, I spoke on the gift of prophecy basing my message on Jehoshaphat's army in 2 Chronicles chapter 20, an amazing military victory inspired by prophecy. After teaching, we always went to prayer, and on this night, three people prophesied for the first time. One of these, the aforementioned Tony Hares, developed a very significant gift of prophecy in the coming days.

We had now begun to meet as a church, eventually called Blackhorse Christian Fellowship. We dropped the 'Baptist' name as many of us were from different denominational backgrounds. Prayer became increasingly significant and one of our prayer meetings provided the backdrop for our first miracle.

As the Holy Spirit was given freedom to move among us, all sorts of remarkable things began to happen. The first, as I recall, was a dramatic healing. One of our new members, Sid Feltham, a man in his early fifties, was stricken down with a cerebral haemorrhage, which almost killed him. He was left paralysed down one side, bed-ridden and could scarcely recognise his wife Olive, who was deeply concerned for her sick husband. A number of us were due to meet for prayer on a Tuesday evening. While I was preparing at home for this gathering, I felt the Lord speak very clearly to my heart: 'Why don't you do what it says in James chapter 5?'[25]

I was familiar with this healing text that involved calling for the elders and anointing with oil, so I determined to mention it at the start of our meeting. When I arrived at the house of one of our members, talk was immediately about Sid's situation and two of the other men said exactly what I had thought. This passage, like so many in the New Testament, is familiar to us, but we rarely do what it says!

We had some discussion about the type of oil we should use and decided anything could be used if applied with the prayer of faith. We decided to meet again the next night for prayer while my father went with another of our elders, Stan Bidmead, to Sid's house. Olive was thrilled to see them and said that Sid was upstairs in bed very much 'out

25. James 5:13-16

of it'. The doctors said it would be some weeks before he could try to walk.

After talking with Olive, Dad and Stan went upstairs, anointed Sid and prayed over him. The next day, Olive contacted us to say she walked into the bedroom the following morning and Sid was sitting on the side of the bed, asking for a cup of tea. Within days, he walked around the block unaided, and was completely restored apart from a slight slurring of his speech! Our faith went through the roof – this was just the beginning.

Still teaching, coaching Bristol Boys Soccer Team and playing rugby for Kingswood Grammar Old Boys, I began to trim these activities to the point where I left my job to devote myself to my growing Christian ministry. I developed a door-to-door ministry on the estate, visiting every home, giving out Gospels of John and seeking to speak to everyone as I was able. I trained others in this work, and I believe every home in our community received a personal visitation. I would estimate that at least fifty adults were converted in two to three years, and some of these were truly remarkable. Remember, everything was being watered in prayer.

Tony and Margaret Hares had a home open to everyone. On the end of the block where they lived was a hopeless alcoholic, Ivor Jenkins. Everyone in the area knew him because he was often in the gutter, just completely overwhelmed by his drinking. Tony and Margaret and others shared with his wife and Ivor that he really must get help. We encouraged him to go to a specialist centre run by the Salvation Army in Swindon called The Harbour Lights.

Ivor went and we all prayed earnestly. I will never forget the night he returned from Swindon and strutted into Tony and Margaret's house with a flourish, saying, 'I'm cured.'

Unfortunately, none of us had a witness in our hearts that this was accomplished. Not long after this, he returned to his old ways, and we prayed on. One lunchtime, he popped into the King William IV on Staple Hill High Street and came out after his liquid lunch very much the worse for wear. He was so drunk as he tottered down the High Street that he fell over a pram and knocked the baby out of it. Mercifully the baby wasn't injured, and this proved to be Ivor's wake-up call! He managed to get home and asked to be driven back to Swindon.

He later told me what happened. On the Sunday morning, he went along to the Salvation Army service at their Corps, and when the lady officer who had been preaching invited people to come to the 'Mercy Seat' he rushed forward, fell on his knees and began weeping like a baby. He rose up that Sunday lunchtime completely delivered from a life of addiction and with a determination to share the gospel with all who would listen. He got a new job as a soft drinks salesman and his territory included pubs all over the West Country.

On the occasions I have met Ivor over the ensuing years he has always encouraged me by his faith and determination to honour God in everything. One of his friends, John, who we had a lot to do with, came out of a terrible gambling addiction that had controlled his whole life. They made a great team as they went out wherever they could, sharing how Jesus had set them free!

Another lady, Mavis Bushell, had a dramatic encounter with the Lord, and, like Lydia in Acts chapter 16, when God opened her heart, she opened her home. I used to go to her house where many young mums would gather, put their children on the floor with very noisy toys, and I would teach them from the Gospel of John that I was giving out on the estate. At one time, we estimated that seventeen of Mavis's relatives had come to the Lord.

While all this was going on, I was working with other like-minded people across the city of Bristol in a ministry we called Tell Bristol. This consisted of a number of important events: a monthly day of prayer and fasting at the WEC[26] Missionary Headquarters in Redland, regular teaching events – often hosting visiting charismatic leaders from all over the world, special evangelistic outreaches and sometimes, social action.

The first major event that Tell Bristol hosted proved very significant. I had felt that we should host a conference on revival with the renowned author and speaker, Arthur Wallis. When our team met to discuss this, I was concerned that we get the right venue. Someone suggested that I contact a young Anglican priest named Malcolm Widdecombe who had recently arrived at an old Anglican church called St Philip and St Jacob, in the heart of the city, right by the Old Market. He graciously agreed to let us use the church and also got his team to help manage the event. On the final night, when we had been delayed praying with people until nearly midnight, he was there to lock up the church.

26. WEC Worldwide Evangelisation Crusade

Three days after the conference, he asked me to visit him and his wife Meryl, at the Old Rectory where they lived. He had been sent by the bishop to close the church down as only a handful of elderly members remained. Instead, God began to work his wonders and Pip'n'Jay, as it was affectionately called, became a remarkable centre of renewal and revival. Malcolm and Meryl asked all about the baptism of the Spirit and spiritual gifts, and we became firm friends. So many of our Tell Bristol events were held there, and Malcolm often invited me to preach and teach his congregation. It was not unusual for him to ask me to come early on a Sunday evening, when I would sit with him in the vestry and recite Evensong, required by canon law. Then he would say, 'Right, Peter, let's get in there and do what we want to do!'

Preaching in that ancient pulpit, where once John Wesley had preached and been thrown out, only to continue his ministry standing on the gravestones, was a huge privilege, and to see this church, so often packed, particularly with young people, is such a wonderful memory. Although the bishop had sent 'Wid' to close the church down, God had other plans! Early on, Malcolm set a distinctive goal for the church:

Seek first

literally, from Jesus's favourite words in Matthew 6:33.

His plan was that this church would always give away more than it spent on itself. And this is what it did, supporting mission and evangelism all over the world on a scale that I have never seen in any other church.

Some time ago, I was invited to a very special event at the church, their own version of the popular TV show *This is Your Life*, I think for Malcolm's sixtieth birthday. I had been living in New Zealand for many years, frequently travelling back to the UK, and I was pleased to be one of two 'mystery guests', with a voice coming out from behind the curtain. The other mystery guest was Anne Widdecombe, Malcolm's famous sister, a well-known politician, and more recently a celebrity on the popular TV show *Strictly Come Dancing*. It was a great night to honour Wid, and sadly for me, the last time I would see him, as I heard of his passing not long ago. His was a friendship that I will always treasure.

We had so many excellent speakers at Pip'n'Jay, from Michael Harper of the Fountain Trust to the cross-carrying Arthur Blessitt, who packed the place out. Larger events were held in the Colston Hall, with people such as David Wilkerson and David Watson with The Fisherfolk, Jimmy Owens with Pat Boone and *Come Together*. At this latter event, we had almost as many people outside on the steps as the 2,000-capacity crowd inside. I was impressed that Jimmy and Pat went to the people outside before hosting their great musical. We were so inspired by this that we gathered our own band and chorus and took it on the road around the West Country, to Bath Abbey, Malmsbury Abbey, Gloucester Town Hall, to name a few of our dramatic venues.

Just a few months ago, I was present at an Assembly of God church in Santa Barbara, California; the speaker had been present at the late Jean Darnall's memorial service at the Church on the Way, Los Angeles, and assuming that no-one present that Sunday morning would remember her, he paid a special tribute to her, but, of course, she had been a great favourite of ours in Bristol. I remember when this lovely American lady first preached in Pip'n'Jay. She said: 'Great Britain, I've never seen so many chimneys and so little fire!' Then, 'I'm an American, a woman and a Pentecostal!'

In spite of this, she was a great favourite in many of the more orthodox churches.

Writing during my eightieth year, there are so many stories to tell and inevitably some oversights. During my last years at Blackhorse, some of the leaders involved in a fresh move of the Spirit arising out of Buenos Aires, Argentina, had a huge impact on us. Initially, Ivan Baker came, then Keith Benson, followed by Orville Swindoll, brother of the famous American teacher, Chuck Swindoll. What a gracious man Orville was, one of our first guests at the beginning of our married life. These men carried such a vision of the gospel of the Kingdom that they greatly impacted me personally, long before the books of the prolific N.T. Wright popularised this approach to the New Testament. Most famous among them, Juan Carlos Ortiz, set the Billy Graham Congress at Lausanne alight with his teaching. I had the privilege of hearing him preach at Christchurch, Clifton in Bristol. Later he would lead the Spanish-speaking congregation at the Crystal Cathedral in Los Angeles.

All these brothers carried something in the spirit that made a deep impression on us. Many years later, Neil Edbrooke, a gifted teacher in the Bristol church, wrote to me and expressed his thanks that I had taught such a clear foundation of the gospel of the Kingdom. I am sure that my involvement with these great men had profoundly influenced me in this.

Chapter 8

University Challenge

So I was at college for three years at the beginning of the Sixties, a decade of enormous change. From 1961 to 1964 I studied Physical and Religious Education and I have already described the spiritual pilgrimage I was on through this time. Having come to faith as a student and eventually become chairman of the Christian Union, it was only natural that I became very involved in ministry to students in the early years in Bristol and then much further afield.

It was customary in those days for the Christian Unions to hold important Mission Weeks, when they sought to reach out to the whole of the campus with the gospel. I was invited to be on mission teams at Bristol, Lancaster, Cambridge, Birmingham, Liverpool, and other Further Education establishments, and even led some mini missions which were very challenging.

Let me give you an insight into a Mission Week in Cambridge, for example. I was part of an excellent team led by Michael Green, a prominent Anglican evangelist and teacher. I was attached to Downing College, Cambridge, which involved residing in the college and working with the students there. In the mornings, our team would meet with Michael for planning, prayer and updates of the mission's progress. We then spent the day in the college among the students and faculty, and at night, we would meet in the Guildhall where Michael would give one of the main mission talks, tailored to those wanting to know more about the Christian faith.

On those nights, up to a thousand students packed the Guildhall, an exciting prospect for the future impact of the gospel. I would go with students and come back to further gatherings in their rooms, which could continue late into the night. It was fairly unique that a Christian organisation could command such crowds night after night.

Many came to faith in this time, and I was invited back to Downing College later to conduct a mini mission specifically within that college. I would dine at the top table in the refectory, with all the college dons. After a sumptuous meal, we would be ushered into a drawing room where a butler would serve cognac and liqueurs, and trundle round with a humidor of cigars.

Some of the most high-powered brains in Britain would be in that room and I had many opportunities to share my faith with them. I was also invited to preach in the college chapel, which was quite an honour. Each college had an appointed chaplain. Remember that all the great universities had a Christian foundation.

I got to know the college chaplain, a remarkable man. The Christian Union had got offside with him, but I befriended him, and we had a great time together. He had come to Cambridge from the Community of the Resurrection in Mirfield and was both a Doctor of Science and a Doctor of Theology. A brilliant man! At the end of each day, I would often be in his rooms at the college, and we had such animated and fruitful discussions. I will never forget what happened on my last day there. He asked if we might pray, and with that, he came across the room, laid hands on my head and brought a powerful prophecy to me! All this from an Anglo-Catholic monk!

On these missions, I had the privilege of working with amazing team leaders, as diverse as Roger Forster, David Watson, Michael Green and David McGuiness. I think Roger Forster had the finest mind of any missioner I worked with. He and his wife, Faith, went on to lead the dynamic Ichthus church network and were good friends. David Watson was the leading charismatic evangelist. His church in York would eventually pack the great York Minster, which is second only to Canterbury Cathedral. His tragic death from cancer cut short one of the most effective ministries we had in Britain.

For many years, the great John Stott, Rector of All Souls, Langham Place – next to the BBC – had been the leading student missioner. But then a new breed of charismatic leader arose. This led to a lot of conflict within the InterVarsity Fellowship (IVF), and I remember being invited to an important one-day conference at All Souls with other university missioners. The IVF wanted to get their growing concern about charismatic issues into a discussion forum. They had asked John Stott to give a more traditional paper, and then David Watson, who was so overtly charismatic, to respond. I will never forget David's response! He spoke from Paul's words in 1 Corinthians 2:1-5, emphasising verse 4,

My message and my preaching were not with wise and persuasive words, but with a demonstration of the Spirit's power.[27]

---

27. NIV

87

David was my hero! I had quite a shock one day when I was driving him from Bristol to York. He had stayed the night with us in Olveston as we were planning a citywide mission with him and a popular folk group from Texas, The Fisherfolk. As we drove along, enjoying an animated discussion, he suddenly said to me, 'Peter, I would like you to take over my student ministry.' I was gobsmacked, as he explained that he now wanted to concentrate on other areas of his ministry. I remember my response, 'I foresee one problem with this, David; I'm not you!'

At the close of the first Cambridge mission with Michael Green, a remarkable thing happened. It was soon after I had met Linda in 1970. At our last team meeting a request was made. 'Michael has to get back to Nottingham, could anyone drive him there.'

I immediately responded, 'My fiancée lives in Derby and I am due to go there tomorrow. Nottingham is en route so I will gladly take him.'

The next day when Michael got into the car, there was only one thing he wanted to talk about: charismatic experience. I think we talked non-stop all the way to Nottingham. I shared with him my own testimony of the baptism in the Spirit and the remarkable awakening we had experienced at Blackhorse in Bristol. I'm sure it helped that I had been so deeply involved with the old Anglican church in the heart of Bristol, St Philip and St Jacob.

When we got to Nottingham, he did a lovely thing. He had just been appointed Principal of a new Anglican theological college there, and he invited me inside. He said, 'Tomorrow is a very special day. Prince Charles is coming to open the college, and I would like to give you a tour beforehand!'

Linda and I met Michael a number of times over the years, mostly at receptions my colleague Gerald Coates organised, as well as at the Evangelists' Conference at Swanwick. The Archbishop of Canterbury, George Carey, a good friend of Gerald's, invited two leading Anglicans to return to Britain, especially to help him 're-evangelise' the Anglican church. He called Bishop Michael Marshall to return from South America, and Michael Green to return from Canada. What a great job they did!

The development of the community in Olveston and, subsequently, Bristol Christian Fellowship, was greatly influenced by the involvement of students from the university, the teacher-training college in Fishponds and the technical college. I remember being on a mission at the university with Roger Forster. I was newly married and we had two young children. I was having dinner in the student refectory one night when I noticed that several of the students sported badges that declared *Stop at Two!* In my naivety, I thought this meant two drinks! Of course, it meant two children, and here I was with Linda expecting our third child!

As our Bristol church grew, great work among the students was spearheaded by Nic and Jenny Harding. Eventually, this arm of the church purchased the Ark, a parish hall near the university. A lot of fruitful ministry flowed out of there in the following years.

I remember complaining once to our mentors, John and Christine Noble, that we weren't a 'proper church' as we had such a huge proportion of university graduates. John's wise answer was, 'You must work with those whom God gives you, Peter. You were converted as a student and have had so much involvement in the student scene, it's only natural that you will attract lots of students!'

Chapter 9

Pastor Duma and Willie Burton

During my years as chairman of Tell Bristol, I had the privilege of meeting many great Christian leaders. Often they stayed at my parents' home and I was responsible for their itinerary and driving them everywhere.

With Pastor Duma and Willie Burton there was a strong connection with Africa. W.F.P. Burton was the apostolic leader of the Congo Evangelistic Mission. When he finally left the Congo, 1,500 churches remained. Pastor Duma was an incredible Zulu leader of the Umgeni Road Baptist Church in Durban, South Africa. This was at a time when Apartheid was a strong political force, but such were his gifts that he transcended all man-made barriers.

His biography *Take Your Glory, Lord* was originally published by the South African Baptist Missionary Society. It wasn't very well written but an Australian publisher got hold of it, improved the writing and graciously invited me to write the foreword. It is one of the most remarkable testimonies to the supernatural that I have read.

Duma was invited to join the South African contingent to Billy Graham's World Congress on Evangelism in Berlin. From there he came across to the UK and Dennis Clarke asked me to pick him up in Manchester and host him in Bristol for several days, an experience I will never forget.

In our house, he was as quiet as a mouse. In the pulpit he would often roar like a lion. He was old but still a striking, formidable Zulu Warrior; not tall but of a square build, with very powerful shoulders. I drank deeply at his well and I have often described it as rather like having Jesus in the house.

He told me that early in his ministry he became deeply dissatisfied with his own spiritual state. To rectify this, he determined to seek God and so rose early to walk up a nearby mountain and devote himself to prayer and fasting. On the third day, as he walked up the hill he became engulfed by a cloud of God's glory, whether in his body or out of it, he scarcely knew. As darkness was falling he came to his senses and began walking down towards his home. All he could say was, 'Duma was a different man!'

Almost immediately, remarkable miracles began in the unpretentious Baptist church. Many stories he told me personally; too many to recount here and so unpredictable that you knew it came from someone distinctly led by the Holy Spirit. One of the two instances of resurrection from the dead is as follows: Nicholas Bhenghu, the famous African evangelist had a teenage daughter who died. When Duma heard of this, having had a friendship with Bhenghu, he determined to go to the family home, which was some distance away. The first part of the journey was by taxi, then he had to walk into the bush, feeling strangely constrained all the way.

When he arrived at the house, he was taken into a room where the body was laid out on a table, surrounded by serving women. She had been dead four days! He asked for a basin of water and began to wash the body. The women began to whisper, saying, 'We've already done it!'

Next, Duma anointed her with oil and felt the Lord say, 'Stretch yourself on this girl.' As he did so, life poured out of him, the girl coughed and sat up. The women fled in terror. Duma himself had to be carried out and seemed to be unconscious for three days. For a month, he had no strength, then suddenly his faculties were fully restored.

Duma told me that often strength drained from him when he prayed for people. Every Wednesday at Umgeni Road was a day of prayer and fasting. The prayer team were people trusted, trained and appointed by Duma; you couldn't just turn up. They saw every kind of miracle imaginable, but often he was so weakened that he had to be helped home by the deacons.

People came from far and wide. Often, men and women in high office sought his counsel and prayer. At the end of a service or prayer session when people had been helped and sought to thank him, he would just bow his head and say, 'Take your glory, Lord.'

The Apostle Paul in Romans chapter 8:14 says

> *Those who are led by the Spirit of God*
> *are the children of God.*[28]

Not long after this, I was speaking to a packed lecture theatre at Birmingham University. I was leading a student

28. NIV

mission and felt constrained to share Duma's resurrection story recounted here. Many lives were deeply touched that night.

Many of Duma's experiences made a deep impression on me. Once he had been asked to conduct a wedding for a lady in his congregation. He was not at all sure that it was a good thing and sought to dissuade her but she was determined to marry this man. On the day of the wedding, after some singing, he began to speak but instead of leading into the marriage vows, he began to preach fervently. He went on and on as the congregation became more and more restless. After nearly an hour of his preaching, the bridegroom fell to his knees and shouted out, 'Stop the wedding. I am a married man!'

Another time, he was travelling on a bus into the city of Durban, when suddenly the Holy Spirit said to him, 'Get off the bus.' He still had some way to go but simply began to walk down the pavement. After about a mile, he came on a scene of chaos. The bus had been in a crash in which several people had been killed or injured!

Sometimes he was involved in physical healings and sometimes more serious demonic possession was involved. One day he was asked to go to a palatial home owned by a wealthy family. They had a distressing situation with a child who could not be controlled or educated. He was taken inside the house to a padded room with a very solid door with a sliding panel. When he looked in, he could see a pile of blankets on one side. The child was like a wild animal that only ate off the floor. Duma said, 'Please let me into the room' – something the helpers were not keen to do.

As they shut the door, there was a terrible scream as the child raced from under the blankets and picked him up as if he were a soft toy and threw him onto the ground. Duma leapt to his feet and spoke to the demons in the name of Jesus and a miraculous, total deliverance took place. They had to educate and train the child, but complete peace was restored to this troubled household.

My lasting memory of Pastor Duma was how he loved my mother's father, recently widowed and living with us. I can still see them peeling oranges and whispering together, enjoying each other's company. It was not long after he returned to Africa that my grandad died and I had the privilege of sitting through the night with him as he passed peacefully into the presence of Jesus. The fragrance of Duma's life has never left me, and greatly encouraged me in my faith.

Willie Burton's stay at my parents' home had another dramatic outcome. Now in his eighty-fourth year, he was like the Winston Churchill of the church, minus the cigars! He had quite an austere, portly appearance, and wore those half-lens glasses on the end of his nose, that I have always found quite intimidating. A man of letters, highly intelligent and a very gifted water-colour artist. He answered all of his correspondence in a beautiful copperplate hand, and was not afraid to answer difficult theological questions from his vast biblical knowledge.

On first meeting my mother, he went straight to the mantelpiece and took down a postcard that depicted an elephant banging a bass drum, with the inscription *Let everything praise the Lord*. He said, 'You don't really want that, do you, sister?'

He scarcely knew me, but at breakfast on the second day, he turned to me and said, 'Young man, when are you going to get married?'

I may have choked on my cornflakes but I managed what I thought was a smart reply, 'What do you think about Paul's comments in 1 Corinthians 7, especially verses 32-38?'

There followed a long, pregnant pause. Then finally he said, 'One greater than Paul said, *"It's not good for the man to be alone."*'[29]

End of conversation! However, later the next day as I was driving him through thick fog to the coastal town of Clevedon, he suddenly said, '...but whatever you do, make sure it's the right one!' as though he was continuing the conversation from the previous morning's breakfast table. I must confess that this conversation had a dramatic impact on my thinking and prepared the way for so much that was to follow.

Willie himself told me that as an enthusiastic young missionary, he had made his mark in the Belgian Congo and had gone on to South Africa, with the intention of finding a wife. With tears in his eyes he said, 'We had thirty blissful years together before I buried her in the Congo where we had faithfully served the growing churches.'

In his remarkable book, *Signs Following*,[30] he records the fact that he had seen every kind of healing miracle

---

29. Genesis 2:18 NIV
30. W.F.P. (Willie) Burton, *Signs Following* (Revival Library Reprints, 2017)

recorded in the New Testament. The book included copies of x-rays taken in a South African hospital, having been sent there with a life-threatening illness. Before the surgeons could operate, two Christian women came into the ward to pray for him. He never made it to the surgeon's table, the two sets of x-rays testifying to his complete, miraculous healing.

I loved the stories he told me of his early days in the Pentecostal Movement in Britain and of his call to the mission field. One night in Bradford, he had been working with the extraordinary healing evangelist, Smith Wigglesworth. It became very late as they had been praying with people, so Smith invited him back to his house to stay the night. At 4am the bedroom door opened with Smith marching up and down with a glass of water, and declaring, 'Willie, we have been sent to preach the gospel, heal the sick, cast out demons and to wake the sleeping ones.' With that he sloshed his glass of water over the sleeping Willie!

A growing burden for Africa had come upon him, so when news reached him that the great missionary pioneer, C.T. Studd was planning to take a team with him to Africa, he arranged an interview as a prospective candidate. In the course of the interview, Willie felt he should share his own Pentecostal experience with C.T., including his belief in all the spiritual gifts. C.T. Studd said to Willie, 'Come and bring your box of tricks with you.'

Willie said to me, 'How could I work with a man who called the precious gifts of the Holy Spirit a box of tricks!'

And so, rather like Paul and Barnabas separating in Acts 15:36-41, the Congo Evangelist Mission was born. Initially, four men undertook the arduous journey to the Congo. One died on the way and another turned back finding the challenge of even the journey too much. When Willie began to travel through the villages and towns in the Congo with his companion Jimmy Salter, they often came upon places where human meat was hanging in the dwelling. Cannibalism was rife in the country. He said to me that the only thing that saved their lives was that when they preached and prayed for sick people, miracles of healing repeatedly happened. It was often disconcerting to see men licking their lips and staring at them when the young evangelists spoke.

One day during our visit together, I had the privilege of taking Mr Burton to the main Pentecostal church in the centre of Bristol, the City Temple which was led for so many years by the charismatic Welshman, Ron Jones. Between the morning service and a Sunday school which Willie had asked to speak at, we sat alone in the pastor's vestry. He began to tell me of an incident that occurred on a visit to Australia.

He had been invited to a massive conference as the guest speaker at a big campground. They had given him a trailer for his accommodation. He said, 'I was feeling quite overwhelmed: me, a tramp preacher from the jungle, with the responsibility of speaking to these thousands of Australians who had gathered. I knelt by the bed, feeling overwhelmed and inadequate, when suddenly Jesus stood in the caravan.'

As Willie spoke to me, tears began to flood down his face! He said, 'The Lord stood behind me and spoke to me words of tremendous reassurance. I didn't see his face, but I saw his feet, and he laid his hand on me, imparting his blessing on me.'

Needless to say, the blessing of God fell upon that convention. Shortly after this very personal encouragement to me embarking on a life of ministry, as he approached the end of his, he was out among the children, holding them spellbound with his conjuring tricks. Yes, he was a conjurer as well. He really did have a box of tricks!

During the latter half of the twentieth century, Dr Martyn Lloyd-Jones was the minister at Westminster Chapel in Buckingham Gate, just a stone's throw from Buckingham Palace in London. To my mind, 'the Doctor', as he was affectionately known, was probably the best biblical expositor it has ever been my privilege to listen to. One thing that he would often say was that along with the Bible, the greatest encouragement in his Christian life, had been the biographies of great Christian men and women throughout the ages. This observation I would wholeheartedly endorse, having been enriched by so many testimonies myself. However, I have had in addition to this, the privilege of knowing many such people, which is why I have included some of their stories in my own story.

Having mentioned some of the men, it would be remiss of me not to mention some of the women. Gladys Aylward, the 'small woman' of China, had tea at my parents' home when I was a young boy. Among her many achievements was stopping the barbaric practice of binding women's feet in China. In my early twenties, I went to hear her preach one night at the Congregational church in Hambrook,

Bristol. You could scarcely get in because of the crowds who gathered to hear this diminutive woman ablaze with the gospel!

I met Corrie ten Boom one day, almost by chance, on the drive of a conference centre in Holland. It was wonderful to talk with her as her life story and books had a great impact on me and I was just embarking on extensive travel behind the iron curtain.

Irene Webster-Smith, of the Japan Evangelistic Band, took the gospel to the heart of the Japanese royal family. I drove with her from a conference near Birmingham in the centre of England and was so enriched with everything she shared with me.

Pat Cook, the great pioneer of Afghanistan, has been a close friend of ours for many years. She set up medical centres for the oppressed women of Afghanistan at no small risk to her own life. We still regularly talk on the phone, although we live on opposite sides of the world.

Jean Darnall, the great American evangelist, shared so much with us in Bristol. She was the link that brought Jimmy Owens with his *Come Together* musical that had such an impact across the UK. Linda and I loved it when she stayed in our home and laid hands and prayed over each of our children.

Some commentators say that a legitimate rendering of Psalm 68:11 is,

The Lord announces the word,
and the women who proclaim it are a mighty throng.[31]

---

31. NIV

Certainly, the New Testament demonstrates this, for example when the prophet Simeon arrives at the consecration of the baby Jesus in Luke chapter 2:22-40, hot on his heels is the prophetess Anna.

Dennis Clarke, Campbell McAlpine and Arthur Wallis were three mentors who had an early and significant impact on my ministry, and I have to say that Beth Clarke, Shelagh McAlpine and Eileen Wallis were equally important. It was through Shelagh that I received a remarkable prophetic word to step out into my future ministry.[32]

---

32. Shelagh's prophecy is on page 71, Chapter 7 of this book

Chapter 10

The Festival of Light

It was during a committee meeting of our Tell Bristol ministry that my attention was drawn to a front-page article in the *Bristol Evening Post* newspaper. It announced the grand opening of the first sex shop in the Broadmead shopping centre: 'Anne Summers'. Many dignitaries and members of the press were invited for the 'cutting of the tape' the following day. I immediately felt prompted to turn up, even though uninvited.

As I drove along the Inner Ring Road around lunchtime, I noticed a crowd and reporters on the pavement, so I swiftly parked and joined them outside the shop. I approached two reporters and gave an impromptu interview on the pavement. They both said, 'Why don't you go inside? The TV cameras are in there.' I said I didn't have an invitation, but they encouraged me to push my way in through the crowd and I managed to achieve a clear view of the proceedings.

The very attractive Anne Summers was introduced, a beautifully dressed blonde in her late twenties. She explained to us that this was a sparkling new development, not to be confused with the down-at-heel cinemas and shops in back streets inhabited by men in grubby raincoats. No, this was a fantastic educational project, designed to help people in their relationships.

The brief talk over, the host invited questions, so I immediately took to the floor. I pointed out that this was in fact a money-making enterprise, not an educational project, and that a lot of people were concerned that it was simply the thin end of the wedge, preparing the way for more sinister pornography, as was currently being experienced in Denmark and Sweden.

Pandemonium broke out. The two TV crews homed in on me, both BBC and ITV. The host had to stop the questions, and Anne Summers came off the platform and pushed her way into the interviews I was doing for our national TV networks. The front cover on the *Evening Post* read, *Anne Challenged by Evangelist!* I also managed to get on the television evening news, and a door opened for me with the media, with regular opportunities in the coming days.

An interesting postscript to this incident was that some months later, the *Daily Express*, one of our national newspapers, devoted the whole of its back cover to a detailed story under the caption: *Anne Fights for Her Name!* It had gone the way I said it would, and she now desperately wanted to disassociate herself from it.

This was all a fitting prelude for events that would hit us at the beginning of the Seventies and lead to the Festival of Light. This is what happened: a missionary friend, Peter Hill, had returned from service in India and was alarmed to see the moral landslide engulfing Britain in the wake of the Sixties' liberation of 'sex, drugs and rock and roll'. He began to call for action and soon came to the attention of some powerful media figures. A prominent commentator in the British media, Malcolm Muggeridge, got right behind him and I believe it was Saint Mug, as he was often called, who coined the title Nationwide Festival of Light. Equally prominent Mary Whitehouse, a moral crusader that the media loved to hate, also got on board, as well as many other national Christian leaders.

The main event of the Festival of Light was to be a huge demonstration in the heart of London in Trafalgar Square, followed by a massive march to Hyde Park and then an even bigger festival in Hyde Park. But there was so much more. Public meetings were held all over the country and countless newspaper columns and radio and television interviews were generated. Opposition was strong which simply added fuel to the fire and there was much public debate.

I was drawn onto a steering committee, meeting in an East End Anglican church, hosted by the vicar, Eddie Stride. Our chairman was Colonel Orde Dobbie, son of the British General Sir William Dobbie. Malcolm Muggeridge pitched an idea which was enthusiastically taken up, 'Why not light the original Armada beacons all across the country?' This was to happen before the main London events and had a lot of important symbolism and enthusiastic support. The original beacons had been lit from county to county as a warning when the Spanish Armada was coming up the English Channel to face Sir Francis Drake's fleet.

This would all culminate in a massed march, public rally in Trafalgar Square and a huge open-air event in Hyde Park. As we prayed and planned, the whole project developed a life of its own, beyond anything we had even imagined. I was all over the country, addressing public meetings, having radio interviews and appearing on TV. Linda and I had married on May 15th, 1971 and our first baby, Amanda, arrived a year later on April 19th, 1972. Thus our married life got off to a tumultuous start as I had to travel all over the country. Orde Dobbie had pulled strings to get a special telephone line put into the accommodation where we rented two rooms in an elderly lady's house. Linda was pregnant and we had very little money but somehow we managed. In fact, we prospered because the project caught the public imagination – and not just the Christian public. I had several months of incredible opportunity.

There was also a lot of opposition! The night we publicly launched the Festival of Light in Westminster Central Hall, opposite the Houses of Parliament and Westminster Abbey, it seemed that all hell broke loose. All of us speakers, which included Cliff Richard, the Bishop of Stepney and a host of other prominent people were on the platform, when groups of Gay activists in all sorts of chains and fancy dress rushed among the crowd of some 3,000, yelling and screaming!

I remember being summoned to a TV studio in Plymouth to defend the Festival of Light in a debate with an Anglican vicar who had called us a 'Festival of Darkness'. Another time, at Lancaster Town Hall with the Lord Mayor, the Bishop and various dignitaries, I had to quieten a man yelling abuse from the front row. The mayor leaned across and said to me, 'Pray for us. He's one of our city councillors.'

Not all our encounters were hostile. I was invited to address the Gay Liberation Society in both Bristol and Bath universities; I was well received and we had some positive debate. It was clear to me that through the Festival of Light, we Christians were well and truly out of the closet and into the public arena.

Operation Beacon was a huge success. I was present at the lighting of the beacon on a prominent hill behind Portsmouth, one of Britain's important naval bases. We had a great crowd of around 2,000, and we joined in very specific prayer for our nation. At the same time, beacons were lit all over the country, some at large gatherings and others in smaller rural communities. Either way, it made the national news again.

Any of us who were present on the great day at Trafalgar Square will never forget it. We later received a Christmas card with an amazing panoramic photograph of the crowd that brought London to a standstill. The incredible march to Hyde Park was led by the cross-carrying Arthur Blessitt, whose arrival in the UK coincided with our events. Probably as many as 100,000 people gathered in Hyde Park, and a highlight for me was when Arthur, in his inimitable way, preached the gospel, and at his appeal people everywhere, including a number of the police on duty, got on their knees.

As I reflected on all these events, I knew something significant had happened. We were initially there to protest about one thing, the moral degeneracy that we were witnessing. But I feel the Lord had another agenda! I believe something in the spiritual realm over London and our nation was broken, which we are still benefiting from today.

Just think of the incredible numbers of churches that have sprung up across the capital, many of them with thousands of members. They range from the great initiatives inspired by Holy Trinity Brompton, the birthplace of Alpha, to many of the black Pentecostal churches that are dramatically impacting our communities. When asked by one of the guys in his squash club how many members his church had, Revd Nicky Gumbel told him, 5,000. The guy said, 'Jesus!'

Quick as a flash, Nicky acknowledged that, 'Yes, Jesus is there too.'

I have mentioned that as a result of all this, many great opportunities came our way. We learned how to handle all sorts of situations wisely and creatively. My friend, Malcolm Widdecombe (the vicar of Pip'n'Jay) and I were frequently approached by *Points West*, a popular news programme on the BBC.

I remember fondly how Malcolm demonstrated such a fantastic gift for turning a potentially difficult interview to great advantage. A petrol station near the Bristol city centre decided to use a new approach to increase their market share; they employed some attractive girls as topless petrol pump attendants. Initial footage of a long queue of cars waiting to get onto the forecourt then switched to Malcolm in the studio. The presenter said, 'Well, Reverend Widdecombe, what is your church doing about all this?'

Wid's answer, 'We're praying for a sharp frost.'

Even the interviewer couldn't stop laughing.

Chapter 11

Travelling Man

After leaving my employment in 1966, I immediately formed a close friendship with Hugh and Rosemary Thompson. Hugh was a well-known children's evangelist and a gifted Bible teacher. He had abandoned a promising career, training to be a doctor – and they were now living a life of faith, as I was. We had a lot in common.

He and his wife, Rosemary, had a burden for the council housing estates around Bristol, and when they moved onto the Patchway estate, next to the huge Rolls Royce Aero Engines plant, I was a frequent visitor to their home. His growing family meant I had first-hand experience of the life of being responsible for young children while I was still single. We worked together on special missions during the summer, one based on the Patchway estate where they lived, another based in the Little Stoke Baptist Church nearby, and another on my own Blackhorse estate.

Interestingly, I have just been corresponding with one of our first converts from the mission in Patchway. We had pitched a tent adjacent to the Youth Centre, and I lived in a caravan on site. Glenys was in her late teens, and she later met her husband, Simon Hart, through our work. As a brand-new Christian, when the mission was over, she used to meet with us in the home of an older lady who lived opposite the Youth Centre. To renew our friendship after all these years and to see all that she and her husband have accomplished for the Kingdom of God has been a great encouragement to me. It's what the New Testament calls *fruit that remains* . . .[33]

It was through Hugh that I took my first trip outside the British Isles. He wanted to go to Holland for a week-long conference with a Dutch ministry that published a magazine called *Power from on High*. This group was majoring on the restoration of spiritual gifts in the modern church and taught us a great deal about healing and deliverance. Not long after the conference, we were invited to return at their expense so that they might record all the teaching tapes in the English language.

It was while I was there that I met, very briefly, one of my heroes, Corrie Ten Boom. Also, I heard a great deal about another Dutch pioneer, Brother Andrew, of the Open Doors ministry. This extraordinary man was deliberately targeting all the closed countries in the world, especially those that at that time were behind the Iron Curtain. I lapped up everything I could about his ministry. It was through Andrew that I learned about spiritual authority, the power of 'binding and loosing', that enabled him to penetrate some of the most closed countries in the world. Later, I would connect with members of his team as I travelled down into Eastern Europe. I was also privileged to host him at one of our big events in Bristol. His book *God's Smuggler*[34] was a game-changer!

---

33. John 15:1-8 NIV
34. Elizabeth Sherill, *God's Smuggler* (John Murray Press, reissued by Hodder & Stoughton, 2002)

However, the first country that I became deeply involved with was Norway, a place that I knew nothing about, and I don't think I had ever prayed for. Some extraordinary factors took me to this amazing country. Out of the blue, a letter came from a young Bible college student in London called Tore Lende. He had been listening to some lectures from my friend, Roger Forster, who later headed up the Ichthus network of churches. Roger's teaching so inspired Tore that he asked him if he would consider coming to his home country of Norway. As was usual in those days, Roger was booked up into the foreseeable future, without a window of opportunity. Instead, he gave him my name and address as a possible alternative.

So one day, I received a strange letter which I wish I had retained. It said something like, 'I am a young Bible student in London with very little money or influence. However, I feel we need your ministry in our country. I can't promise you a lot of engagements or any money to help with your travel, but I feel it is important that you come.'

I'm ashamed to say, I laughed when I read this. So much so that when I met my prayer partners that evening, I read the letter to them, and we all laughed together. I really didn't take this unusual request seriously. The next morning, I had a huge surprise! (How does the Lord orchestrate these things?) A copy of our newspaper, the *Daily Telegraph*, landed on our doormat along with the new, weekend colour supplement. This magazine was spread out on my desk, and I was just flicking through the pages when I reached the back cover. The whole of this cover was a magnificent, Alpine-like snow scene with the bold words emblazoned across it: *Consider Norway for a minute!*

In moments I was on my knees by my bed with the picture spread out before me as I asked the Lord for forgiveness that I had treated this matter so disdainfully. I knew that I must make a tentative response so I sent a reply to Tore saying it would be good if we could meet up sometime. I mentioned that I had a series of holiday conferences in front of me in Cornwall and Devon over several weeks. His response was could he come immediately and, with that, he hitch-hiked to Newquay, a journey of some 250 miles and we met for the first time.

Tore and I instantly bonded and I knew the Lord had a specific purpose in this. I encouraged him to come and see what my team was involved in, to get a better idea if I would be suitable for his country. A mission was planned after my holiday conferences based at the Little Stoke Baptist Church, north of Bristol. Tore joined us for a week and was quite blown away by all that happened. We got together with our diaries, and I said my first opportunity was the month of November.

He agreed to meet me in the southern city of Stavanger, and I began to explore my travel options. When you have no money or even potential fixed income, it's difficult to make plans! The cheapest way was on a Bergen Line ship from Newcastle to Stavanger. The one-way ticket was £10, sharing a 10-berth cabin in the bowels of the ship. I shared this cabin with a group of drunk guys rushing in and out all night and was relieved when we berthed in Stavanger. A new adventure was about to begin!

Tore first apologised that he couldn't take me to his home as his parents wouldn't approve of me. Norway, back then, was a Lutheran country. To be Norwegian was to be Lutheran. It didn't mean that they were all dedicated Christians, but they were very wary of anyone who didn't fit into their traditional mould. So Tore put me in a lonely motel – I was the only guest – and it was winter like I had never experienced before. Deep snow and very, very cold. He had arranged two meetings with the Student Christian Union from the University of Stavanger. It was my first experience of speaking through an interpreter and, at first, the students seemed very suspicious of me.

The next night, things warmed up and I felt I was making some headway. Then we had to leave and begin a very uncertain journey across the south of the country to the capital, Oslo. This took several days as Tore was trying to open doors for us and we slept on various relatives' couches. Nothing happened, and I started to feel quite anxious. Fortunately, before I had left for Norway, God had given me a promise from Psalm 37:5,

> *Commit your way to the LORD, trust also in Him,*
> *and he shall bring it to pass.*[35]

I had received this three times from different sources and was convinced it would happen. Tore had one more tentative engagement, at a school further north on the west coast, in a place called Volda. When we came to Oslo, which was so bitterly cold I got a headache just walking down the street, we went to the largest Pentecostal church in Oslo and not one individual even spoke to us. Then we were to drive to Volda, a two-day journey, the next morning

---

through very difficult winter conditions. We were living on bananas, and the truth is that any money spent on fuel or accommodation, Tore didn't have. He was borrowing to do this – something that really troubled me.

When we arrived at Volda, I really thought I had come to the end of the earth. We met Jorunn Verlo, the leader of the Christian Fellowship, and she said we were to meet with them the next day, which was Sunday, at 3pm. No accommodation had been arranged and there was no food! Tore put us into a pension house, and I had a very frank talk with him. I said, 'If nothing opens up tomorrow, you must get me back down to Bergen to see if I can get a passage on a ship.'

The next morning, when I awoke, Tore was nowhere to be seen. I had some time in prayer and the Word and felt strangely encouraged. When Tore returned, he said that he had found a church in the town that would like us to visit them and bring a greeting at their morning service. This was a group called *De Frie Evangeliske Forsamlinger* – the Free Evangelical Assemblies, a kind of unusual mix of Christian Brethren and Pentecostal. They also had one of their special evangelists, Knut Selvaag, visiting them for ministry over six weeks. I went with Tore, and although I didn't understand a word, I felt a positive atmosphere.

After Knut's message, I was invited to bring a greeting, so I stood with my interpreter, Tore, and spoke for about five minutes. As I made to sit down, they asked me to continue, and the breakthrough began.

At the end of this service, the elders asked me if I would come back that night and minister to them. A lovely couple asked, 'Where are you staying and where are you going for lunch?' We replied that we had nowhere. So they prevailed upon us to go home with them.

That afternoon I ministered to a group of the students in the teacher-training college, and immediately I knew we must have more time with them. Many of them came to the church where I was speaking, and the elders asked me afterwards if I would stay for the whole week. The Holy Spirit began to move powerfully. We had special student meetings during the daytime, and we packed the little chapel at night.

When we got to the end of the week, we baptised a number of people, but the one who most impressed me was Jorunn Verlo! She knew she was to be baptised but faced immense conflict. She could no longer be the president of the Christian Fellowship and she wouldn't be allowed to teach Religious Studies, her main subject in Education. Her parents pleaded with her on the phone not to do this as she had been baptised as a baby in the Lutheran tradition. But she was determined, and although it was like conducting a funeral, she went ahead. Her life was transformed and in letters sent to me in England, I was thrilled to hear of her spiritual progress.

Sometime later, I was a guest speaker at the Baptist church in Bergen and in the middle of my talk, the Holy Spirit fell on Jorunn, and she began to speak in other tongues for the first time. These things didn't usually happen in a Baptist church!

During our week in Volda, at the Sunday evening service, the elders again approached me and asked if I could stay for another week. I agreed but pointed out that the next Sunday had to be my last day as I had commitments in the UK the following weekend. They took the main Town Hall in the community for three nights and invited all the churches. I will probably never know all the outcomes of my time there, but what happened on the last Sunday was very special. Mathias Stove, an elder statesman of the church network, had returned home. He had been a pioneer missionary and still ministered across the nation. He hadn't been present during my meetings but he came onto the platform and embraced me in front of everyone. He said to them, 'I want you to know that I will open the door to all our churches across this country.'

Then he prayed a wonderful prayer of blessing over me and Tore, who had done a great job of interpreting for me. At the end of the service, the elders gathered round and blessed us. They reimbursed Tore for all his costs; gave me a very generous gift; then said, 'We have arranged for you to fly to Bergen, and you will be met at the airport by friends from our main church there. They are booking you a passage on the ship from Bergen to Newcastle, but they would like you to speak at the church, mid-week, before you go.'

Little did I know that the members of the Kristing family who met me would become our good friends and we would have many happy times of ministry with them. I was even invited to speak at the Bergen 600 citywide celebration in the King Håkon's Hall, when the meeting was preceded with a great torchlight procession through the streets of the city!

Another bonus was unforeseen. A very gifted Bible teacher from London was also in the city, and he arranged to meet me at his hotel before I embarked on my voyage home. His name was Lance Lambert, founder of Halford House, Richmond, and subsequent expert on Israel, ending his days living in Jerusalem in prayer partnership with Derek Prince. Lance and I became firm friends and I was invited on numerous occasions to speak at Halford House. (In the next chapter, I describe the impact of his ministry on the churches in Bristol and on me personally.)

In the years that followed, I travelled frequently to Norway, often supporting existing churches and many others built on a house-church model. We had at least two joint holiday conferences, where we took a group of people from the UK to link up with groups of Norwegian Christians. Early in our married life, Linda, and later our children, travelled with me to Norway, sometimes with other members of our community.

We often had people from Scandinavia join us at special conferences in the UK. We had the privilege of hosting The Børud Gang, a remarkable family group of musicians. This tradition has continued through our New Generation Church in Sidcup, who frequently host the Euroclass team and also work at their Apostolic Centre in Denmark.

Two incidents in Norway and Denmark had a deep impact on me. The first happened in the south of Norway as I was returning from a trip into the Communist Bloc. My friend and colleague, John Noble, and I had been travelling together and we took a ferry from Poland into Sweden. When we arrived in Oslo, we parted company as he needed to drive back through Europe to get to England. I had a series of engagements across the south of Norway, and everywhere I went, people wanted a report of the progress of the Church behind the Iron Curtain.

When I arrived in Flekkefjord, where Tore, my interpreter, was living at the time, a large public meeting had been arranged in the Town Hall. I spent the day in fasting and prayer as I sensed the Lord wanted to say something very significant. I walked up into the densely wooded hills and entered into a dialogue prompted by the Holy Spirit. It all centred in the account of the church in Antioch in Acts chapter 13, and the release of that powerful apostolic team under Paul and Barnabas. The dialogue went like this: 'What is the real need of the Church behind the Iron Curtain?'

I had plenty of illustrations from my travels in Yugoslavia, Romania, Czechoslovakia, Hungary and Poland, so I said, 'Do they need money?'

The answer of course, is yes, as Communism had impoverished most of them. Imagine being, as I was, the only person in a church of 500 people in Romania who drove a car!

'Do they need clothes and equipment?'

Of course they do. I had risked my neck smuggling a consignment of short-wave radios from Richard Wurmbrand's organisation. Jim Dixon and I had taken a printing press for the Russian Church right up to the Czech border with Russia.

'Do they need Bibles and Christian literature?'

Yes, they do.

On my first trip into Eastern Europe I was travelling through Romania. Everywhere I went, the churches would assign someone to travel with me, if they could. A delightful young doctor named Nick Gorgitza told me he was busy translating an English book by a prominent Christian author. I knew that this particular book would not be very helpful to him, so I asked him why he was doing this. He said, 'It's the only book I have.'

I made sure I got some great books sent through to him on my return to England.

Later, my friend Barney Coombs translated a very helpful book on the Holy Spirit for Czechoslovakia. We managed to secrete 5,000 copies of this in Peter Tophill's VW Corvette. Great for the job! I couldn't help but say that, in Britain at that time, virtually every home had a Bible, but had that brought revival? What of the shelves of unread Christian books in many homes?

That night in Flekkefjord, I gave the people the answer that the Holy Spirit gave to me. God wants you to become an Antioch! He wants our churches to become a breeding ground for future apostles and prophets who can reproduce powerful New Testament churches all over the globe. We must not imagine that if we give generously to the offering tonight, that we have absolved ourselves! The miraculous growth of the Early Church was fuelled by men and women of the stature of Paul and Barnabas.

When I returned to the UK, I carried this message everywhere. I remember sharing it at Basingstoke Baptist Church where my friend Barney Coombs was the pastor. They took it seriously and Barney later testified in his biography how much the development of the Salt and Light Ministries network had been influenced by this.

The second incident happened on my way home from Norway with Linda and the children. I had decided we should return briefly through Denmark, as a special conference had been arranged with Brother Andrew and Loren Cunningham, Head of Youth with a Mission (YWAM), as guest speakers. I remember the one word that I felt was crucial to our future. It came from the great Loren Cunningham, 'So many people concentrate on the breadth of the ministry; consequently it is shallow. If we will take care of the depth of our ministry, God will take care of its breadth.'

This word was to shape so much of our ministry in the coming days!

Chapter 12

Lance

My dear friend Lance Lambert died in 2015 in Jerusalem where he had made his home during the latter period of his life. For many, he was a leading authority on Judaism, as well as a phenomenal Bible teacher. We lost touch in later years, apart from a special lunch in Auckland that Linda and I held in our home when Lance was on a speaking tour in New Zealand. But for me, he was always the Apostle of Halford House in Richmond, London, and a huge influence on my growing faith. Following our meeting in a hotel in Bergen at the end of my first visit to Norway, we agreed to meet up in Richmond on his return; and a rich and, I believe, mutually edifying relationship was established.

He regularly invited me to stay at Halford House and speak to its growing congregation. We loved hanging out together and sharing with the many international students living there. Also, I encouraged him to come to Bristol and several visits stand out in my memory. Over two nights I got him to share the Halford House story which completely blew our minds. In our sceptical society it is such a remarkable account of faith in God.

I also introduced him to the congregation at Pip'n'Jay and he became a firm favourite there. One occasion particularly stands out in my mind. Malcolm Widdecombe, priest in charge of Pip'n'Jay, and a few chosen leaders, met with

Lance for the day in the old vicarage at the top of the Old Market. Lance expounded the opening chapters of Genesis and the concluding chapters of the book of Revelation in a way that I had never heard before or since. There was also intense discussion and an unfolding of Paul's understanding of the Jewish question in Romans, which is still foundational to what I believe today.

As for Halford House, let me whet your appetite. The story has been written down, but never published, to my knowledge. He told me that publishers who approached him felt it could be more successful than David Wilkerson's *The Cross and the Switchblade*, probably the biggest grossing Christian book of all time, but Lance and his elders felt a restraint in proceeding with this.

The story begins with Lance himself whose parents were evidently anti-Jewish and anti-Christian. He told me that at twelve years of age, he didn't even know the Lord's Prayer. There followed a remarkable odyssey to faith throughout his teens. He began to have angelic visitations. After some years, he said that the Lord told him, 'I will no longer speak to you in this way', but by now he was firmly established in his Christian faith.

At Duke Street Baptist Church in Richmond, under the mentoring of an outstanding leader, Dr Alan Redpath, he began to prepare for missionary service with a focus on China. During this time, he began to re-think his understanding of the Church and was greatly influenced by the teaching of T. Austin Sparks and subsequently the great Chinese teacher, Watchman Nee. With a like-minded group of young people, he began to meet in a more 'church in the house' context, and so the Halford House adventure began.

One incident which is especially relevant in the light of Lance's own angelic visitations, happened in this earlier period. He had cause to visit an elderly Christian missionary who was busy sewing at the table in her parlour as Lance talked with her. Without warning, her sewing machine broke down, much to the lady's consternation. She said to him, 'Lance, what can we do? I am an elderly lady who knows nothing about fixing sewing machines and you are a young man in a similar plight. We must pray!' With that, she began to call on the Lord's name, invoking the angels according to the promise in Hebrews 1:14,

> *Are not all angels ministering spirits*
> *sent to serve those who will inherit salvation?*[36]

As the prayer was quite lengthy, Lance began to interrupt her, but she interjected, 'Shush, Lance, give the angels time!'

Dumbfounded, Lance watched as a few minutes later she began sewing again as if nothing had happened. This kind of supernatural intervention is characteristic of the extraordinary happenings that seemed to occur frequently in the development of Halford House.

When Lance and the enthusiastic young people surrounding him first became aware of Halford House, it was a decaying Queen Anne mansion in the heart of Richmond, fronting onto the street but with a substantial garden, developed as

36. NIV

allotments for growing vegetables. After much prayer and negotiation, the house was purchased for £400. In later years, I could not believe that such a valuable asset was purchased for such a meagre sum!

Lance was a tall, distinguished and cultured man who became well known to the trades people in the town and especially the antiques dealers. Under Lance's leadership, the emerging church determined to restore the old house to its former glory. This was how I came to know it. One night, I was invited to speak at an evening Bible study held in the library. This was a glorious room with a full-size grand piano and almost the whole of one wall was dominated by a huge gilt-framed copy of Constable's *Corn Field*, the original of which is in the National Gallery. Lance told me that while he was walking through the town one day, he met an antiques dealer who said, 'I've got something for you.' Against a wall at the back of the shop, hidden away behind some heavy furniture was this painting. The dealer sold it to Lance for just £10. Later investigation found that much of the painting was by Constable's students under his supervision. It was very valuable but approaches by various art authorities were firmly rebuffed.

The house was developed on two sides. One held the library, a beautifully restored meeting room, a dining room and Lance's unique study where I spent many happy hours. The other side of the house had rooms available to international students doing special training courses, and, as a guest speaker, I often stayed there.

The main builder, a classic Cockney who I will call Bill, was not a Christian, but was happy to supervise the many different projects because he was convinced that his employers were well-off, if somewhat bizarre, Christian people. He was accustomed to saying, when a bill fell due, 'I'm sure you'll pray about it'.

One day the truth was revealed! A substantial invoice for subcontracted work had been received for £1,500, a lot of money in those days. Lance called for an emergency mid-week prayer meeting at lunchtime in the library. They didn't have the money and their prayers carried a particular urgency. Bill, who was used to coming in and out of the house at will, opened the front door and whistled his way up the stairs. He opened the door to the library where they were praying and suddenly everything became clear: they really didn't have the money and they were on their knees praying for it!

Ashen-faced, he stumbled down the stairs. Inside the front door, on a carpet behind the letterbox, was a pile of pound notes. He scooped up an armful, dashed up the stairs, through the library doors and declared, 'You can stop praying. It's come!'

It was the needed £1,500.

There were so many stories like this. I must tell you one or two that stand out in my memory. Lance and his colleagues didn't believe in having insurance; they went to a higher power. On at least two occasions they had divine protection on what could have resulted in serious injury or fatality. Lance was working in his study one day when he heard a tremendous crash on the paving stones outside his window. Bill had fallen from the roof while repairing the

Queen Anne chimneys. He fell some seventy feet, picked himself up and dusted his trousers without any sign of injury.

Something similar happened in the final stages of restoring the meeting room. There was a large pile of bent back chairs inverted on one another and standing like a pyramid in the centre of the room. Another contractor, who needed to speak to Bill, came up the stairs and called him, as he had climbed out through a skylight in the centre of the room to do a roof repair. Lance heard a commotion and ran up the stairs to find the contractor, open-mouthed, gazing at Bill sitting astride the top-most chair in the pyramid. He said, 'I called Bill, and he stepped back in, onto the ladder, missed his step and fell, but he didn't fall normal. He just floated like a feather!'

Everywhere you looked in Halford House seemed like a glorious representation of the Kingdom of God. Everything was birthed in prayer. One day, in the beautifully restored gardens, Lance proudly showed me three delightful swing couches with canopies over them. He had been concerned for the retired missionaries who used to enjoy the garden, so he prayed for special chairs. In a matter of days, not one, but three of these arrived from an anonymous donor.

One Sunday morning, I was speaking at the morning service and met a TV actor from the popular *Z Cars* series on the stairs. He said to me, 'Every time I walk into this house I want to worship.' That's how I felt. Uplifted, edified, before a hymn was sung or a word spoken. For someone like me from a new church tradition, who often had to use school halls and the like for our meetings, it was such a refreshing experience.

126

My last memory of Halford House was somewhat tinged with sadness. Lance had become increasingly involved with Israel and happened to be there during the dramatic events of the Six-Day War when Israel so expertly rebuffed the attacks of the nations surrounding it. During this time, Lance was part of some intensive intercession with a like-minded group of prayer warriors. One of them brought a prophecy that was largely accepted by the group he was with.

On his return to England, he was so concerned about this word that he asked reputable Christian leaders to gather with him at Halford House to weigh it. In essence, it said that the Six-Day War was just the prelude to an imminent all-out confrontation with Russia. There must have been more than a hundred leaders present and it fell to my lot as a recognised prophet to challenge what was said. I fully understood what it must have meant for Lance to be present during the intensity of those days, but I felt a definite check about spreading this message in the nation as I had no witness that it was true. It did prove to be a substantial red herring.

I mentioned earlier the help I received from Lance's teaching on Romans, especially with regard to the place that the nation of Israel holds in the purposes of God. I had been troubled by the phrase *And in this way all Israel will be saved.*[37] I felt this could not possibly be true historically or futuristically if taken as an absolutely literal statement. In response to this, Lance took us first to Romans 2 to define what Paul meant by Israel. There are several surprising statements in this chapter, but the essence of what Paul says is that true Jewishness is not based on external

---

37. Romans 11:26 NIV

qualifications, but inward responses – that is, circumcision of the heart. Gentiles who walk righteously can be included as much as Jews who do the same.

A man is not a Jew if he is only one outwardly,
nor is circumcision merely outward and physical.[38]

Some commentators speak of so-called 'Replacement Theology', proposing that God's purpose is not centred on the Jews anymore, but the Body of Christ, the Church. The term I prefer to use is 'Inclusion Theology'. Charting Paul's teaching through Romans 9, 10 and 11, he talks of the tragic loss of his own people, and says that as Gentiles, we have been grafted into this amazing vine. But then he declares what the inclusion of the Jews might mean! It is all conditional as in Romans 11:23,

If they do not persist in unbelief, they will be grafted in,
for God is able to graft them in again.[39]

We know that in Galatians 3:28 Paul says categorically,

There is neither Jew nor Greek . . .
you are all one in Christ Jesus.[40]

In summing up his argument in Romans chapter 11, he declares,

For God has bound everyone over to disobedience
so that he may have mercy on them all.[41]

When I read this, I can only feel that Paul has much more faith for humanity than I do!

38. Romans 2:28 NIV
39. NIV
40. NIV
41. Romans 11:32 NIV

Chapter 13

Eastern Europe

Having begun to travel in the late Sixties to Norway, my attention was drawn to a new challenge – the Iron Curtain countries of Eastern Europe. This was initially inspired by the ministry of Dutchman, Brother Andrew. I was impressed by his team's cassette tapes and subsequently his remarkable biography *God's Smuggler*. Eventually I had the privilege of meeting him in Bristol and hosting a big gathering to hear his amazing story in the Methodist Central Hall. He is one of those people you will never forget!

Andrew's philosophy was this: the barriers that society has erected, particularly those epitomised by the Berlin Wall, are no obstacle to the gospel. He majored on spiritual warfare, showing from the New Testament that we don't wrestle against flesh and blood, but principalities and powers in the spiritual realms,[42] and we are assured of victory in the name of Jesus and through the power of his Holy Spirit. So, as you approach barbed wire fences and men with machine guns, driving a car packed with Bibles and special assistance for the suffering Church, you come as an ambassador of Jesus Christ, unafraid of the obstacles that confront you. Andrew shared story after story of God's amazing deliverance in these circumstances. Later on, his reach went far beyond the Eastern Bloc to oppressed countries all over the world.

---

42. Ephesians 6:12

I was soon to put all this to the test! I felt I should make my first trip down into Europe with my focus on Yugoslavia, Romania and Czechoslovakia. The British and Foreign Bible Society supplied me with a lot of Romanian Bibles, but my main concern was to see for myself and report back to churches in the West, the situation as I found it, with suggestions of how we might help them.

My first challenge was transport. The little Minivan that I had owned since leaving college was not equal to the demands of this journey, so I prayed a great deal about God's provision for me and the costs of the journey. At this time, I had a growing relationship with Malcolm Widdecombe, the priest in charge at Pip'n'Jay in Bristol. One day I was in the city and pulled up at a favourite spot on the Durdham Downs at lunchtime, to pray and read my Bible. I had been invited to speak to Wid's young people in the vicarage that evening, and I wanted to be prepared. I have already explained that I read the Bible consecutively each year and have received remarkable guidance from Scripture. This lunchtime was no exception.

I was reading in the Old Testament book of Numbers and came to the passage at the start of chapter 7 that describes an unusual gift. Each of the leaders of the twelve tribes of Israel brought to Moses six carts with twelve yoke of oxen to pull them. The purpose of this gift was to help the three priestly families who were responsible for the tabernacle that Moses had been commanded to build. It was a special tent for the purposes of worship and sacrifice, and in its centre was the Holy of Holies containing the sacred Ark, which housed the tablets of stone engraved with the ten commandments.

The three priestly families – Gershon, Merari and Kohath were responsible for the care of the tabernacle and also transporting it through the wilderness. However, an important distinction is made: Gershon got two carts and four oxen; Merari, four carts and eight oxen; but the Kohathites received no carts as they were responsible for carrying the Ark and the other sacred objects. As I sat in my car on the Downs, I felt that the Lord clearly spoke to me! Effectively he said, 'You see, son, if you need a car(t) you get one.'

With this, I was able to pray the prayer of faith and knew that he had my need of transport in hand. That evening, I shared with the youth group in Pip'n'Jay's vicarage. At the end of the evening there was much prayer and then they gave me an envelope. It contained the largest gift I had received up until then. I think it was £300, this was in the late Sixties. A friend who owned two garage businesses on the coast near Southsea, Ted Kent, located a suitable upgrade for me. Ted himself had begun to travel into Eastern Europe and gave me excellent advice as well as a very reliable car.

One thing I hadn't thought about was insurance. When I contacted my broker, he assured me that I wouldn't be able to get insurance for those countries and tried to dissuade me from travelling. I knew enough of God's leading to ignore this and continued making my plans. Many people gave me gifts towards the project and when I crossed the Channel to Calais, I thought I had all I needed to accomplish my first missionary journey into Eastern Europe.

I travelled to Holland and met with a member of Brother Andrew's team who gave me an important contact in both

Romania and Czechoslovakia. The first part of my plan was to travel down through Germany and then head to the Operation Mobilisation base in Vienna. It was a long trip, but I eventually managed to locate Dale Rhoton and his team, who gave me a warm welcome. Dale and his wife were leaders of the European division of Operation Mobilisation. What remarkable, sacrificial people they were!

They had a young missionary with them preparing to go into ministry in Turkey at this time, a very dangerous place to go. I felt to give him a gift from my trip funds, which actually would deplete my resources for getting back to the UK, but I knew the Lord would help me when the time came. I just had no idea what a challenge this would prove to be!

My first step was to go into Yugoslavia as a staging post for Romania, my main focus. Remember, my car was packed with Romanian Bibles among other things. I spent a long weekend with a group of young people led by Dr Branco Lovrec, Billy Graham's interpreter there. They travelled with me to a church on the Adriatic coast, but unknown to me, we had to go over a mountain range where deep snow had fallen. I nearly lost the car and perhaps our lives, as we slid on the icy road in front of an oncoming truck. I managed to correct the slide but hit ice at the side of the road, which damaged the right front side of the car. Fortunately, it was still drivable, and I ministered at a church there for the first time in Eastern Europe.

At this time, Yugoslavia was much more open than the rest of Eastern Europe, but then I travelled from Belgrade across the border to my first and only contact in Romania.

When you cross the border for the first time, it's a heart-stopping experience. I had the car full of Bibles! Would they impound them and me as well? Actually, the Bibles remained untouched, but they made a fuss about my car damage. Had I reported this to the police? No, I hadn't, but then, no one else was involved in the accident. In the end, they let me go and I advanced with some trepidation into the centre of Timişoara.

I booked into a modest hotel and wondered how I would make contact with the Christian pastor there. After prayer, I decided to go that evening, asking a taxi driver to take me to the street written on a piece of paper I gave him. He led the way through the darkness to the street in question. I proceeded on foot to find the actual address in a block of flats. With trepidation, I knocked on the door and it was opened by a man who broke into a big grin. He embraced me and whispered into my ear, 'Have you any Bibles?' I knew I was in the right place. We walked back to my car and drove it into a garage space near the flats. 'I'll see this gets unloaded,' he said, and took me back to his simply furnished apartment.

It was such an amazing beginning. I told him that he was my only contact in the country. He responded that they would provide me with someone to go with me across the country. That night I slept well and, in the morning, they introduced me to pastor Simeon Cure. What an amazing man. He had spent several years in prison for the gospel. They gave me a young doctor named Nick Gorgitza to travel with me. He was a great companion, and together we travelled to a city called Cluj, a main student centre. We met with student leaders and arranged a special two-day visit on our return journey.

Then we travelled on to Bucharest and visited the Baptist seminary, a very dark place. The president wanted me to visit his home church in the north of the country, but I had no peace about this and distrusted the man himself. Nick and I travelled on to a big church in Constanţa on the Black Sea coast.

When we returned to Cluj, I was looking forward to my meetings with the students. I was housed with an elder of the church who was a lawyer, and his daughter was a gifted interpreter. We met that afternoon so I could discuss my planned talk with her, then I retired for a couple of hours to get some rest. As I lay on the bed, there was an urgent knocking on the door. It was my interpreter. She said, 'There is much trouble. The police have been driving around the streets, surveying our house, and they've been to my father's office. They know about the plans for your meetings.'

I was temporarily thrown by this; then made a rapid decision. I asked her to drive with me quickly to the main road that would lead me to the border with Belgrade in Yugoslavia. I didn't want to put them in any difficulty or danger. She was reluctant to do this and even was willing to travel the whole way with me, but I insisted she didn't. I drove through the night with a brief rest stop.

The next morning, full of apprehension, I drove to the border crossing. Amazingly, I passed almost immediately through without being apprehended. Some weeks later, I received a letter from my new friend Dr Nick Gorgitza. He had written a letter to me in an envelope that had a tiny postcard inside with small, but legible, English writing. He said, 'We were sorry that you had to leave us so suddenly. It was good that you did!' Often, I have reflected on the implications of this statement.

The road from Belgrade across country to the border with Austria is a very difficult one but I felt as free as a bird. More than 400 kilometres of constant potholes and various hazards. You know that you have left Communism behind when you arrive in Austria! I returned to another warm welcome from my friends at the Operation Mobilisation base, and a fresh challenge: Czechoslovakia!

I had been following developments in this important country with some alarm. Under the inspired leadership of Alexander Dubček, the 'Prague Spring' had occurred in which the plucky Czechs had sought to throw off the yoke of Russian oppression. Sadly, this was short-lived. The tanks rolled in, and a progressively ruthless domination of the country took place. Vienna is close to the border city of Bratislava. I had planned to go there as Dale had given me a large consignment of Russian Bibles that they were keen to see safely delivered across the border, but with the cost of my journey and my diminished funds, I thought I had only enough to get me back up through Europe and across the Channel again. I waited for two days, praying for God's provision to arrive, but nothing happened. On the third day I felt: 'You must go and trust me to provide for you.'

Feeling quite anxious, on a very wet afternoon, I headed for the border. I had one contact in Sukrova Street, Bratislava, and had no idea where this was in the second largest city in the country. My crossing of the border, with all its customary intimidation, passed without incident. I drove into the city and sat in a car park praying for guidance. If you ask for directions, you must be very careful as you don't know who you may be talking to. So I simply joined the traffic and on my way from the city centre, I suddenly looked up and saw a signpost – Sukrova Street! I was overjoyed. I parked carefully and made my way to another apartment block.

When I rang the bell, an older man opened the door and immediately smiled at me. He had perfect English as he and his wife had once studied at the Glasgow Bible Institute in Scotland. When he learned that I was carrying Russian Bibles, he was even more thrilled. He told me that the Czech people hated the Russians and to try and improve relationships, they were offered cheap tours on special buses to Moscow. This industrious pastor was using the opportunity to get many of his key people to travel and help the churches there. My consignment could not have been more appropriate.

I spent two delightful days with this couple and visited outlying churches who welcomed us with open arms. On the third day, I planned to leave and head for Prague, the capital. There was only one problem, I had no money to buy petrol and it was quite a long journey. After breakfast, the pastor asked if I could help him. He had some parcels that needed taking to the post office and if I could assist him, he would then point me to the right highway.

When we left the post office, he suddenly turned to me and pushed some Czech currency into my hand. Also, he gave me the address of Christian leaders in the centre of Prague. To stress the uniqueness of this, let me emphasise what had just happened! I have never, ever, received financial support in Eastern Europe, coming as I did in a nice car, European clothes and a watch on my wrist. Coupled with this, I could not change any of this currency at the border. They want marks, dollars or pounds, not Czech korunas! What it meant for me was that I could fill up with petrol and get safely to Prague, then fill again before I crossed the German border.

Writing all this as I am, it must seem strange to younger people who have grown up with smart phones, computers, Google maps and all the technology that we take for granted today. I was raised in a family that had no phone or television! My dad refused to have a phone at home as he was on it so much in his business. As a busy pastor as well, he would say, 'If they really need to be in touch with me, they will come and see me.' And they did. So as I travelled across Europe, I relied on signage, basic maps, and especially God's guidance.

As I approached the beautiful city of Prague, I had no idea how significant this night would be. I had already become painfully aware of the Russian occupation. Driving through forested roads I came across huge encampments of troops and tanks. In fact, I brought back some of the first photographs of the Russian occupation to England. Arriving in the city, I found my way to a central apartment block not far from Wenceslas Square. A Christian family invited me in and made me feel very much at home. They said, 'Tonight is a very important night and we are all going to be watching television.' Apparently, the Czech international ice hockey team was engaged in a game against Russia, I believe in Sweden. They said to me, 'We can't compete with their guns and tanks but if we can beat them in this all-important game before the eyes of the world, it will mean more to us than you can possibly understand!' The dream came true as the Czech team triumphed over the Russians.

What happened next has been imprinted on my memory ever since. I've never witnessed anything like it. We were on the third floor of the apartment block and after the final whistle, windows were flung open and the people began to shout and sing. The most popular song was top of their charts. Essentially, it translated, 'Go home, Ivan. Go home. Natasha is waiting for you.' With that, we all joined the crowds pouring out into the streets and headed for Wenceslas Square. Traffic was at a standstill and as I managed to squeeze into the square with my new friends, I witnessed what it was for a whole city, and indeed the whole nation, to be in an uproar. The singing and swaying, shouting and dancing went on and on.

Then things came to a head. The top of the square was fronted by the National Museum, now pockmarked by Russian machine gun fire. On another side of the square, flanked by smart shops, was the Russian-owned travel agency, Aeroflot. The crowd cheered as they burnt it to the ground and daubed the street with these words: 'Revenge for our Museum.'

Alas, this was the final straw! The huge Russian army took control, and the country was brought to its knees. Dubček was ousted and every department of life was invaded by Russian imperialism. For example, in education, all teachers had to sign statements such as, 'I agree with the Russian liberation of the country' and 'I renounce all religious faith.' My friend, John McFarlane, a Cambridge graduate and brilliant linguist, who worked on the translation of technical books and studied at the University of Prague, told me, 'My professor became a road sweeper and his chair at the university was taken over by a man with no university degree!' This process happened at every level of life. I had witnessed the brave 'Prague Spring'. Now and in subsequent visits, I met a people bowed down by totalitarian rule, with their spirit crushed.

I drove out into Germany the next day, filling my car before I left the country. I still had insufficient funds to get home and, of course, no mobile phone or computer. I had no credit cards either. Before I left Vienna, Dale Rhoton asked me to consider stopping off for an afternoon where he was holding a training conference, I believe in Frankfurt. I was on the ring road, passing near the given address, and somehow managed to locate where they were meeting. Dale was pleased to see me as he had a team of students from Cambridge University, planning to go into Czechoslovakia on a mission trip. He asked me to address the conference, and we had a great time sharing about what was happening there and in the other countries I had visited.

We had afternoon tea and then I hit the road as I was keen to reach England for scheduled meetings with some of the churches that had supported my venture. I said goodbye and left the house, walking to my car parked some way up the street. As I was climbing into the car Dale came running up the street and pushed a hundred deutschmark bill into my hands saying, 'Buy some good German petrol!'

So I made it to the Channel Crossing, landing in Dover, not far from my first meeting with the Christian Fellowship in Canterbury. My reports and ministry were enthusiastically received there, and in other places, and they gave me generous gifts, which greatly facilitated my return to Bristol.

Before my marriage and subsequent call to New Zealand, I made a number of other trips. My first adventure was on my own, perhaps an important step as I had to face the possible outcomes of such a journey. Without going into too much detail, let me mention some of my different travelling companions and some of the things we accomplished.

My great friend, Barney Coombs, head of Salt and Light Ministries, who is now with the Lord, had written an important book on the Holy Spirit, which he had specially translated for the people of Czechoslovakia. We managed to get 5,000 copies safely into the country and engaged in ministry in a variety of places. There was such a desperate need in Eastern Europe for an outpouring of the Holy Spirit.

I made my first trip into Poland with my lifelong friend, John Noble. Then we came home via Scandinavia, addressing meetings in Sweden and Norway, envisioning the churches in the wake of Brother Andrew's book, *God's Smuggler*.

Another old friend, gifted writer and raconteur, Maurice Smith, accompanied me to Hungary. I remember us travelling fairly lightly across the Channel, only to arrive at the home of one of Brother Andrew's team in Holland where our car was loaded to capacity with helpful goods and materials for a leader in Budapest. We laughed a lot as we drove as there was no way of concealing the amount of stuff that we had!

On another trip, I was given a large consignment of bulky short-wave radios by Richard Wurmbrand's organisation. I had to lay them on the back seat of the car and cover them with blankets. I kept one out on view, sitting on the top of the blankets. I shall never forget the border guard, opening the back door of my car and lifting this one radio out with admiration. I believe he said something like 'Great radio', then put it back on top of the hidden pile and waved me through.

A more dangerous adventure I can date accurately, as I was now married and our baby daughter Amanda was just a few weeks old. I was to accompany a new friend, Jim Dixon, who was the managing director of a large printing company in Basingstoke, in transporting a printing press for the underground Church in Russia. This was hair-raising! Linda went to stay with Jim's wife Jean, as we travelled into Poland. We spent a key time with a very gifted woman who had a number of youth groups; she wanted us to stay but we were on a mission, and we travelled on to a town strategically near the Russian border. At night, in an enclosed courtyard, we unloaded the press for Christian leaders who had a border guard in their fellowship. He undertook to make sure the press would travel safely into Russia. I remember our journey on to Warsaw, the Polish capital, because somewhere in a town en route, two men in heavy official overcoats, stepped off the pavement and flagged us down! We were completely clean. Had this happened a couple of days prior to this we could well have ended up in prison. On our way home we went through

East Germany into West Berlin where Jim's company was negotiating to buy the latest presses.

On all of these journeys, significant things happened that I will never forget. In Kraków, John Noble and I stayed with a fine Baptist pastor who was also a gifted scientist working for a state company. He welcomed us to his house and immediately, he and his wife moved out of their bedroom for us. They had family and others staying there too. When they had all gone to work, John and I scoured the kitchen and opened the fridge door. We photographed the contents: one carrot, one stick of celery and a glass of water. It humbled us to be able to give gifts, support and encouragement to such sacrificial leaders. In Kraków, I also visited the Catholic seminary and received an enthusiastic response from the students. I was able to give them a number of important theological books.

In the chapter entitled *Travelling Man*, I have recorded the revelation that God gave me on my way home from Poland through Norway when I asked, 'What is the real need of the Church behind the Iron Curtain?'

Some years later, Linda and I were invited to speak at a conference in West Berlin. We were billeted with a remarkable American army officer, Colonel Eugene Bird. Our time with him was so special. He and his German wife were living in a house built by Albert Speer, Hitler's architect. After the liberation of Europe, Eugene became the Commandant of the Spandau Allied Prison, personally responsible for its most infamous prisoner, Rudolph Hess. Eugene took us all over Berlin, East and West, including a memorable visit to the site of the bunker where Hitler died. (Situated in the hallway of Eugene's house was an icon in a specially protected cabinet. It was an American flag, from the moon landing, given to him by one of the original astronauts, Buzz Aldrin. Eugene told us that this flag was more valuable than the house itself.)

Linda's father was a German paratrooper that she never met and we have never been able to locate. Incarcerated in a prisoner-of-war camp in Derby, he met Linda's mother through a repatriation day-release programme, prior to his return to East Germany. Linda was named after the linden trees on Lindenstrasse, the main boulevard through Berlin. Our time in Berlin was especially significant for Linda.

There is an important footnote to this chapter, in the light of the international conference in Jerusalem in 2020, addressed by Prince Charles and other world leaders. The event was to mark the seventy-five years since the liberation of the Nazi death camp at Auschwitz. During my travels in Eastern Europe, I twice visited this horrific place where the Nazis murdered a million people, most of them Jews. The chill of Auschwitz has never left me, and many times, I have described this to classes of school children and church congregations, highlighting its terrible implications.

I passed one glass show case after another, full of prosthetic limbs from the disabled, spectacles, tresses of women's hair. The displays are overshadowed by the notorious gas chambers. When I was there, busloads of school children were coming from all over Europe, but here is the disturbing finale. We were led into a movie theatre and shown historic footage of the camp and the liberation by the Allied Forces. A pertinent message was given to us.

Remember, these school children were coming from Iron Curtain countries, dominated by Russia. The Russians were keen to tell them, 'This is what we – yes, Russia was part of that liberating army – delivered you from.' As I drove away from Auschwitz, all I could think of were the subsequent atrocities that Stalin inflicted on his own people.

Prince Charles said,

Hatred and intolerance tell new lies, adopt new disguises and still seek new victims. All too often, language is used which turns disagreement into dehumanisation. Words are used as badges of shame to mark others as enemies, to brand those who are different as somehow deviant. All too often virtue seems to be sought through verbal violence. All too often, real violence ensues, and acts of unspeakable cruelty are still perpetrated around the world against people for reasons of their religion, their race, or their beliefs. Knowing, as we do, the darkness to which such behaviour leads, we must be vigilant in discerning these ever-changing threats, we must be fearless in confronting falsehoods, and resolute in resisting words and acts of violence. And we must never rest in seeking to create mutual understanding and respect.[43]

---

43. From the speech by Prince Charles at the World Holocaust Forum staged at Yad Vashem, the World Holocaust Remembrance Centre, January 2020.

Over the years as I have travelled and served in many nations, it's not often that I become aware of the blessing that has followed these endeavours. For example, I felt the most important of my published books was *Baton Change – Releasing the Next Generation,*[44] as it tackles the critical issue of transition in leadership. This book has been published in Indonesia, and also in Argentina for the Spanish-speaking people of South America. More recently I was told that Operation Mobilisation India had published it in English for the Indian continent. I have yet to receive a single report of how these books have fared.

Some years after my adventures in Eastern Europe I received an encouraging follow-up. I have spent a lot of time in California, staying with friends and also ministering in some of the Vineyard churches. Our friends John and Carol Gombos were keen for us to meet some friends of theirs who lived in a beach community south of Los Angeles. We went to stay with Tim and Samona Taylor and the amazing thing was that Samona was from Timişoara and the church where I had made my first delivery of Bibles. In fact, Samona's parents, who were there at the time of my visit, had subsequently come out to live with their daughter's family. They couldn't speak much English, but they were overjoyed to meet me and Linda!

There is a great promise in Ecclesiastes 11 verse 1,

Cast your bread upon the waters, for you will find it after many days.[45]

---

44. Peter Lyne, *Baton Change – Releasing the Next Generation* (Regal Books, 2001)
45. NKJV

And then later, in the same passage it says,

Sow your seed in the morning, and at evening let your hands not be idle, for you do not know which will succeed, whether this or that, or whether both will do equally well.[46]

In the next chapter, Linda has recorded her own amazing story. Our backgrounds could have not been more different. I was part of a happy, stable Christian home where our parents loved each other and loved us. Linda, on the other hand, had a childhood full of instability and uncertainty. You will read how we found each other, and I proposed in three days. We married on May 15th, 1971, a decision we have never regretted. My father married us, and my brother Eric was best man. Our older brother, Alan, played the piano, Barney Coombs led worship and Arthur Wallis preached. On the way out of the service, a friend pushed some money into my hand to spend on the honeymoon. Our life of faith together had begun!

---

46. Ecclesiastes 11:6 NIV

Chapter 14

Linda's Story

I have always been fascinated by doors – the size of them, their shape, the thickness, the colour. The older the door the more fascinating they become. I love nothing better than walking the streets of old cities and towns and communities just looking at doors. Italy was a highlight for me, along with Jerusalem and many parts of France. Not only is it the look of the door that intrigues me, but the stories of lives lived behind those doors, both past and present.

There are four doors that I have walked through that have had a profound effect on my life and future: the first two with some fear and trepidation, the following two with eager anticipation. Let me explain as I pass straight through the second door.

The year was 1965, halfway through the decade of Cliff Richard, The Beatles, Beach Boys, Cilla Black, Sandy Shaw, The Rolling Stones, Chuck Berry, Elvis Presley, and so the list goes on. The incredible music of the time! However, music was far from my thoughts as I was living a nightmare. Just before my seventeenth birthday I discovered I was pregnant! I could not believe this was happening to me. I had previously been going out with a boy whom I had known for two years. The first year we were just friends as he already had a girlfriend. However, the following year our relationship became more serious, and we even talked of marriage.

Although, at the time, I was deeply in love with him, I decided I needed to end this relationship as it had gone beyond where I was feeling comfortable, and I could see a conflict between what I wanted for my life and the reality of where it was headed if I continued down this path. In this, my judgement proved correct as he went on to sire at least seventeen children in the course of his life, taking responsibility for none of them as far as I am aware.

I had taken a job in the town of Rocester in Staffordshire at a place called Barrowhill Hall. I had been hoping to sit my City and Guild Certificate in Cookery there, as it was a subject in which I seemed to shine, according to my teachers at school. They had encouraged me to go there upon leaving school but as I did not want to leave home at the time, I didn't pursue this opportunity; but now seemed the right time.

It turned out that Mrs Drabble had decided to retire from any formal teaching but had happily agreed to take me on to work in her exclusive afternoon tea rooms which served two of the most prestigious private schools in the area. Every weekend, parents would visit their children, and this was the perfect place to bring them. It had the most beautiful rural setting, with immense gardens and lawns. I learned to make fudge and marmalade and use an abundance of beeswax which we made for polishing the tables and the floors. Mealtimes were very lively affairs, especially when their son returned home from university; then there were sparks flying everywhere.

Mrs Drabble had a permanently downturned mouth and a wonderful way of appearing to be looking down on us mere mortals from her lofty perch. I came unstuck a few times. One such occasion was when her very diminutive, mild-mannered husband complimented me on my delicious porridge. She took this to mean that he preferred mine to hers, which led to the silent treatment for some time. Mind you, I was used to that kind of treatment at home, so nothing new there.

Another time she made the unfortunate comment at the table that she was gentry and we were peasants. The next time I was home I shared these thoughts with my mum to get her take on things. I also mentioned the fact that she served lump sugar at the table. My mum replied in typical fashion, 'You tell Mrs Drabble, only horses eat lump sugar.' So I did and she was not best pleased! However, I am grateful that she did teach some wonderful skills which have stood me in good stead over the years.

It was during this time that the harassment from my ex-boyfriend began. It's a funny thing looking back. You wonder how you could allow yourself to be so manipulated and intimidated. Why would you keep everything to yourself and not ask for help? I think shame has a lot to do with it, and somehow feeling you are to blame. After all, you are the one that got into this relationship in the first place, so you have no-one to blame but yourself. You try to manage the situation but the fact is, you often can't!

I came to dread my two days a week at home. I would take my greyhound Philip out for his walks, and I would often be confronted by my ex-boyfriend hiding behind a tree or just seemingly popping up out of nowhere. One time he became so aggressive he almost strangled me. The next day I went to the police station and reported the incident. A statement was taken, and a young police officer was assigned to take me home. He actually asked me for a date but of course I refused; I was too scared of the consequences.

One of the things I loved to do in the evening was dance at the Locarno in Derby. In fact, it was there that I first met my boyfriend. He was the disc jockey and whenever I walked into the room, he would play my favourite song, 'Nadine' by Chuck Berry. He would often leave the platform and come and dance with me. It was during that time that our friendship grew and I began to hang out with him and his friends. I was fifteen years old at the time. But now he had become a different person. At least, he showed a side I had never seen before. My mother always described him as a lovable rogue.

One particular night he cornered me and pulled off my hairpiece, threatening that if I did not meet him at his house the following Wednesday, he would travel to Rocester and cause a scene and humiliate me in front of my employers. I was terrified of this scenario playing out so I agreed to meet him – a decision I would later come to regret. I did meet him outside his house and talking was not on his agenda. I felt like a scared rabbit in the headlights. Walking home later I remember telling God that no matter what he threatened in the future, I would never put myself in that position again. Later, I discovered that he had had to visit the local hospital having damaged himself in some way during our encounter.

This took place on a Wednesday in the middle of February 1965. It was two months later I discovered I was pregnant. I had no idea what was wrong with me; it came as a total shock. The next few months were a nightmare! I moved out of my home into a rented room because my family were ashamed of me, and the neighbours shunned me. I became very sick, bent over in pain; I just wanted to die. In fact, I asked God on more than one occasion to take me to be with him.

As a child I had prayed this prayer many times. I thought how wonderful it would be to be with my heavenly Father who I knew loved me so much. However, he seemed deaf to my pleas for which I am truly grateful. In all my darkness and pain, I never imagined for one moment all that God had in store for me, that he would take me through that 'valley of the shadow of death' and bring me into his glorious presence, but not in a way I could ever have expected.

I often think about people who take their own lives, especially young people. I feel such sadness that they have come to the place where they feel there is no other option but to end it all. If only they were able to trust somebody else with their emotions and seek help to bring them through the dark times. They get caught up in the immediacy of the situation where it seems the only way ahead is to end it all. I totally understand this emotion. I have been there; I have lived through it and I have come out the other side with God's help.

I seriously considered suicide when, after realising I was pregnant, I went to tell James that I would marry him, as I could not think of what else to do. He had previously met me in the street and sensing I was pregnant offered to marry me. He had given me his address as I had no idea where he lived. Later, I stood on his doorstep, only to be humiliated even further when he informed me I was too late, as he had since discovered his girlfriend was also pregnant. I walked away devastated. I just wanted to end it all. I lay on my bed in agony asking God to take me. In fact, I had decided I was just going to lie there and die.

Eventually I was so ill I asked someone to get my mother. She sent the doctor instead, who immediately admitted me to hospital. I couldn't stop throwing up, which lasted for days. The excruciating pain was caused by acute kidney infection. After a week in hospital my mother came and took me home and I was reunited with Philip, my darling greyhound. I was in deep distress. My hair had begun to fall out and the future looked very bleak. I had become huge very quickly and every time I ventured out, I knew I was being judged by those around me.

We had a wonderful friend called Kay Morley, who had been our education officer, and who had visited us on a regular basis when we were children, due to the fact that I had to have so much time off school looking after Mum when she was sick. She suggested I went away to the city of Lincoln in the East Midlands. It is a beautiful cathedral city, not that this meant anything to me at the time, but it did have an Unmarried Mothers' Home which was run by the Anglican church.

It was all arranged and early in 1965 Mrs Morley and I embarked on a journey that, little did I know, would change my life forever. The home was called 'The Quarry'. It was a big daunting Victorian Building. As I stood looking at the imposing door before me, it felt like I was about to enter a prison where there was no escape and, actually, I had no choice in the matter. I had no option but to be there. It was the second door I had no wish to enter.

Once inside I discovered this was a typical institutional place. However, the staff were amazing. I loved the matron; she was so kind. I also became friendly with a lovely elderly retired missionary called Sister Downing. I was placed in the laundry under the care of Mrs Tinker who had lovely twinkling eyes. She was a wonderful caring person. She talked a lot about Jesus as we went about our work.

The girls continually had discussions as to who was a Christian and who was not. I remember being very offended one day when one of the girls suggested that I was not a Christian. That was not how I saw it at all. I had always loved God and wanted to follow him. My grandma was my earliest influence in giving me Christian values and a love for Jesus. It was in her home as a four-year-old, lying in her big scary bed, that I had fallen in love with a picture of Jesus on her bedroom wall. He was surrounded by sheep and carrying a little lamb. I remember asking Jesus if I could be one of his little lambs. I grew up knowing that God was my heavenly Father, even though I had no earthly father. I talked to him every day and I knew he answered my prayers. Well, almost all of them!

It took nearly five years for him to answer my prayer concerning my stepfather Bill, who brought nothing but misery into my life. It was just before my ninth birthday when he finally left. I remember getting down by my bed and thanking God for answering my prayer. When he left, he sent removal men to take all the furniture from the house, leaving us with nothing. However, my four-year-old sister was determined they were not having the blanket chest, so she sat on it swinging her legs. Needless to say, it remained in situ and the men, who were disgusted with the job anyway, were very happy to oblige her. My sister, Karen, still has it to this day, and we often laugh over the incident.

He left our mother broken and sick after months of taunting her over the woman he was seeing, even showing her a present he had bought Mavis for Valentine's Day and asking Mum if she thought Mavis would like it. There was a lot of mental cruelty going on at the time, both for me and Mum. She was having difficulty sleeping at night, so the doctor had prescribed sleeping pills – Bill had even suggested that she might like to take the lot. His best friend, Peter Hicks, on hearing this, was horrified and made a plan to come by every night on his way home from work and give Mum one pill at a time. It was a wonderful act of kindness, looking back. The relief was immense when Bill finally left. We all sighed a corporate sigh of relief!

Mum set to work with a plan and the help of Mr Brooks who owned a second-hand furniture shop on Normanton Road. She was able to furnish all the rooms which she planned to rent out and reduce our own living space down to two rooms: the kitchen and the living room, in which she put a bed-settee which the three of us were to share. It worked wonderfully. Later Karen moved into a box room and very much later I also had my own bedroom. Mum's plan to rent out rooms to paying tenants was a great success and got us through our childhood. We had next to nothing to live on, but we were happier than we had been in years.

Karen, Mum and Linda

Another time that God clearly answered my prayer, apart from all the little ones, was when I was eleven years old. Mum had been terribly sick for ages, suffering from asthma and bronchitis. She would lie down at night and be fighting for her breath. I sat up with her night after night as she struggled to breathe and coughed up all sorts of vile stuff. Many times, I would run to the doctor in the night trying to get him to visit.

This particular time he arrived at 11am as I was preparing the Sunday lunch. He took one look at Mum and immediately went off to arrange for an ambulance to take her to hospital. Of course, in those days there wasn't the convenience of mobile phones; you had to rely on the nearest telephone box, usually located on a street corner.

As the ambulance drove away carrying Mum, I remember falling on my knees crying to God, begging him not to let Mum die, as she was all we had in the world. By a miracle she survived the night, which I later learned she was not expected to do. They had even brought in a lawyer for Mum to sign a will making sure my sister and I were looked after in the event of her death. Wonderfully, she survived! She spent a month in hospital on this occasion and I visited her every night at 7 o'clock, which was the official visiting time. Weekend visiting took place in the afternoons when we were allowed two hours. It was in the days of the matron and rules were very strictly observed.

Karen and I continued at home. Karen remembers one of the tenants agreeing to watch over us, but she obviously couldn't have played a very significant role as I don't even remember her. Apparently, she had suggested sleeping with us; Karen's recollection is that she told her she was too fat. Anyway, I collected the rents, and at one point I actually rented out one of the empty rooms. I felt very grown up, even though I was only eleven. My darling sister

Karen was seven at the time. What a childhood we had, the pair of us!

After a month Mum returned home, although still quite weak. As a reward for all my hard work she bought me a beautiful purple bike. I was so proud of my bike; it was something I had dreamed of for ages. I used to stand outside the bike shop looking in longingly, hoping that the man behind the counter would take pity on me and give me one. Finally, I had my own and I was ecstatic!

A month later, Mum was back in hospital. This time we were not so lucky, as we were sent to a children's home. I remember quite vividly sitting in the office with the man who was running the home as he questioned me as to who had been doing our washing. When I said I had been doing it, he told me that it looked grey. I remember feeling hurt and deflated as I had tried my best – clearly, for him, that was not good enough. I hated that place and was relieved when the time came to go home. I hadn't been allowed to visit Mum in hospital and the independence I had enjoyed previously was gone.

Mum wasn't faring much better as one day I remember her ringing me from a convalescent home where they had sent her, begging me to get her out of there, but what could I do as an eleven-year-old child? Finally, they let us all go home and mercifully we were together again. From that time on, Mum was a semi-invalid, hibernating for much of the winter for fear of being sick again. I was continually having time off school to look after her. It just became the norm.

So why am I saying these things? Because God was as much a part of my life as breathing. I would never have made it through my childhood and teenage years without his help, so for someone to say that I wasn't a Christian made me feel indignant, but it also made me think again and consider my life as it was at this point broken and hopeless. I had no idea that in the next few days my life was going to change dramatically. I was about to step through the third door that would change my life forever and the course of my whole future.

I had agreed to go and see a Billy Graham film with Mrs Tinker and some of the girls. Billy Graham was an incredible American evangelist, very gifted in sharing God's Word in a simple way that everyone could understand. Of course, when I agreed to go I had no idea who he was.

The previous week I had received a great shock, which I guess accounted for my size. It was in the days before ultrasounds when doctors and nurses used something that looked like a metal cone as a listening device to pick up the baby's heartbeat. This particular day, three weeks out from the birth, they picked up two heartbeats; yes, I was having twins! I couldn't believe it. In my heart I had already decided to somehow keep my baby, even though I had no idea how. In those days you were very much on your own, which is why so many babies were put up for adoption. Twins, who would have thought it?

The following week, Mrs Tinker and some of us girls went into the town to the local Baptist church, which was putting on the special event. It felt so great to be doing something different for a change, so we were very excited but also very conscious of our situations. It was obvious where we had come from, but Mrs Tinker set us down at tables together in her usual reassuring way as we waited for the film to begin. Right from the start I was enthralled by Billy Graham's passion for God, his clear message, the words ringing in my heart,

For all have sinned and fall short of the glory of God.[47]

He went on to share how God had sent his only Son into the world to die for us. He said that though our sins were red like scarlet, they would become white as snow,[48] because of Jesus's sacrifice on the cross. John 3:16 says,

For God so loved the world that he gave his only Son,
that whoever believes in him should not perish but
have eternal life.[49]

He said that we could be free from sin and the power that held us captive, that we could have a personal relationship with him. This was everything I had always longed for, to know God in this way. I thought I did but somehow something was missing. As the film came to a close, Billy Graham invited people to get up out of their seats and go forward and receive Christ. I asked Mrs Tinker to pray with me and some of the girls joined in. I felt too conscious of my size to go to the front so I prayed in my seat for God to come and cleanse me and forgive all my sins so I could come into his eternal Kingdom.

I was to discover that this was not just a prayer but a life-changing event. How could a few words spoken from the

---

47. Romans 3:23 NIV
48. Isaiah 1:18 NIV
49. John 3:16 ESV

heart change a life? But it did! I walked out of that place a different person. I felt like I was walking on air! I wanted to shout from the rooftops that I was saved, that I belonged to Jesus! Not even my circumstances could dampen the joy that was filling my heart. I couldn't stop talking about what God had done for me. It was incredible! Yes, I still had to go through all the pain, the humiliation of my circumstances, the disdainful treatment of the staff in the local hospital when I was finally admitted there. I still had to go through the overwhelming sense of loss at the thought of giving up my babies and feeling the decision was being taken out of my hands, regardless of my feelings, but inside my heart was leaping with a sense of inner joy and peace and hope. Yes, for the first time in the midst of all that was happening in my life, I felt hope!

There is a Scripture that says, if we draw near to God, he will draw near to us.[50] Another tells us that he will come as the Comforter, that he will never leave us nor forsake us.[51] I would like to share two incredible experiences that took place at this time.

The first happened around the time I was giving birth. Because I was having twins I wasn't allowed to stay in the caring, safe environment of the home but was sent to the local hospital. The attitude of the staff was very much in keeping with the times, sadly! There were no kind, reassuring words – in fact just the opposite. I was alone and had to bear the consequences of my situation alone.

---

50. James 4:8 ESV
51. Hebrews 13:5 ESV

After trying various ways of inducing me, which would seem archaic today, they finally broke my waters. The intense pain was almost immediate. I didn't realise what had hit me. As for the staff, they pretty well ignored me, even though I was throwing up for most of the night. I remember feeling embarrassed as expectant mothers around me were having visitors. In the end I was too sick to care. At one point during the evening, I called to a nurse as she was passing by the bed and told her I needed to push. She told me not to be so silly, it was far too early for that. However, on examining me, they whipped me off to the birthing room. This was about midnight. It became obvious that it was not going to be a straightforward birth. Both babies were breech and would be coming out bottom first.

As I lay there on my own – the nurse having gone off to find a doctor – I realised I wasn't alone in the room. It was as if the Lord himself had come into the room and was standing beside me. I had an overwhelming sense of peace and his presence. I can't explain the full extent of my feelings or what I experienced that night, but it is as real to me today as it was then, and still brings tears to my eyes as I think of my compassionate Saviour not allowing me to be alone in the extremity of my circumstances.

Shortly after the doctor arrived, he did an episiotomy, making it easier for the babies to be born. At 2.30am David arrived weighing in at 6lb 12ozs and fifteen minutes later Tanya made her way into the world weighing in at 6lb 3ozs. Wow, such big babies for such a little body! They were quickly taken away – something to do with the fact that they were breech and needed special care for three days. From memory I think I had at least fifty-six stitches.

It was agony every time I moved or tried to walk. I had to be taken in a wheelchair to see the babies. It took weeks of pain before I was able to walk normally again.

I decided I wanted to breastfeed my babies, which thankfully I was able to do. I remember when I was finally released from the hospital to be taken back to the home, getting into the ambulance I said to myself, 'I will never let you go!' Back in the home, just to get to the bathroom for me was an absolute mission, as the stitches were so painful, and any kind of movement was excruciating. The babies would be brought to me to breastfeed. They were such special times! While I was recovering in bed, I was given the task of making sanitary towels. Very inspiring!

The next incredible experience happened late one night. By this time, I was now sleeping in a dormitory with all the nursing mums. The only difference for me was that I had two babies to feed. Fortunately, David was a guzzler but Tanya was a slow feeder, so I was always the last to bed and the first one up at 4.30am.

This particular night at midnight I was totally exhausted, and I crawled into bed and started to pray. At that moment, it was just like the Holy Spirit came and enveloped me with his love. I was overwhelmed! The Lord knew exactly what I needed. I had been feeling like I was at the end of myself. I just bathed in his presence and, as it lifted, I put my light on and wrote in my diary: 'the Holy Spirit visited me tonight!' Being a new Christian I really didn't know anything about the Holy Spirit but again the great Comforter was there in the midst of my extremity.

Eventually, the day came for me to leave the home. Many had already had their babies adopted out and gone back to normal life. For me, it wasn't so straightforward. Not everybody wanted twins and to complicate things, their father had African-American blood due to his mother's liaison with an American soldier during the war. Anyway, I was not planning to adopt them out. I wanted to keep them. However, the home had arranged for my babies to be transferred to a children's home in Lowestoft in East Suffolk. Sister Downing accompanied me on this journey.

I won't lie. In one way I was relieved. I was so exhausted, both mentally and physically. My face was full of boils, and I needed sleep, lots of sleep! But it wasn't easy leaving my babies. How could it be? The nurses who took them were lovely and seemed genuinely excited to have them. Later, sitting on the train, heading home to Derby, I mulled over all my mixed emotions. I asked God for help as I didn't know any Christians in Derby and needed to start afresh.

It was strange being home, but I was relieved at the same time. Philip, my greyhound, wasn't there to greet me as my mother had had him put down the week before. I wasn't really able to share my experiences with her or talk about the twins. In fact, I spent the next six months secretly crying for the babies I no longer had, pouring over the beautiful photographs taken days before leaving Lincoln. God was not going to leave me to myself though. He had plans and another miracle was about to take place.

I found myself walking down Normanton Road the following day. I have no idea why on this occasion except to say that much of my life revolved around this incredible road, which I loved and where I felt so at home. This was the road that led to my school and I walked the length of it most days. It was where my mum bought her second-hand furniture after my stepfather left. Mr Bottom's fruit shop was also there, where I acquired my beautiful black and white cat Bunty, and Karen, her tortoiseshell cat Pinky. Annabel's was the shop where I bought a brooch for my mum, after accidently knocking over and breaking one of her ornaments when playing with my balloon. My punishment from my stepfather was a week without television but Mum relented when I gave her the brooch. I can still remember his harsh words as he came through the door and heard the television, 'Why has she got that on?'

Close by, was the Bible and book shop where, as a small child, I had saved my shilling pocket money each week to buy my first Bible, which I still have to this day. It cost 21 shillings and when I had paid 18 shillings the man who owned the shop gave me my Bible. I was so excited I ran all the way to Grandma's to show it to her. Way down the bottom of the road was our favourite cake shop called Bird's. Every Saturday we would go with Mum and pick out one of our favourite cakes. One week it would be a cream puff; another, a chocolate éclair or one of their delicious little trifles. Bird's is an iconic cake shop and can only be found in Derby. Whenever I go to Derby, that is one of my first ports of call. Unfortunately, this particular one has finally closed its doors. I drove by a few years ago with Peter and my sister Karen, not realising that this would be for the very last time. I have never tasted better cakes – a wonderful tribute to my home town, for sure! There was Clark and Pearce, a small department store where every year Mum allowed us to choose two dresses for summer, two dresses for winter and a pair of sandals or shoes depending on the season. We loved that tradition.

Yes, this road held so many wonderful memories. It was the road I walked up and down almost every day of my life. This day was to be no different. There is a wonderful verse in the Bible which says,

I being in the way, the LORD led me.[52]

This particular day he led me to Muriel. She had lived in our home several years before, with her gorgeous little boy Simon. She had since moved into her own home with her growing family of boys. I was so excited to see her again and even more excited to hear what she had to say. She had recently renewed her faith in Jesus and told me about a little Pentecostal church she was attending, Whiston Street Assemblies of God. She asked if I would like to join her there.

Oh, I couldn't believe it – my first full day back home and I had met someone as passionate about their faith as I was. God had provided for me in such a miraculous way. Muriel became my lifeline. I spent night after night with her in her home talking about Jesus. Some nights I would feel like I was floating home. We talked about Jesus returning and when that might be. Could it be tonight? I longed for the moment to come! Somehow, there was a wonder in it all. I still feel that wonder today, as I draw ever closer to the day when I will see 'The One' who in his compassion drew this broken heart to himself. Oh, they were heady days!

52. Genesis 24:27 KJV

I threw myself into everything available. I spent all day Sunday at church, even having lunch there. Sunday morning kicked off with the Breaking of Bread service. After lunch we had outreach into the community, bringing children into the Sunday school. At 6.30pm we would move into the gospel service and often stay on until late into the evening. No-one seemed eager to leave! Wednesday night we had the Bible study, and Thursday the prayer meeting would take place. We were all expected to attend the meetings and were eager to do so. To begin with, I was the only young person. Later, a lovely family joined us who had a son who just happened to be a youth pastor. This was to play a crucial part of the plan that was later to unfold.

The nights when I was not attending church, I would spend either with Muriel and her four boys or with my new-found friends Tom and Iris Sherlock. They were an older couple, full of faith and wisdom concerning the things of God. Night after night we would talk about Jesus and what it meant to follow him. Tom would expound his end-time predictions which would enthral me. Over the course of the years my theology has somewhat changed but nevertheless he gave me a good understanding and grounding in Scripture. Iris would talk about the need to lay our lives down daily for others and showed me practically how this worked in the situations we found ourselves. Her insight has been invaluable to me over the years, especially when confronted by difficult situations and less than charitable people. She was a saintly woman and dearly loved by everyone who knew her.

What a privilege it was for me to be surrounded by such godly women as Muriel and Iris. Finding them was like finding treasure. Both Iris and Tom have since gone to be with the Lord but my dear friend Muriel, now in her eighties, continues to be a light shining brightly. No matter what trouble or hardship she has faced in life, her love of Jesus has remained constant. Her words are always words of encouragement, always life-giving, always filled with thankfulness to God, always looking forward in hope to 'The Day'! Her love and her enthusiasm for God have been her hallmark, and over the years she has had that ability to draw people along with her into the presence of God.

How thankful I am for that day in January when our paths crossed and, taking me by the hand, she led me along the path of life, helping me to continue my journey of faith. How important such friends are. They are our treasure!

My hope is that I too might be a treasure in some way in the lives of people around me; that I might be a source of hope, a source of joy, a source of infection, leading people to seek the God who loved them so much he willingly gave up his life, to bring freedom from sin and take us into relationship with our heavenly Father through his sacrifice.

Along with my church life I was working very long hours as a receptionist for a television rental company called Telefusion. I loved meeting people, so this was the job for me. I was there for three and a half years until I eventually joined the Derbyshire Royal Infirmary as a Clinic Clerk (having done the customary four months in the Records Department, where everyone started off before taking up their position of choice).

I had originally thought of going into nursing but I loved the administration side of things and I decided this was a great fit for me. I got to work with doctors and nurses, interact with the patients and run the very busy outpatient clinics. All very rewarding! In later years I was able to continue this passion by working in the more intimate setting of a doctor's surgery where you knew your patients by name, where they lived and some of the stories and challenges they faced. When I worked at Maungakiekie Clinic in Auckland, we had a wonderful elderly patient called Miss Wilson. She would ring me daily for a chat and sometimes more than once a day. She was very interested in world politics and really felt she had some answers. She was keen to share her views with various world leaders such as presidents Ronald Reagan and Gorbachev, and *Time Magazine*. One day she showed me a letter she had sent to each of them and, to add weight to her thoughts, she informed them that Dr Trotman agreed and so did her nurse Linda! These memories are really priceless.

When I eventually retired, I was working in another wonderful surgery called Balmoral Doctors, in Auckland. It was hard leaving them all behind. By this time I was travelling two hours to get to work and working ten or eleven hours a day. I loved it but my family felt enough was enough and I reluctantly bowed out, aged sixty-nine. At the time I was also doing some nannying for a wonderful family in the village where we lived. For nearly five years both Peter and I had the joy of caring for a beautiful little girl called Honor, a couple of days a week. She was our absolute joy. We couldn't wait for 'Honor Days'! She called me La La and this seemed to stick. She had two older siblings who were also gorgeous but most of our time was spent with Honor as they were generally at school.

But coming back to those early days, days of discovering my new-found faith, days of turmoil and mixed emotion concerning my babies, decisions had to be made. It was June 1966 when I made the journey back to Lowestoft to visit my twins. A Christian leader had agreed to accompany me, and I was thankful not to be taking the trip alone. Walking through the door I was greeted very enthusiastically by the matron. Apparently, a lovely couple had been taking David and Tanya out for walks and were very keen to adopt them. I was assured they would be going to a wonderful home and that they would even have an uncle who was a bishop.

Now came the decision. Would I selfishly hang on to the thought that one day I would be able to care for them myself or would I release them into a loving, caring family where all their needs would be met? After much thought and prayer, I decided reluctantly that this was in their best interest, so papers were signed and I walked away with a heavy heart, but also with the assurance that I had made the right decision.

Of course, you can't just turn off your emotions at will. My twins were never far from my heart as the years rolled on. Where did they live, what were they doing? However, I had given them into God's hands and he would take care of them. And he would fill the big void left in my heart.

Having written briefly about the second and third door, perhaps it is time to venture through that first door, which was of great significance to me. This took place when I was two-and-a-half. My mother had just taken a job as a housekeeper for a man called Mr Disney of 2 Avondale

Road, in Derby. I remember us getting off the bus on Normanton Road and walking up Mill Hill Road. It was a very long road and seemed even more so for someone my age. Finally, we arrived and clutching my hand tightly my mum announced that this was going to be my new home.

Mill Hill Lane and the corner of Avondale Road, Derby.
A historic photograph of the house where Linda and Karen grew up.

For a start, I wasn't very popular with the children of the house and probably neither was my mum. Who can blame them! Their mother had left their father, running off with another man, leaving them behind. To say that it was a hostile environment for me would be an understatement. Until the day Mr Disney left, seven years later, I lived in fear of his constant disapproval. However, I would like to point out that I met him again when I was about eighteen and had become a Christian. He was visiting Derby and offered to give me a lift home. Before I got out of the car, he asked me if I could forgive him for his past treatment of me. I was able to tell him that I had already forgiven him. It was an amazing moment and brought some healing and closure to something that had been so destructive in my life.

Getting back to those earlier events, his daughter, Christina, eventually went to live with her mother in Canada and his son, David, was taken in by the grandparents. Again, for David that must have been quite devastating, as a young boy, to be ripped away from both parents. For me, at the time, though, there was such a sense of relief! I was too young to realise how this must have affected him. In later years I met David again and we became friends. It was so exciting to discover that he, too, had found a living faith in Jesus.

David, Linda and Karen in 2019

After being in my new home for a year and a half, my baby sister was born. Not without some trauma though, as before giving birth my mum contracted pneumonia and pleurisy and was very ill indeed. I was sent to live with my grandma and only allowed home after the baby was born. My grandma, of course, was wonderful. She would take me to her little chapel and her idea of an outing was to visit the cemetery to look after Grandad's grave. I would fetch the fresh water for the flowers from the tap which was nestled somewhere amidst the angels. I loved those times playing among the graves. If I was very good and we had time, we would go across the road to the old cemetery where the Gypsy Queen was buried. To this day I still love graveyards.

I learned so much from my times with Grandma. I learned to iron with the old-fashioned iron that you heated up on the stove. I helped her with the washing on Monday mornings, putting the clothes and sheets through her big mangle in the scullery before helping her hang them out. I broke down the salt that came in big slabs – not in fancy containers as they do today. One of my favourite jobs was blacking the old-fashioned grate in the living room. I would also cut up the newspaper and thread it through string to put in the outside toilet for the men. If you were a female, you got to enjoy the very hard shiny toilet paper produced in those days. Most of all, her faith had the biggest influence on me.

As soon as Mr Disney was free, he and my mum were married. Life didn't get any easier for me though. I don't remember a word of encouragement coming from his lips towards me in all those years. I do remember the thrashings. I do remember the harsh words and the fear he instilled in me. I dreaded him coming home at night. I would get a tight knot in my stomach.

I remember one classic moment that really sums it up. Mum had gone out shopping one Saturday afternoon leaving me behind with him. He had the bright idea that he would teach me to tell the time. However, it didn't go to plan and the harder he tried to teach me the more frustrated he became at my lack of understanding. I was only four years old at the time. The whole thing turned out to be a complete disaster. It was then that he posed the proposition that when it came time for me to go to school, they should send me to the school for backward kids up the road.

When Mr Disney fell out of love with Mum, his treatment of us and his destructive words came against us with full force. Karen was thankfully protected somewhat from this as she was his own child and, you could say, the apple of his eye. However, she wasn't totally immune to the situation, especially when he decided to take all the furniture when he left, as previously mentioned. Those months of tension before his leaving were almost unbearable but we came through and afterwards felt a huge sense of relief. Mum had fought to keep the house for us, so we still had a home, in spite of all the challenges ahead.

In those early days Mum's resilience got us through, even though she had become very sick and only in later years recovered fully. I don't know how she did it, but with all the rooms fully furnished, she began to let them out.

Did we have some incredible characters staying over the years! For instance, there was Fiery Jack from the circus who insisted he couldn't stand children. There was the famous actress Pamela Lane who was married to John Osborne the playwright who wrote *Look Back in Anger*. We had swathes of wonderful Irish people with their incredible sense of humour, and if a first cousin came to stay it wasn't long before second and third cousins followed in their wake.

Many actors came to stay when they were performing at the local playhouse, which was great as we were always given free tickets which I took full advantage of. As a child I would often be on the front row, on my own, watching some Shakespeare play or another. I especially loved the pantomimes, of course. Two of the actors, Alec Linstead and his friend Patrick, shared a room. I could hear Alec telling Patrick not to forget to plunge the eggs in cold water. Whenever I boil an egg, I still hear those words ringing in my ears. Poor Alec, one day he came home and passed a man going out of the door as he was coming in, carrying carrier bags full of stuff. 'Gosh', he thought, 'That man has a suit just like mine.' In actual fact it was his suit and his stuff. This man had shimmied up the drainpipe in the middle of the day and robbed him and Patrick of as much stuff as he could carry.

We also had the joy of accommodating musicians from the Ray McVay band who, at the time, were based in Derby. I remember Ray himself picking my sister and me up from the bus station once, when we had just come back from a week spent in a children's home in Skegness. One of my favourite people in the band was Jerry who played saxophone and wrote many of the arrangements. Jerry was famous for throwing his hands in the air and saying to my mother (Elsa), 'It's all happening, Els, it's all happening.'

Obviously for him it wasn't, as he left the band shortly after that. Terrible timing, as the band broke into the big time just after he left. Another one of my favourites was Richard, the very handsome thirty-six-year-old piano player who lived on the top floor. As a thirteen-year-old I had a crush on him and admired him from afar.

I cleaned many of their rooms for extra pocket money. Jerry's room was always disgusting. Then there was the Irishman I called 'hairy Johnny'; with him there was always a lot of ducking and diving as he would try to grab me whenever I was close by. The key to that situation was to make sure I was never alone with him.

One time my Mum let a room to a young man who seemed very nice but later robbed our electric meter in the cellar. It turned out he had just come out of prison for having broken into most of the houses in our road. Having missed ours, he must have thought this was a good opportunity to put that to rights. However, he was mortified to realise that Mum would have to pay the money out of her own pocket, so before leaving he gave her the envelope with the money still intact.

There was also the prostitute who stole all the new clothes we had been given just before we went off on yet another supposedly great holiday at the children's home at Skegness. We didn't want to take our new stuff with us and were looking forward to coming back to try it all on. Mum was also away in Mablethorpe at a convalescent home quite close to Skegness. Anyway, this girl made the most of the opportunity and along with our clothes she stole Mum's treasured marcasite ring. We could never prove that she was the thief. Mum did confront her with her suspicions. She also felt she was lying about her whereabouts during the day, so Mum decided to play detective and follow her. She soon realised what kind of work she was really doing, and that was the end of her.

I think the worst was the poor young man brought to Mum by the Social Services. He had had a very troubled past, having watched his father murder his mother. He slept on the floor with an axe by his side and at one point his bedroom was next to Karen's, which then became mine. Later, we found that he had drilled holes in the bedroom wall – a very disturbing scenario! How my sister and I survived all this is a mystery.

Another stand-out memory was from the early days when a man who rented a room asked Mum if she would help him write a letter to his estranged wife. Everything was going fine until he got to the part which talked about his impending suicide. Immediately the pen went down, and Mum quickly took control of the situation, 'You are not doing it here, duck; I don't want any mess!' He was quickly dispatched from the premises.

Another time there was the man who was renting one of the rooms overlooking Mill Hill Lane, quite a busy road with buses frequently passing by. We were unaware that he had a habit of exposing himself, and people on the bus must have been shocked. The first we knew of it was when the police turned up on the doorstep to arrest him. As he was being taken away, Mum very astutely shouted after them, 'Remember, duck, no fixed address!' Later she was very pleased to read in the paper about this unfortunate man who lived at no fixed address.

My mum was very popular with the local constabulary and especially the CID. They would regularly pop in for a cup of tea when passing. In fact, everybody seemed to make a beeline to our house for a cuppa and a chat.

Every day, Albert the milkman would come bringing his bottles of milk. On Saturdays he would always give us a free bottle of cream to go with Mum's delicious apple pie. She made the best pastry ever! For some reason she also had an early milkman called Mr Rogers. He said the same thing every day for years, 'What's it going to do today, Els?' One day, she could stand it no longer and blurted out, 'I DON'T KNOW, MR ROGERS. WHAT IS IT GOING TO DO TODAY?' As far as I know, he never ventured to ask that question again. Mum could be quite scary at times and woe betide you if you got in her bad books.

The other regular visitor was Mr Ken Yates, who came once a fortnight with his cartload of fresh vegetables pulled by his beautiful shire horse. She knew the drill well and would stand outside the house untethered until she felt Ken had had a long enough break, at which point she would set off up the road at quite a pace, with Ken running along behind trying to catch up with her.

When it came to letting rooms there was one golden rule which we were prepped for very carefully, should someone from the National Assistance Board ever turn up and ask us how many rooms we let. The answer was to be: 'Two, duck, we let two rooms.' Fortunately, we were never put in that position. Of course, it was totally untrue, it was closer to five rooms. We could never have survived on less. As it was, after bills were paid, we lived on thirty shillings a week

– the equivalent of £1.50 or NZ$3. Even though money was worth more in those days, this was still a meagre amount to live on, especially as it had to feed and clothe us and take care of any other expenses. Everything got entered in Mum's little red book. Once a month I would pop down to the local building society to deposit £9 10s 8d.

Our food was always plain but delicious and in small quantities. It was nothing to be sent to the greengrocers for two hard tomatoes, and woe betide him if we came back with soft ones. We were sent back very quickly to exchange them and to make it clear that Mum was not happy.

I would often take my pocket money and visit the Polish shop and buy salami and black seeded bread. The smell of the salami would drive Mum mad but I loved all that tasty food. It's only recently that I discovered that I likely have Polish as well as German blood in me, which makes it easier to understand my love of ethnic food. We once had a Nepalese Gurkha staying in our home. I'm not sure how a Gurkha from Nepal managed to find himself in the middle of Derby but that was the moment I tasted and fell in love with curry. Many years later, while visiting Nepal, I couldn't get enough dhal bhat. I think we ate it every day for fourteen days. Often it was prepared on the ground by cleansed lepers. That's another experience and another story tucked away in my memory.

In August 1970, four months after I turned twenty-two, I found myself headed down to Devon with our youth group to a Christian hotel called Haldon Court. Little did I know that within hours I would meet the man I would spend the rest of my life with! I was about to walk through the fourth door, but this time to actually run through it with eager anticipation. When I think of how close I came to nearly missing the whole thing, I just stand in awe at God's timing.

I had been planning on going to Spain with my neighbour and her family. Mrs Neale was paying for my holiday. I was aware that our youth leader, Peter Boyd, was taking the young people from the group down to Devon for a week's holiday, but as they were all younger than me, I wasn't sure I would easily fit in. Also, I understood there were going to be nightly meetings with a guest speaker and early morning Bible studies. It didn't sound much like a holiday to me. Spain sounded much more exciting. However, the closer it came, the more uneasy I began to feel. I thought I had made the wrong decision. So, with just one week to go I asked our youth leader if there was a chance of fitting me in after all. Almost immediately it was agreed that by swapping the girls' and boys' dormitories there would be room for me to join them.

The night before the trip I thought, 'What have I done?' It seemed a stupid decision! I got down by my bed and cried to God for a husband. I was lonely and longed to be loved, to have someone to share my life with. It's not that I hadn't had offers, I had received three that year, but I knew that for me it would have to be love at first sight.

The following day as we all piled into the minibus, Peter Boyd made a very unusual comment, especially coming from him as he was such a serious kind of person, 'Well, Linda, we have one spare space in the minibus. You never know, you might meet somebody!' We all laughed.

We set off with great excitement, anticipating the week ahead. A great bonus for me was that we would be passing through Bath, that beautiful historical Georgian city. I had immersed myself over the years in books by Georgette Heyer. Her novels are mainly set in and around Bath. There would be the dashing hero, in his long Hessian boots, riding his magnificent horse and the beautiful woman who would eventually become his bride. Their relationship would always get off to a rocky start, usually both despising one another in the beginning. There would be misunderstandings and dramas until the day when they could no longer ignore each other. They would realise that their passion for each other was such that they couldn't remain apart. They would have their happy-ever-after scenario. The perfect ending!

After many hours of travel, we finally arrived in Devon at the beautiful little seaside town of Exmouth. It was almost dinnertime, so we quickly unloaded our luggage, found our dormitories and headed downstairs for dinner. As we walked into the dining room my eyes were drawn to a very handsome young man with black hair and glasses. He was seated at one of two tables. However, to my disappointment, we were ushered to the other table. Our host, John Cunningham, introduced us all to each other and in that moment, I discovered that this gorgeous person was none other than the guest speaker. Suddenly, I became very excited at the thought of all those meetings. Bring them on!

Our first meeting was straight after dinner. I sat enthralled as Peter began to share some of his story and his journey with God. The thing that struck me most of all, apart from his good looks, of course, was his absolute passion for God. I was hooked; I fell hopelessly in love with him immediately. That was nearly fifty-two years from writing this account. I have to say our love has never wavered from that very day.

Little did I know at the time that Peter was feeling exactly the same about me. Three days before, he had prayed in faith for a wife, on the headland above Polzeath Beach in Cornwall. God somehow had miraculously brought us together from two different parts of the country and the attraction was simultaneous for both of us. Only God could do such a wonderful thing!

The following morning I rose early, a miracle for me, and made my way downstairs to the lounge where I heard someone playing the piano. Approaching the door, I realised that the pianist was, in fact, Peter. In that moment I heard an audible voice in my head saying, 'This is the man you are going to marry.' My response to this was, 'Well, Lord, you've only got a week'. It was in that moment I was struck with the fact that I would be Linda Lion as I had not heard his name clearly. I was relieved later when looking at the notice board to discover his second name was in fact Lyne. I thought it sounded quite wonderful. I was to become Linda Lyne.

With time being so short, I felt I needed to give the Lord a helping hand. That opportunity came during breakfast time. Our host announced that we would be having a meeting later that evening, but before that, we were encouraged to find a local church to go to. I suggested to my sister Karen that as we had a spare seat in our minibus maybe Peter would like to come with us. She dutifully passed this message down the table to our youth leader, who popped over to ask Peter what he thought about the suggestion. The message came back that he was speaking at a house-meeting in Pinhoe and also that he had his own car. 'Gosh,' I thought, 'he has his own car.' I was very impressed. Coming from Derby, that seemed quite a novelty to me, as I didn't know too many people with their own cars.

Anyway, all was not lost, I had a counter-plan. My next message was to suggest that we had always wanted to go to a house-church meeting, which were becoming all the rage in those days, so perhaps we could go with him. To my relief he thought this was a great idea, so he would join us on the minibus.

Everything was going according to plan until Peter Boyd asked me to give my testimony. Great, which part should I start with first? Should I mention the circumstances of my conversion? How would this godly man react? I was in a panic and so I decided to give a sanitised version of the truth. I just didn't mention the twins; how could I? I thought if there was any chance of being with him, this could completely put him off. Knowing him as I do now, I know that would not have been the case. However, my insecurity did not allow for this possibility. That settled in my mind, I waited with eager anticipation for late afternoon when we would set off together.

It worked out far better than I could have imagined. By the time Peter came to get on the minibus there was only one seat left, which just happened to be next to me. As he sat down, I held my breath; I couldn't believe my luck! He made some comments about the orange hat I was wearing, saying he wasn't sure why I would need to wear it when we were going to a house-meeting. I informed him that in the Assemblies of God we always wore a hat during meetings and especially if we were taking part. We had quite a funny exchange about this and clearly our opinions differed at that time.

Somewhere along the journey our arms touched, and it was just like electricity shooting up my arm; it was an incredible feeling! Being so close to him was truly wonderful, I could hardly breathe! The meeting was great, so refreshing! My testimony seemed to go down well and before long we were back on the minibus sitting beside each other again and I experienced that same lovely feeling as our arms once more brushed each other.

We went straight into another inspiring meeting and, as I had already anticipated, Peter had got caught up in counselling. The night before, standing behind him in the queue for our evening drink, I watched carefully to see what he would order. My plan was to look for an opportunity in which I might be able to swoop in and serve him his favourite drink, which at that time was Horlicks. I reasoned that people would be queuing up to talk to him after a meeting and what better way to show my servant heart. It worked like a dream! As Mr T from *The A-Team* used to say, 'I love it when a plan comes together.' Oh, how devious we women can sometimes be, but also so resourceful!

Early Monday morning, before 8am, found me sitting on the front row of the meeting, pen and paper in hand, wearing my round 'owl' glasses, looking very studious and spiritual, waiting for the Bible study to begin. I was not disappointed as Peter had a wonderful way of bringing Bible characters and events to life. Later, my mother was to remark that Peter was the only preacher that didn't send her to sleep, which coming from her was quite a compliment.

Well, things progressed over the next two days. Of course, I only knew how I felt about Peter but had no idea how he felt about me. On Tuesday afternoon all was to be revealed. We were taking a trip to a local wood and Pete Boyd had asked Peter to join us. I actually contemplated not going as I was feeling quite miserable about the whole situation; it seemed that Peter was blissfully unaware of me. In the end, though, I reluctantly boarded the minibus and made my way to the back in quite a tearful state. I just could not imagine life without Peter. As the minibus came to a halt, we all piled out. I had already made the decision to set off by myself. But Peter had other plans.

He started walking alongside me, which made me a bit annoyed at first. Didn't he realise that he was making my life a misery! As we walked into the wood, we had to cross a little stream. Peter took hold of my hand to help me across. Later he confessed that he wished he hadn't let it go. However, as we plunged deeper among the trees, he suddenly pulled me close to him and kissed me passionately. My head was spinning. I began to reason in that moment that here was a man of God, so he must mean something by kissing me in this way.

At that very same moment the heavens opened, thunder and lightning bolted across the sky and my heart leapt as I reasoned, Yes, even God is giving his blessing! We ran back to the minibus thoroughly soaked. Everyone else had already made it back and began clapping and cheering as we ran towards them. They must have guessed something momentous had just taken place.

The following day he took me to see the movie *Oliver* and afterward, standing by a farm gate, he posed a question. 'If I asked you to marry me, would you?'

Well, obviously, I said, 'Yes!'

By that evening I realised things were getting quite serious really quickly and I began feeling very nervous as Peter still knew nothing about my past. That night, as I shared these thoughts with the Lord, I opened my Bible to my daily reading which happened to be Psalm 112. Verse 7 shot out of the page at me,

> *He shall not be afraid of evil tidings;*
> *his heart is fixed, trusting in the* LORD.[53]

I love the way God does that, when we need encouragement or guidance. It could not have been any clearer if the Lord himself had been standing in the room. With those words ringing in my heart, I lay down in peaceful rest.

The following day, Peter had arranged to take me to Exmoor. I was very nervous as I realised this was crunch time for me. I could not let him propose properly without sharing my past with him first. Not very romantically, he asked if I would mind him having a rest in the car before going for

53. Psalm 112:7 KJV

a walk, as he had been up early preparing for the evening meeting. Of course, I agreed.

For the next little while I sat next to this sleeping figure while my mind was in turmoil. My stomach was also in an uproar; it would not stop rumbling no matter how much I held my breath. Finally, he woke, and we went for a walk along the river and I began to pour out my heart concerning my past.

Peter was absolutely amazing! First of all, he was not at all fazed by my revelations. And secondly, he began to minister to me from the life of King David who had come home with his men from the battlefield to discover that everyone who had been left behind, including his wives and children and those of his men, had been taken into captivity by the Amalekites. They were desperate and enquired of the Lord what they should do, as his own men were turning against him.

But David found strength in the LORD his God.[54]

David and his men, having received God's word to pursue them to victory, set out on this daunting task. And then in 1 Samuel 30:18 it says,

David recovered all.[55]

Peter said to me, 'I believe you will recover everything you have lost.' That was such a special moment for me, to feel

54. 1 Samuel 30:6 NIV
55. ESV

his love and concern, but also the faith that he imparted into my spirit. He went on to ask me to marry him. Obviously, my answer was 'Yes', although I had one other thing I needed to mention at this point. I had agreed to buy my mother a fridge and wondered if that would still be okay, which of course it was. Later, after we were married, Mum told Muriel that if I hadn't got married, I would have bought her a cooker also! So Mum! Anyway, it all seemed like a wonderful dream. Who needs Georgette Heyer!

The following day saw us sitting on the grass in the grounds of Haldon Court with Peter's diary open, pouring through dates to see when he could fit our wedding into his busy schedule. This included a month-long trip to Norway, university campaigns, tent missions and finally a citywide mission in his own city of Bristol the following April. Interspersed with these events were numerous speaking engagements around the country. After much deliberation we settled on May 15th the following year. Looking back, we wished we had married immediately. Today we would have done things differently but in those days, protocol and family expectations played a great part in our decision-making. We really just wanted to be married and together, now that we had found each other.

That evening Peter shared with the group our plans to marry and there was much excitement. John Cunningham and his wife actually came to our wedding the following year, along with more than a couple of hundred of Peter's friends from all over the country. I think I managed to muster eleven in all which included my mum, who typically kept us on tenterhooks as to whether she would be coming or not; even though we had bought her wedding outfit, it was not a given. My sister Karen was my bridesmaid and dear Tom Sherlock agreed to give me away. However, I am running ahead of myself here, as at this moment only the date had been agreed. The logistics were still to be sorted.

The following day Peter took me to meet his parents. We had to drive through Bristol on our way home to Derby, so we arranged for the minibus to pick me up later. I do wonder what his parents must have thought at the time. Peter brings a complete stranger into his home and tells them we are going to be married. It must have blown their minds, although I must say, they were very gracious. Peter had actually written a letter to them earlier in the week to prepare them somewhat.

I was dreading the moment we had to part, which came far too soon. I arrived home in Derby later that day and broke the news to my mother. She, too, was very impressed with the fact that Peter owned a car. However, the following months proved to be quite difficult and at times she could be quite hostile about the whole thing. Looking back, I think she was probably dreading me leaving. It wasn't as if I was just going down the road. I was moving to a completely different city, miles away. She was also worried as to how she would manage to feed all her cats once I was gone as I took care of buying their food. I think we had seven cats at the time. Mum couldn't help taking in strays who soon became part of the family. Peter decided to pray about it. Mum got wind of this and when the third cat got run over by a car, she asked Peter if he would mind not praying anymore.

I must just mention one more incident. The following week Peter's brother, Eric, was getting married to Christine and I had been invited to the wedding. I was to arrive at Bristol Temple Meads by train the evening before, and Peter was coming to pick me up. I was so nervous wondering if he would change his mind when he saw me again, or would he still feel the same. As the train pulled into the station, Peter was standing in full sight on the platform watching every carriage go by, holding a big bunch of red roses.

I was so struck by this wonderful act of commitment and kindness. It spoke volumes to me of who this man was, so openhearted and honest and honourable. Maybe, like me, you have experienced in your past, someone arranging to meet you and suddenly stepping out from the shadows at the last moment – not my Peter! Over the coming months we saw each other almost weekly. I would either go to Bristol to his home or he would divert and come through Derby on the way to or from one of his many speaking engagements.

I do laugh now when I think about our courtship. Most people would have found it quite strange, and it would not have been everybody's idea of romance. For instance, a typical weekend consisted of the Friday half-night of prayer, followed by a day of prayer and fasting at the WEC Missionary Society. Saturday evening would find us in the old Anglican church, St Philip and St Jacob, fondly known as Pip'n'Jay! The minister, the late Malcolm Widdicombe, a great friend of Peter's, let him use the church for his Tell Bristol citywide evangelistic meetings, of which Peter was the chairman. Then we would move on to Sunday. Ah, yes, Sunday! Well, that started with the early morning communion, followed closely by the all-age Sunday school. Peter and his brother, Eric, ran a Bible study in the home of Roger and Joyce Booth on the Blackhorse estate. It was like watching a game of tennis as they bounced questions and answers back and forth. They both had very strong opinions and were not afraid to share them.

We would then head home for one of Peter's Mum's delicious Sunday roasts, followed by an equally delicious steamed pudding which was served with custard as well as cream. His mum was a great cook. Her chocolate *éclairs* and cream puffs could even rival Bird's cake shop in Derby, which is really saying something. If I remember rightly, we had the afternoons to ourselves before plunging into the evening meeting. Often, we then went off to an after-church meeting at some other church where Peter would be speaking. Not for the faint-hearted, I have to say, but I proved I was up to the task.

How I loved Monday mornings when I would have Peter all to myself. We would take a leisurely drive home along the Fosse Way, the old Roman road leading right up through the Cotswolds – always such a romantic journey! The first time Peter suggested we stopped for elevenses, I thought he meant a cup of tea but actually he just wanted a good old-fashioned snog. Yes, I was even up for that too!

The girls I worked with at the hospital were incredible. They thought our romance was a fairy tale come true and did everything they could to support us, even to the extent of giving me their spare days off so I could spend as much time with Peter as possible.

The whole of October, Peter was away in Norway. I found it really difficult being apart for so long. On the day he returned, docking in Newcastle, he made his way by car and arrived at the Derbyshire Royal Infirmary around lunchtime. One of the girls had kindly given me her half-day and so Peter whisked me away into the city centre to buy me an engagement ring with the gift he had received in Norway. On arriving home, we knelt by my bed as he slipped the ring on my finger. That night we went to the Berni Inn, an iconic steak house in the middle of Derby, to celebrate. Just the two of us together, lost in each other's love, so content to be in each other's company.

Wedding of Peter and Linda, May 15th, 1971

Over the years, we have shared our lives and our homes with too many people to count but always the thing that has kept us constant is our love of being together, never tiring of each other's company. Even now, fifty-two years later, we are still enjoying our 'togetherness'. I thank God every day for the amazing gift of bringing Peter into my life and for the love that has transcended all the difficulties life throws at us, and we have had our fair share. I think the secret is not just our love for each other but our love for God and our desire for his Kingdom. This has been the motivating factor in everything we have tried to do. I am sure we have made mistakes along the way. Perhaps we could have handled some situations differently, but we have always been passionate in our desire to serve God and his people, to see God's Kingdom established in people's lives, to see people set free from bondage into living lives full of purpose, and for the Church of God to thrive in the midst of great opposition which surrounds us on every side.

If I had to sum up what I have been trying to say, it is that the hallmark of our lives has always been our passion for God, for each other, for his Church and for this world which God loved so much he was willing to die for it. I long that people would know this amazing truth and that they would discover the gift of God I discovered all those years ago. It completely changed my life and continues to be my source of strength every day.

Another part of the story I would like to share happened in 1984. We were living back in Britain and Peter was away at the time, when I received a phone call from my mother. She had a terrible confession to make. It must have taken a huge amount of courage for her to make this phone call and was certainly long overdue. The reality was that a whole lot of secrets and lies which she had hoped would never come to the surface were about to be exposed. She began her confession by announcing that although I grew up thinking I was her first born, in reality I was actually the fourth born. Gosh, demoted just like that! By this time, I was shaking, wondering what on earth was coming next.

Over the course of the next few minutes Mum began to unravel the truth. She had always told us that she had been engaged to a man called Philip but broke it off after seven years as she had become bored with him. Now the story was coming out that in fact she had been married to him for that length of time. I learned later that the night before the wedding she had tried to get out of going through with it, pleading with Grandma that she didn't love him. She was told it was too late to back out now, although Grandad said, 'Don't marry him if you don't love him'.

However, the pressure was too great to change things at that late stage, with everything set in motion. The following day she actually fainted at the altar, such was her anxiety. These facts only came to light much later. However, on this night she shared how she had given birth to a little boy called Barry. When he was about two years old, she left him playing in the garden and never went back. She had decided to run away with a soldier who had been stationed in Nottingham. He took her up north to his home in Sunderland to live with his mother. This proved to be a complete disaster as he had quite a violent streak and living under the same roof as his mother was very challenging, to say the least. He was a fisherman and was away for periods of time.

On one such occasion Mum put on as many clothes as she could and went to the local police station to ask if they could help her get a ticket for the train back home to Derby. We knew that story well. The part we did not know was that she had her little girl, Sandra, with her and was also pregnant with her next child. On arriving home Grandma made it very clear to Mum that there was no way she could stay there with two children as the house was already filled to capacity. The only answer was to have them adopted out. I can't imagine what she went through at this time. Sandra was eighteen months old; her adoptive parents later changing her name to Pamela. Mum's new baby was born on Christmas Day, inspiring her to call her Carol. She was adopted straight from the hospital, avoiding too much of the bonding process. Nevertheless, it must have been a traumatic time for her.

I began to understand now why she wrapped herself in hardness. She was just trying to protect her fragile spirit. She lived with the consequences every day of her life. She carried this whole burden alone. No wonder when I once asked her why she wouldn't give her life to Christ, she said that there were reasons that I couldn't possibly understand.

The other bombshell she dropped at this time concerned my father. I already knew that he was a German soldier in a prisoner of war camp in Derby. For some reason only known to the authorities, they had decided, before repatriating the POWs, to allow them out into the community at weekends to mingle with the locals . . . and mingle they did! The inevitable happened, of course, as my mother discovered when she found herself pregnant after an afternoon picnic in Darley Park under a rhododendron bush with a handsome young German called Paul.

However, she had always told me that his mother was Dutch and his father German. I lived with this fantasy over the years of having a Dutch side to me, which I was quite excited about. Another illusion was about to be shattered. For some reason the revelation she was about to share really affected me when she said, 'You know I told you your father was half Dutch and half German; well, he was all German'. He wasn't a *van* he was a *von*!

The following March, Paul and the other POWs were repatriated to Germany. Somehow, his best friend, Fritz, managed to escape and made his way to America, where he became Fred. I well remember the day when Fred came to visit, standing in the kitchen, all very clandestine, wearing his raincoat and dark glasses. That was the nearest I ever came to knowing my father, by meeting his best friend.

I was born in April 1948, a month after my father left. My mum once again had to forge a new life for herself, but this time it included me. She would do everything possible to keep me with her, for which I am truly grateful.

The final part of her confession was to do with her daughter Carol, the one given up for adoption at birth. Somehow Carol had managed to find her and had turned up on her doorstep many years before. She had been visiting Mum all this time without our knowledge and at times had been very unkind to Mum, which we were later to witness first-hand. Now I understand why at times Mum was seemingly distressed without a clear explanation. Even to the point of moving to be near us in Bristol, which didn't work out at all as she was really a Derby girl.

One day, Carol rang my sister, Karen, out of the blue to inform her that she was her sister. Karen, of course, was shocked and told her that I was her sister. Then Carol went on to explain the situation to her. Poor Karen was equally shocked, not only to discover that, but all the other forthcoming revelations. That was the reason for Mum's phone call. There was nowhere to hide; it was all finally coming out into the open.

This reminds me of a prophecy I was once given by our dear friend and colleague Dave Day. In prayer he shared with me that things that had long been hidden would be brought into the open. At the time I had no idea what this entailed.

When Mum had finished telling me everything I just shook uncontrollably. I tried to phone Peter but I could not even dial the number. My mind was racing as I tried to process all this new information. Finally, I managed to reach him. I was desperate for him to rush over and see her there and then, but that was not possible. When he finally managed to go, she had closed down again. A missed opportunity, I felt, but at least the truth was out.

There was no condemnation on our part, just a sadness that Mum felt she had to carry this burden alone for all those years. Dear Mum, what she must have suffered. I realise now why she found it so hard to show love, to gather us in her arms, to give us the enveloping love we longed for. She had been hurt so many times, had so much loss. She had built a wall around her heart which was hard to penetrate. Through her own rejection she often rejected others, especially if they had crossed her in some way.

It is easy to judge someone with this kind of life-story, but society is different today. It seems everything is laid on: homes are provided, welfare given, and attitudes have changed. In those days, life was hard; they were just getting over two World Wars and women were still trying to find their place. Attitudes were still very Victorian.

To understand how she became so damaged you only had to look back into her past. She had never known her real mother, Charlotte, although she often asked who the lady was, standing on the corner of the street staring at her. At such times she would be hustled quickly through the door. Charlotte had taken in a lodger while her husband, Arthur Eyre, was away fighting in the First World War. Charlotte and Arthur had three children during the course of their married life: Ethel, Billy and Vera. In 1917 along came another baby, Elsa, who was my mum. It was always rumoured that Elsa actually belonged to the lodger. Aunty Grace visited the house one day and the lodger was standing by the fireplace. Aunty Grace looked at the baby and then looked at the lodger and remarked how much the baby looked like him, which caused a smile to appear on his face.[56]

Mum always says that he was a true Romany gypsy, but again that is hearsay. Mum's skin was swarthy, as is mine.

---

56. My sister Karen did some research into War Records at the library and found a form written in 1919 in which Arthur Eyre states he has three children – therefore denying that Linda's mum was his child.

I have a rare photograph of myself as a child on one of our school trips to the Blue John mines. It shows one little brown face in a sea of white faces. For my seventieth birthday I decided to have a DNA test to finally ascertain my roots. The results that came back were very interesting. I was surprised to discover that only 18% was indeed British whereas 46% was Eastern European and 26% Western European with a smattering of 6% from elsewhere. On the back of this test, I received an email from a lady living in the States; she had been adopted and had discovered that her birth mother was Polish and her birth father German and that she had the same DNA as me.

I never cease to be amazed at what turns up! It certainly answered some questions for me, though, as I never felt like I really belonged. I was always down at the Polish shop buying salami and black bread with seeds. I loved going there! I loved all the smells, the different kind of food available. This was before ethnic food became popular in Britain, when fish and chips and mushy peas were on the menu big time, when you had chicken at Christmas, and roast beef and Yorkshire pudding was the favourite Sunday roast, rivalled only by roast lamb and mint sauce. It was always my job to pick the mint and make the sauce. Food in those days was delicious but plain.

Returning to Charlotte, whatever the truth may be, on hearing that Arthur was coming home and had been alerted in a letter by a neighbour about the alleged affair, Charlotte did the unthinkable thing. She and James, the lodger, packed their belongings and left the house in Stanton Street which was just along the road from her brother, Will, and his wife, Annie, who I would later come to know as my grandma. Charlotte pushed a letter through a neighbour's door informing her that she and James had gone away together and that they had left the children sleeping in their beds. How does somebody do such a thing? No wonder Mum suffered from rejection!

Annie and Will took all the children home with them, but the authorities soon stepped in and removed the children into care, but they were allowed to keep one child, so they chose Elsa. A lady called Phoebe Crow, who lived just around the corner in Clarence Avenue, took the other children. Consequently, Mum grew up thinking her cousins were her brother and sister and that her actual siblings were her cousins. The truth only came out on Mum's first day at school when one of the children told her that her mum (Annie) was not her real mum. What a shock! She ran home crying, having heard the truth in such a cruel way.

Many years later, when Mum was older, she went in search of her mother Charlotte, who was living in Blackburn, a few miles from Manchester. Mum says she found her way to the house and knocked on the door, only to be turned away by Charlotte who did not want her children knowing anything about her past life. She even named one of her children Ethel, the same name as one of the children she had left behind all those years before. I cannot imagine how Mum felt as she walked away. Yet, many years later, she did the same thing to her own son Barry, when he turned up out of the blue one afternoon. He didn't make it across the threshold as she informed him, 'You can't come in here, duck, not with a cold like that!'

Poor Barry was never seen again! Lest she be judged too harshly, I believe she built a wall around herself for her own protection and this wall was very difficult to penetrate. Also, the guilt must have been enormous. It is my belief that she just couldn't face the truth and live with it. It helps me understand her rejection of our own children whom she hardly ever acknowledged as they were growing up.

One wonderful thing that did take place, however, was that Carol found her real sister who was living in Australia, and when visiting the UK, she brought her to see Mum. Mum had been so upset with Carol's treatment of her that she would not let them come into the house and made it quite clear she did not want to see them. However, Pamela quickly assessed the situation and wisely suggested Carol wait in the car, and that she would try again.

This time Mum opened the door and opened her heart to her. She threw her arms around her and held her tightly, crying into her shoulder saying, 'I never wanted to let you go!'

I believe that was a wonderful healing moment for both Mum and Pamela. Sadly, Pamela was never to see her again, but sent a lovely message to be read out at Mum's funeral. Both Karen and I have since connected with Pamela, which has been a real blessing. On the two occasions we have been together I could not believe how much like Mum she is, in both her mannerisms and her likes and dislikes. Scary really!

I want to record the last few, remarkable days Karen and I got to share with Mum before she passed away. It was truly incredible, and I hope that anyone reading this story who is facing a similar situation with their own family and friends would take heart from this and believe for the impossible.

Mum Elsa and Linda

During this last week with Mum, I began writing a letter to my dear friend Jeffrey who was now living in the States and working with YWAM in Tyler, Texas. Jeffrey knew all about Mum, Grandma, Stanton Street, Clarence Avenue and my childhood, and over the years would refer to these places and the people as if he knew them; that's why it was important for me to write especially to him. We had actually introduced him to Vicky, now his wonderful wife, when she visited us in New Zealand.

He had been a close friend for years and had continually come to my rescue on the many occasions when Peter was away on ministry trips. We used to laugh because it always appeared to coincide with us moving house, which happened quite regularly, as we were often in rented homes. We would come to the end of yet another move and, having unpacked the beautiful champagne glasses that Jeffrey had bought us at one time, we would break out the champagne and congratulate ourselves on our accomplishment.

I wanted to share my heart with Jeffrey at this traumatic time in my life and I have always found the act of writing helpful. So after a few personal remarks I began to write the events as they unfolded.

Well, Jeffrey, these last few days have been absolutely amazing, and I thought who better to write to than my friend Jeffrey! My sister Karen and I have been through many emotions in these last few days. It's unbelievable! We have been shocked, we have cried, we have laughed. I wish I could tell it all to you as it has happened, but I don't expect I can. It would take far too much paper and be too involved to really capture the scene but I will try to give you a little glimpse.

The subject is my mother. Last week I got a phone call from the Home, to say that she was quite poorly. She has been going downhill for some time and hadn't eaten properly for months. We see her every two or three weeks but certainly I was not prepared for my encounter this last Thursday. I was so worried after the phone call that I decided I had to come down.

When I arrived, I was totally shocked to see the state of Mum. She was like a pathetic little rag doll with no strength to do anything except hold a glass to her lips. Someone has to hold her up and after a couple of sips she falls back exhausted. She has no control of her bowels now and has to wear a nappy. It takes two to lift her onto the commode. She is so terribly thin, like pictures you see of Sudan or even the dreaded camps.

This person did not look like my mum at all. It was the most distressing thing to experience. We didn't expect her to live the night and so I moved into her room. Big mistake! I think she is enjoying the attention so much she has decided to stick around.

So, Jeffrey, this room has become my world. It is amazing how little you can survive with. A mattress on the floor, a sink to wash your hair in, the odd glass of wine. Having got through the initial shock, Karen and I have settled down to quite a routine. We take turns to sit on the chair or on the bed. We reminisce and discover all sorts of things we didn't know about our past.

Yesterday, Mum's friend Muriel came and we had a lovely day together. So many things to talk about. Muriel lived with us through quite a chunk of our childhood and so there were many shared experiences. What a wonderful day we had together on Monday. That was, incidentally, the day Mum said she was going, but when it got to about 10 o'clock at night, we thought that was pushing it a bit, so we all retired for the night.

So here we are, Jeffrey. I am sitting in the armchair, Karen on the commode (the seat that is, not using it!) and Mum is having a little nap. It is now Tuesday afternoon. I have been here day and night since last Thursday and Karen since Friday, although there is only enough room for one of us to sleep here, so Karen pops round to stay with her brother, David Disney.

Although it has been tragic seeing Mum in this state, it has also been a great blessing because Mum has clearly trusted in Jesus and is looking forward to seeing him.

I have had some lovely times of prayer with her, and we have talked a lot about heaven and what a wonderful place it will be and how fortunate she is to be going first. We've also talked about the people she will meet there like Grandma Crooks, Uncle Harry, Abraham, David and, of course, Jesus. 'Oh yes! It's Jesus I want to see.' She often prays and asks Jesus to take her. 'Please take me, Jesus.' Yesterday she said she wanted to go to bed. Karen said that she was in bed. 'No!' she said, 'I want to go to the real bed.'

Saturday afternoon was very special when Muriel first came. During the afternoon she went and sat on the bed with Mum. She said, 'Elsa, Jesus is my Saviour. Is he your Saviour too?' 'Oh yes', said my mum, 'He's my Saviour and I love him.' She also asked the Lord to forgive her for the things she had done wrong. After Muriel had ministered to her for quite a while, drawing such a positive response from her, we all prayed. There was a wonderful sense of the presence of God in the room. It was one of those moments that you wish you could suspend in time. Certainly, the memory will always remain with the three of us: the day I felt Mum's salvation was clinched, as it were.

It is funny how the enemy then comes to snatch away such a precious time. Just as Muriel left with Karen and Peter, in walked Carol, the half-sister we hadn't known about. The next hour was horrendous, with Carol holding forth in a loud voice. Karen later said, 'It was as if she was pleading her case in a courtroom and was totally insensitive to the occasion.' After all, let's not forget the occasion was the potential passing of our mother to glory, and it was so out of place to air one's views and bring up the past. One thing Mum does have is acute hearing, and even though she is lying there looking dead, she is well aware of everything that is being said. Anyway, the hour progressed, and I want you to picture the scene. I am now sitting at the head of the bed, Karen at the bottom. We managed to manoeuvre into this position by asking Mum if she would like a drink. Carol is now sitting on the chair. Peter has heard her plea for photographs and is avidly looking through one of the albums. Somewhere in the room is Carol's twelve-year-old son.

Now here it comes. Mum suddenly raises her hands in the air and starts to pray fervently that God will forgive her and take her to heaven. Carol, hearing this heart-cry from Mum's lips bursts into tears. In the middle of the prayer, which Peter is totally oblivious to as he tends to be very focused on what he is doing at the time, starts to show first Karen and then Carol some photographs. Only, Carol is not looking; as tears are pouring down her nose and cheeks, still the album is pushed under her nose. Eventually, Peter begins to realise that she is not responding and moves it away. At which time I can stand it no longer, as I proffer, 'Nice timing, Peter!' Like a scene out of a farce. Unbelievable! I just can't capture it in words. Anyway, Carol came back the next night, but I had a word with her and asked her only to talk about nice things in future, which she did.

I don't know where we are going from here. Sometimes Mum seems quite lively, and other times it looks like it is all over. Her memory has become very clear, and we have had renderings of her favourite songs like, 'Going to take a sentimental journey' and 'Falling in love again, never wanted to, can't help it'. This was complete with Marlene Dietrich's voice. We have also had 'How much is that doggy in the window?' and 'All things bright and beautiful'. For days now she has been saying that she is going; at first it was easy to believe but now we are not so sure. She has been making us laugh because she'll say, 'I haven't got long now, you know. I will soon be going' and 'when you've got to go, you've got to go'. Five days later we are still hearing these words and getting less and less convinced as time goes on. In fact, when she said she was going on Monday, Karen said, 'Well, Mum, if you could firm up whether it is morning or afternoon, that would be very helpful.' As I say, she is very weak but still has a wicked sense of humour which she draws out of us.

Yesterday when Dr Fowler came, she confirmed that Mum could go on for ages like this, unlike the doctor last week who only gave her days. The thing is I am committed to staying now and can't really leave her. In fact, I now have a new name: 'Linda-don't-leave-me'! Dr Fowler said she would be back to see her on Friday. Mum said, 'Friday? I'll be dead by Friday!' So Dr Fowler said, 'Well, I'll come Thursday then. Will that be alright?'

Now for the bum news. If Peter's timing is lousy, how about this? Today I am supposed to be on a plane with him to California and Bakersfield en route to Hawaii for our family holiday. The children all leave next Friday. Me, well, I may be spending my vacation in Derby, looking at four walls and being woken in the night to endearing words like, 'I want to go wee wee.' Joking aside, though, I couldn't possibly leave Mum like this. She needs consistent care, and I am so glad of the opportunity of being with her. I feel the Lord has been very gracious to me, to allow me to be with Mum at the end of her life, and I couldn't have wished for a greater response from her towards the Lord. She really is ready to meet him. It's funny, but every now and then she will say, 'Praise the Lord!'

The amazing thing with Mum is that she is not physically ill; she has actually starved herself to death through lack of eating. A few weeks ago she looked about seventy, now she has become like someone in their nineties. The question now is how long will it take? I can't see any purpose in a long-drawn-out process but you can't hurry God either. Karen says he is still trying to work out where to put her! Seriously, though, we have such peace. It is all I could ever have hoped for and certainly what I have prayed for. Although there is obviously great sadness, there is also immense relief that she is going to be with Jesus. I think last week was the hardest to come to terms with, but now it is like we are waiting for the final curtain to fall because the last act has been played.

I don't know if I will send this letter; I may just keep it open. I've got a scintillating night ahead of me. It's 5.20pm. Mum has slept all afternoon, and I guess will continue to as we move into the evening. I'll probably put my bed down about 7.15pm; that's when most residents go to bed. Mum already said, 'Goodnight', to me at 4.15pm. The phase 'small world' is taking on new meaning.

* * * * *

Wednesday 16th November

Well, here we are again, not a lot happening. Mum has slept most of the day. The doctor came and said she could go on for weeks. The holiday is looking less and less hopeful. This morning was funny. One of the ladies who works here came to say hello to Mum. 'I'm going soon, you know. I'm going up soon,' she said, flopping one arm in the air. As the lady started to withdraw from the bed, she said, 'I haven't finished yet.' We all burst out laughing. Mum is still centre stage.

* * * * *

Thursday 17th November

Another day in paradise!

* * * * *

Friday 18th November

Oh, Jeffrey, today Mum passed into the presence of the Lord. What a day! It was wonderful. Mum went so peacefully. The timing was perfect after all. Karen came this morning and Mum's dear friend Muriel. Even my school friend, Colleen, popped in. Mum had a very quiet night, she didn't wake all night and stayed asleep until Karen arrived at 8.45am.

She vaguely acknowledged when we came in by putting her hands out to us. We each took one.

Even then I don't know if we fully realised what was happening until we looked at her legs; one had started to go purple. She started to pant and then her fingers began to go white; later they turned purple also. We read Scriptures to her. We prayed the Lord's Prayer, we sang 'The old rugged cross', 'All things bright and beautiful' and 'To be in your presence'.

She didn't speak today but as Muriel talked to her about the Lord, you felt she heard and responded a couple of times by a slight movement of the forehead. She went to be with the Lord at 2.35pm. As you can imagine we have cried and cried. Cried with sorrow at losing her, cried with relief that she, at last, was happy and with the Lord. All through the time she had her arms outstretched, as if waiting for the Lord to take her. As she kept saying over the week we were with her, 'If you've got to go, you've got to go. I'm ready, Jesus. Please take me.'

On Thursday morning I was reading John 14 to her about Jesus going to prepare a place for her and coming to take her where he is. 'Oh, lovely,' she said. I continued to read more of John 14, then she said in a gentle voice, 'That's lovely, Linda, but can I go to sleep now?'

Later on Thursday, Colleen, my friend, came. Most of the time Mum slept, but at some point, when she perked up a bit, Colleen said, 'You must be fed up of bed and all these visitors.' 'Oh no! I love it. I love people visiting.' That's probably the last real conversation we had. One day this week she said, 'Linda, will you miss me when I've gone.' It was just out of the blue when I thought she was sleeping. You can imagine my answer!

In a funny sort of way, I think this week has been one of the happiest for my mum in a long time. She had her family around her. Her mind was very clear and she was excited about Jesus and heaven. It was wonderful to see her. It was a very precious time. How good of the Lord to give us this wonderful opportunity of being together. It was one of the kindest, most wonderful things he could have done. How like him! He allowed us to have quality time and prepare Mum for eternity. He waited until she was truly ready, and I guess us too.

It is the early hours of Saturday morning and I just can't sleep. I'm staying the night at Muriel's. What a Godsend she has been to us and how appropriate that she would be with us through this time. Tomorrow the children will come and fetch me and on Tuesday I will probably fly to America.

I am so glad to have shared these thoughts with you, Jeffrey. I think it has been therapeutic for me and I wanted you to have the final picture. My very deepest love to Vicky, Aaron and Leslie and to you, my very dear friend.

All my love,
Linda

I think that the day-by-day record of the whole experience in my letter captures something of our various emotions: humour, awe, gratitude to God.

Another couple of funny comments Mum made during that last week I can't help but mention. During one of Muriel's visits Mum said, 'What are you laughing at?'

Muriel replied, 'Well it's quite a happy time really, Elsa, because I haven't seen Linda and Karen for such a long time.'

Mum's response came straight back, 'Happy time? When I'm dying!'

Yet another time just after Dr Fowler's visit, Mum asked if she could have some more orange wine. Muriel said, 'Dr Fowler says you can have anything you like, Els.'

'Did she?' said Mum. 'I must be dying then.'

On the Monday morning, I had woken up bright and early and was wondering about the hymns for Mum's funeral, and just as I thought about 'All things bright and beautiful,' at that very same moment Mum woke up and started singing this lovely hymn which we had all grown up with. Such great confirmation that I was on the right track.

Concerning Dr Fowler, who we had known for most of our lives, it was she who had confirmed in 1965 that I was pregnant and had even considered adopting my twins, but maybe she thought it was too close to home. However, she shared some very encouraging words with me that never left me. She said, 'One day, Linda, you're going to find a wonderful husband. I just know it.' How right she was!

Of course there is so much more I could share, but my daughter, Amanda, has captured it so well and far better than I, in her well researched book, *A Better Ending*[57] which

---

57. A.J. Lyne, *A Better Ending: It's Never Too Late to Begin a Better Ending* (independently published, September 2017)

spans three generations of our family and two World Wars. Some people have named it *The Never Ending* due to its size. I think this book is beginning to rival it. Packing a lifetime between two bookends is a tall order.

In Peter's account of our life story, he mentions my twins and the miraculous way in which, after nineteen years, they came back into my life. Walking into the room when I first encountered them was amazing! Seeing my own flesh and blood standing before me, clutching the little rabbits I had given them all those years before, was like a dream come true. Again, I can only thank God for his kindness. We have had the privilege of being around to see my grandchildren grow up into adulthood and now my great grandchildren, albeit in a limited way due to the distance between us.

The Twins – Tanya and David

Peter has been amazing! He has definitely taken on the role of grandad spectacularly. I think in his travels he has seen them far more often than I have. When we lived in England in the Nineties, we were there during those crucial years when my grandchildren were young children. Although I had missed out on Tanya and David's childhood, I was getting to experience these times with their children. They were very special years indeed. Now to see most of them married with their own children is incredible.

I have to give a lot of credit to our own children, Amanda, Richard and Simon, who never once showed any sign of jealousy towards the twins. It has made it wonderfully easy for me. At last, the cycle is broken of all those secrets and lies that were passed down through the generations.

It was a shock in the beginning when our children first heard about the twins, although I think in Richard and Simon's case, they were more miffed that I had told Amanda before them. For some reason I felt it was important for me to tell her first. Maybe it was because, like me, she was going to discover that she wasn't my firstborn and I wanted to give her time to process the whole thing. I think the secret of their wonderful reactions was that they knew that they were dearly loved and felt secure in that love.

As I draw this part of the book to a close, I would like to include two poems I felt inspired to write. From time to time something will spark me off and inspiration comes. With this first one I was watching an amazing address by Rob Bell called *Everything is Spiritual*, as he outlined the magnificence and wonder of creation.

You go before and yet behind
You stand secure outside of time
The perfect Godhead Deity
And though you're one, you're also three
With such precision this world exists
Breathed on by your holy kiss
Each molecule holding your DNA
Is fused with ours in humble clay
Perfect magnificent awesome delight
You've given day to follow night
The seasons set alongside time
Creation with love so Divine

For this second poem I added my own tune, making it easier to remember and use for my own personal worship. I lay in bed one night recovering from a very painful broken wrist and was finding it difficult to sleep. In these circumstances I usually turn to scriptures which I have learnt off by heart and which I continually like to add to. On this occasion I was rehearsing Psalm 24. I didn't get beyond verse 3 as I contemplated these incredible words,

Who may ascend the hill of the LORD?
Who may stand in his holy place?[58]

I realised in that moment, there is a holy place that we can come into now – not only in the future. I became obsessed with this thought and out of it flowed the following,

There's a place where we can go
Touch the heart of God and know

---

58. Psalm 24:3 NIV

214

He is waiting there for us
He longs to hear from us
In that special place we find
perfect love and peace of mind
There is nothing to compare
with the treasure offered there
A place of mystery, sacrifice through history
A place of majesty where the King will be

There's a place where we can go
Where endless love and mercy flow
A place of awe and liberty
where we can find our destiny
It's a place where we can soar,
touch the heart of God once more
Where dreams are freshly forged,
a place where all our hopes are stored
A place of mystery, sacrifice through history
A place of majesty where the King will be

There's a place where we can come
Touch the heart of God as one,
Pain and sorrow left behind,
where life sits outside of time
A place of mystery, sacrifice through history
A place of majesty where the King will be

Chapter 15

Olveston

In my years pioneering the Blackhorse church, my prayers had become specifically focused. We met in the local primary school and one another's homes, but an increasing burden came upon me. We needed a large house that could offer hospitality and encourage community living. I mentioned the summer of 1973 in Chapter 1 and told how we came to be living in the Old Quaker Meeting House in Olveston. This house was everything I wanted and had actually prayed for, in faith, over the years.

What do I mean by a 'prayer of faith'? It is graphically described by Jesus in the gospels of both Matthew and Mark,[59] that is, you ask, believe and receive it before you actually have it! According to James, it is an essential element in healing prayer.[60] This is not just any perfunctory prayer for healing! It is where God's will has been clearly perceived and received with an assured result.

There is one more thing about this prayer of faith that has been recently revealed to me. In Mark's account, we have graphic details from the beginning of Jesus' passion week. I had always puzzled over Jesus telling us to throw mountains into the sea! Did he really want us to re-arrange the geography around Jerusalem? When teaching on this

---

59. Matthew 21:19-22 and Mark 11:20-25
60. James 5:13-16

earlier in my ministry I would say that he was talking about the mountain of unbelief, always an obstacle to prayers of faith. However, Jesus taught in parables and the setting of this parable is crucial.

At the end of his triumphal entry into the city, he has a good look at the temple and is not happy with what he sees, and he returns to the House of Figs[61] (Bethany and Bethphage) where he is loved and honoured; and the next day, en route to the cleansing of his Father's house, he curses the fig tree. Was this a fit of petulance because he couldn't find any figs? The fig tree has always been an important symbol of Israel and the mountain he is talking about is the Temple Mount, symbolic of religion that was about to crucify him.

The next day Peter draws Jesus's attention to the fact that the fig tree he cursed has withered. Luke's gospel contains graphic prophecies about how this whole religious system is coming to an end.[62] All of which came to pass in AD 70 when the Romans sacked Jerusalem! All of this because,

'You did not recognise the time of God's coming to you.'[63]

Our move to Olveston coincided with my role as a pioneer of the House-church Movement in Britain, subsequently called the New Church Movement, as these networks grew substantially. It was the move away from religious unreality that inspired us in those heady days. Bethany symbolised the fellowship of home and fireside and breaking of bread. Interestingly, the modern names for Bethany and

---

61. The names of the Bethany and Bethphage villages mean *House of Figs*
62. Luke 13:34-35, Luke 19:41-44
63. Luke 19:44 NIV

Bethphage are Azariyeh or Luzarioh, derived from 'Lazarus', whom Jesus raised from the dead at Bethany. All of this foreshadowing a glorious fact: religion may crucify Jesus, but God will bring his body to life!

Looking back, I can see that my Stockwell House burden was definitely God-given, and somehow, heaven has a clearing house for such prayers. In this case, Blackhorse was not to be the location in which my vision was to be outworked. None of my prayer was wasted, and God had a much greater miracle in store for me – miracles, in fact, beyond my wildest dreams. It is against this backdrop that the story of Olveston and the community that shaped our lives would be played out.

With the incredible provision of a beautiful home in The Old Meeting House, our adventure in Olveston began. The Quakers no longer worshipped there and at this time the village had a fairly dead Methodist church and a struggling Anglican congregation. After our initial excitement had worn off, the question to the fore in our thinking was: 'Why are we here?'

The Lord had so supernaturally moved us into this house; now we needed to know his purpose for us. Gradually a clear course of action was revealed to us. After my annual visit to Dennis Clarke's Prayer and Bible Week at the beginning of 1974, I felt clear about four things which Linda and I agreed upon:

1. I would close my diary! A dramatic step, to say the least. I was overseeing the Tell Bristol ministry. I was a frequent student missioner to universities

in Britain. I had an intense programme of ministry invitations and had travelled frequently to Scandinavia, especially Norway, and Eastern Europe.

2. I would give myself unashamedly to my wife and children. Secure them. Their security is in who I am, not what I have.

3. People would come to live with us.

4. We would begin to meet as the Church in our house. This was not to be a prayer group or extracurricular activity; it was to be the Church.

And this is what we did. The first step was difficult. I sent out letters, trying to explain what I was doing, but I'm not sure many believed it. They may have thought, 'He's ended up in a nice house in a very desirable location. Perhaps he's just backsliding.'

The first test came when I had a call from the Christian Dental Association. Would I come as their keynote speaker to their annual conference at the Swanwick Centre in Derbyshire? I was on the point of agreeing to this when I had a prompting from the Holy Spirit – 'You can't go' – so I declined as graciously as I could. I thought I may have to do this for a matter of months, but when it became two years, I wondered if I would ever take up engagements again!

I had never fully realised how important it was to prioritise my family. Back then we had none of the literature that became available subsequently, like how to discipline your children or how to have a great sex life. I was to learn very swiftly how important a secure home base was going to be.

As for people coming to live in our home, this was fast-tracked for us. A call came from John and Christine Noble, our chief mentors in those days. Could we follow up a young woman that they had met through a meeting at a teacher-training college in Cheltenham? She was a new Christian from a non-Christian background and taking up her first job in a nearby town, so we invited her to meet us. She came for the weekend, and within days we asked her to come and live with us. Hazel was the first of many and a wonderful friend and asset to our family.

Richard Burt and Iain McDonald came next from Bristol University, and they have remained lifelong friends and encouragement to us. They were forerunners of a stream of students from the university coming to be a part of our emerging house-church. Very soon, we had four people living with us and frequent visitors, as well as three children.

The fourth issue, becoming a church, was of primary importance. The first time we met, there were just five adults, plus our children. Our three foundation members included Hazel, and John and Margaret Hodges who have also remained our lifelong friends. Almost a year before we moved to Olveston, we had met John and Margaret through some events we were running at Blackhorse. John had only been in a church once, to a requiem mass for a colleague who had died. When we met them, we agreed to drive out once a week to their home at Yate, just outside Bristol, so that we could help establish them in their newfound faith. Eventually, they would sell their house and move into the village so that they could be fully involved with us.

When we first gathered one Sunday morning, I explained that we were going to be a church, but not in the traditional sense. We would worship together, but also eat together and enjoy life together. Our primary theme was described by Jesus in John 10:10,

> *I am come that they might have life*
> *and have it to the full.*[64]

Literally, 'abundantly'. Sadly, much of the Church has interpreted this to say, 'I am come that you may have meetings and have them more abundantly.'

Swiftly, this began to take shape and grow. Not many people have a historic Meeting House as part of their home, so we were able to accommodate more people and, often, that was where we would meet to eat. We understood that communion was originally part of a meal, not the strange 'sip and nip' tacked on to most Christian services. When we grew bigger, the logistics became more demanding. Just to provide refreshments or a meal for fifty people really stretched us.

Like John and Margaret, many moved house to live in the village. At one stage, I counted at least seventeen homes in walking distance of our house. We began to link with other groups emerging in the city, like Redland, near the hub of student life around the university, which was led by Dave and Rhian Day, and the group in Patchway that Hugh and Rosemary Thompson left in the capable hands of Tony and Muriel Pullin when they moved to the north of England.

We encouraged people to have 'extended families' where possible, taking our lead from various translations of Psalm 68:6,

---

64. NIV

God sets the lonely in families.[65]

God settles the solitary in a home.[66]

God gives the desolate a home to dwell in.[67]

In this way we developed community, still retaining the boundaries of the family unit, but extending it, so its benefits could be shared.

---

65. NIV
66. ESV
67. RSV

Chapter 16

Hill House

The Meeting House was at full stretch! Three young children plus four people living with us, constant visitors, and many gatherings in our ancient meeting room. Linda and I had purchased a portable sofa-bed. We could fold it out and slept in different places around the house. To most people this might have seemed crazy, and in a way we were, but no one could doubt our commitment.

Take, for example, the night I was at a meeting in the Mount of Olives Pentecostal Church in Bristol, and on the way out I found a destitute young woman sitting on the front steps of the church. She had seen her father kill her mother and was in desperate need. I spoke to Pastor Robert Fairnie and volunteered to take her home. This was before we carried mobile phones everywhere. So it was quite a surprise for Linda when I turned up with her on a Sunday night. The next four months were as difficult as anything we had ever experienced. She was trouble with a capital T! At one stage, Linda had to go and stay in London with Christine Noble to recover. We even took her on our family holiday for two weeks. The day she left of her own volition, she threw a punch at Hazel, our faithful helper, and storming out the door told us all to 'piss off'. Some years later, Linda had a chance meeting with her in the street, and she told her that we had actually saved her life.

To return to our story, late one night we had a call from a couple leading a church in Bath, that we had been very involved in. Steve and Helen Appel needed to see us urgently and arrived on our doorstep after 10pm. They were very special friends. During the development of the Olveston community, we spent almost as much time in Bath as in Bristol. The group that met in their flat behind the Royal Crescent had grown rapidly into a vibrant church with a dynamic group of leaders, meeting in the Pump Room above the Roman Baths. Eventually, this would become Bath City Church and they purchased the Forum Cinema.

Every week I used to play squash with Steve, and then have time in fellowship and prayer with him and sometimes Helen and Linda as well. Their friendship meant a lot to us. We had a special time together this particular evening and when we prayed for them the Lord specifically spoke to me as well, so much so that after they left, I felt constrained to continue in prayer. Linda went to bed but I remained in prayer all night with an unusual sense of expectation.

Across the road from us, behind a high wall and a bank of very large trees, stood Hill House, a classic English manor house. We had heard a rumour that it was up for sale, even though no advertising was in evidence. As I waited before God, I had an overwhelming sense that we should buy this house. In the morning, I could scarcely wait for Linda to wake up so I could share my conviction with her. She really took me by surprise by saying, 'Are you going to make an appointment to see it?'

It somewhat knocked me back as I thought how can someone like me, who has nothing, make a pitch for the premiere house in the neighbourhood? There was no way out! So before I knew it, we were walking up the drive to meet Mr Parker. The viewing astounded us.

Set in magnificent grounds of approximately two-and-a-half acres, it had a lake with a stream running through it and was flanked by an ancient cider mill with the original circular stone press that a harnessed horse would walk around, crushing the apples. On the ground floor of the house was an imposing lounge with an inglenook fireplace. The bay window at the end looked down on to a lawn graced by a pond with an active fountain. On the opposite side of the hall, a cosy sitting room had a Victorian grate with 'Welcome Home' engraved on the front and standing supports for large kettles. Another sitting room was beyond this.

The spacious kitchen/diner boasted an Aga cooker, and another inglenook fireplace. All the massive windows, in walls about three-feet thick, had mullioned panes and protective iron bars. The iron grate in the inglenook could take massive logs – an impressive sight in winter. Whole carcasses could have been roasted above this! Up the impressive staircase was a delightful, panelled study with a 'priest's hole'[68] under the floor, and on the two floors above were two bathrooms and seven bedrooms. The cellar beneath the house had a stream running through to keep the wine racks at a good temperature. There

---

68. https://www.historic-uk.com/HistoryUK/HistoryofEngland/Priests-Holes/
In the 16th century religious beliefs could be a matter of life and death. Religion, politics and the monarchy were at the heart of how England was governed. Hiding places or 'priest's holes' were built in these houses in case there was a raid. Priest holes were built in fireplaces, attics and staircases and were largely constructed between the 1550s and the Catholic-led Gunpowder Plot in 1605.

were outhouses and four ancient water pumps around the property that meant the lawns remained green in the summer drought that we experienced soon after moving in.

At the time, the asking price was around £90,000, whereas the average house price in Olveston was £8,000–£11,000. By way of contrast, when I visited the village recently, the house had just been sold for £2,000,000! Large ancient trees from the New World surrounded the property. The house dated back to the thirteenth century and was in the Domesday Book.

After our extensive tour, we returned home full of excitement, but wondering how to proceed! Eventually, we made an offer which was sent to the solicitor – £40,000! I was on one of my trips to Norway when Linda contacted me with news from Mr Parker's solicitor: 'Dear Mr Lyne, we appreciate your interest, but is there any possibility you could raise your offer?'

I laughed when I read this, then said to Linda, 'We don't actually have £40,000, so let's raise it to £45,000!'

By the time I returned from Norway, their response had arrived. They had accepted our offer! Now the fat was in the fire! What on earth were we going to do?

As we discussed this, we felt it only decent for us to tell Nigel and Kirstie that we were planning to leave their Old Meeting House that we loved so much. I will never forget driving up to Cheltenham and the response we received from our dear friends. Nigel said he had felt before that Hill House should be purchased, and then made a radical suggestion: could we find someone in the church who might like to buy the Meeting House? We suspected this might be a possibility, as many people loved visiting our home. Then Nigel suggested, 'You find a buyer, and we will give you the proceeds as an interest-free loan to assist with the purchase of Hill House.'

On our way home, our excitement knew no bounds!

Within days, a couple of leaders from another part of the Bristol church, who were close friends, arranged to buy the Meeting House for £25,000. My next move was to call my friend Darrell Martin, of the Halifax Building Society office in the heart of Bristol. At that time, the Halifax was the largest building society in the UK. Sitting in his office, just adjacent to the city centre, Darrell heard our story. We needed a mortgage of £20,000. His response was very clear. At that time, this was the maximum mortgage a couple could apply for. He agreed to make the application but was very doubtful that it would be accepted, particularly because of the unique nature of our faith life! It wasn't long before we heard back from the Halifax.

They awarded us the full amount! We had our £45,000! Our offer was accepted and then we hit a snag! It transpired that in the case of a purchase on this scale, the government imposed a tax called 'stamp duty'. On this property, it was £900 (in New Zealand currency, about $3,000 at that time) – money we didn't have.

In the days following, another miracle happened. A lot of students were coming to our fellowship from the University of Bristol. This involved an eight-mile journey out of the city.

A young surgeon in training, Andy Smith, asked to come and see us. He and his fiancée, Ruth, the chairman and vice chairman of the university Christian Union, were keen to be part of the community. He had been reading in the Bible, the accounts of the Early Church in Acts. Barnabas had sold some land and brought the proceeds to the apostles' feet. He said to us, 'I have received an inheritance from my aunt, and feel as a sign of my commitment, I want to lay this at your feet. Please feel free to use it however you will.'

It was £900! News of our issue with the stamp duty had not been made public, so this was such a huge encouragement to us.

The great thing was that Tony and Muriel Pullin and their family moved into the Meeting House, so it remained in the heart of our Olveston community. We made the move across the road with our limited furniture, wondering how we would be able to furnish it. Another miracle was in store for us! One of the couples in the church, Andy and Gill Luxford, came to see us and said, 'Our aunt is going into a retirement home and is anxious that her house should be cleared. We are responsible for this, so please take a truck and bring back anything you would find helpful.'

There was no charge for any of this, but a surprise awaited us. Her house was full of antique furniture. I will never forget the huge mirror with a mahogany frame that fitted perfectly in the entrance hall as if it had been made for Hill House. You should have seen the massive bed and accompanying wardrobe that graced our master bedroom. Within no time at all, Linda and I, with our three children under five, moved in and nine others joined us.

Just imagine walking up the curving drive, flanked by the cider mill on one side, and the lawns overlooking the lake on the other; up the stone steps to the imposing oak door studded with iron, and enter an oak-panelled hall. A whole new phase had begun! The local people now called me 'the Squire', with tongue in cheek, I'm sure. One of the congregation said to Linda, 'It must be so special to live here.'

With extraordinary prescience, Linda replied, 'I know that if the Lord tells us to move out tomorrow, with our suitcases, we will go!'

We allowed a newly married, young couple, Dave and Annie McGuiness, to live on the top floor. Hazel, the first person to live with us at the Meeting House, continued to be a great support to us in Hill House. We had another key young woman join us, Ruth Crick, from John and Christine Noble's church in Romford. The rest of the household were students from Bristol University, mainly studying medicine. There were always friends and visitors, so we rarely sat down to dinner with less than fourteen people at the table.

It was a time of growth and consolidation of the new church, and with its strong links into the city, initiated by Dave and Rhian Day, it became BCF – Bristol Christian Fellowship. The Meeting House continued to be a vital gathering point and many church members bought homes in the village.

As well as adults, there had been an animal explosion! The lake was stocked with trout that could be fed by hand, and one day we found our neighbour's son, sitting on a stool fishing for them! Linda wanted some ducks, so she contacted a neighbouring farmer, Mrs Pierce, who assisted us. She told Linda to go and collect them with a big sack one night, and the plan was that Donald, the white runner, and his six lady friends could be kept in a duck house to the side of our property for forty-eight hours. Then, when let out, they would smell the lake and head down to the water. Unfortunately, they didn't seem to know about this! They fled in all directions, mostly into a farmer's field at the back of our garden. The last two got stuck under brambles there, and Linda with Peter Cutts, bravely crawled around in this field, rescuing them. Eventually, they got the routine, and were joined later by some Muscovies. There is an interesting footnote to this: I met the farmer down the lane and he wanted a chat with me. In his broad West Country accent he said, "Ere, I seen a couple of your lads crawling about in my field.' (Linda was now 'a lad'!) 'I don't mind, but you should know I've got a bull in there!'

The duck parade to and from the lake became a regular feature, and we had a white rowing boat, moored alongside. However, a complication arose. We also had a Shetland pony, Pixie, pastured in a friend's paddock with Napoleon, their huge black stallion; they were the best of friends. Jo regularly rode Napoleon, and Linda used to walk Pixie through the village on a long lead. One day, a guy called out to Linda from his car, 'Why don't you get a dog!'

Linda, the lover of animals, needed no encouragement! So, Shali, our Afghan hound arrived. Now Linda had Pixie on one lead and Shali on another. What we hadn't factored in was that Afghans are hunters, and now our ducks were in deadly peril. It meant that the door to the front garden had to be carefully closed at all times. This probably saved our children from drowning, as Simon, our youngest, was once found suspended above the deep water at the edge of the lake trying to get into the boat.

We loved Shali, and she loved another neighbour's dog, a beautiful Irish Wolfhound called Tess. Tess used to jump their five-barred gate and regularly come to visit. We built a strong friendship with our neighbours, and the animals proved to be an important point of contact. We made a habit of regularly having friends to dinner who were not part of our church family. To give you an idea of this, let me tell you what happened one evening.

I had been out at some meeting, and when I came home, Linda wasn't there. On enquiry, one of the guys said that Tess had jumped the gate and come to visit Shali. Linda, wearing her wellington boots, just returned from Pixie's field, slipped a lead on Tess and took her back to John and Valerie. They had a huge square table, and a major dinner party was underway. Valerie immediately asked Linda to stay, and when I arrived, she was deep in conversation with a man responsible for selling Concorde, the supersonic aircraft; he was off to Hong Kong the next day. Valerie introduced me to all the guests and asked me to share what we were doing in the community. They were always very open to us and frequently asked me to say grace at dinner parties!

In the first months at Hill House, our marriage came under pressure! We always loved each other, and still do, but things became very tense. We started to argue a lot and found it difficult to resolve issues. We were probably overstretched, which was understandable really, but I began to feel the strain in my spiritual life as well. I had always loved to meditate in Scripture every day and pray, but this was becoming a challenge. We didn't seem to be able to resolve it and I was becoming increasingly worried.

One night, a turning point was reached. Linda was unwell and had gone to bed early. I was due to host our regular household meeting, an important part of our church life. I can honestly say, the last thing I wanted was a meeting, but out of obedience and a sense of responsibility, I made the effort. As I slumped in my chair, Pete Cutts picked up his guitar and began to strum a song we loved, from the book of Ruth: *Cover me, cover me, extend the border of your mantle over me ...*[69]

As we sang, the Holy Spirit spoke to me, so simply, but very firmly: 'This is your problem, Peter! You're uncovered.' In a moment of time, I saw a solution. Tony and Muriel, our fellow leaders, lived just across the road in the Meeting House. We had a good friendship, but I saw we needed to do something more. We needed to invite their covering! When I shared this with Linda, she readily agreed, as things had got quite difficult between us. We made an appointment to see Tony and Mu, and their response was amazing. Tony said, 'We've wanted to share with you for some time but haven't felt free to.'

Now the gloves were off and they didn't pull any punches! I won't go into detail with the issues we got to grips with, but it led to such significant healing in us both, and

---

69. A song inspired by Ruth 3:9

wonderfully secured our future. I know that the term 'covering' has often been abused and, consequently, people fight shy of it. Let me say this, which I think is the key: Ruth provoked Boaz to cover her, not the other way around, and had she not done this, King David would never have come to the throne.

We have always recognised the importance of Paul's teaching on spiritual warfare in Ephesians chapter 6. We really don't wrestle against flesh and blood, but principalities and powers![70] During this phase in Hill House, Linda had a serious headache for three days, but in a time of desperate prayer something was revealed to us. Although Mr and Mrs Parker were living in the house together, it was only until it sold. They had already separated. It was a house of conflict! We came together in prayer, I believe it was with Ruth Crick, an unusual anointing descended upon us. We took authority over a 'divisive spirit' and saw an immediate answer. Linda's headache lifted and so did the spirit adversely affecting our lives.

We had so many special times in Hill House: big barbecues when all the church gathered; a fabulous wedding for Graham and Ruth; the time when a whole group of Danish young people on 'Rent-a-Bikes' turned up at our door. There was never a dull moment at our kitchen table, the conversation sometimes graphic and gory with all the medical students. Not long after this, a member of our fellowship was standing in a queue at the greengrocers and overheard two ladies in conversation. 'There has been

---

70. Ephesians 6:12 NKJV

such a change in Hill House. I used to think it so dark and oppressive, but now it seems light and free!'

Throughout the Olveston years, we continued to have strong links with Bath and were often at Monkton Combe. We did a Bible Week on the school grounds with other leaders from the west. We hosted the first Scripture in Song event with the Garratts in the school hall. We had a favourite restaurant there called Tearles in a boathouse on the Bathampton river. The owners of this unique place, David and Lisa Tearle, came to visit us in Hill House. We took June Sampson there who had become one of our closest friends. She owned Vineyards Farm nearby, just opposite the American Museum. Amanda loved June who taught her to ride and gave her Pixie, the Shetland pony. She painted a marvellous portrait of our three children. We all loved being with her and this relationship continued through the years until shortly before her death. She had been widowed quite young, and later in life married Adrian. We last saw them, living in Bournemouth.

During these four years there was a development, initiated by my friend and mentor, Arthur Wallis. He called together a group of seven at his home in Talaton, Devon, initially to study biblical prophecy. His concern was that there was so much conflicting teaching in the Church at large on these important issues. I was invited, along with Graham Perrins, Bryn Jones, David Mansell, Hugh Thompson and Lance Lambert, who didn't make it because he was sick. What an extraordinary time we had, but not in the manner we had expected. The emphasis became on the making of prophets, not esoteric study. It was the release of ministries that became the focus of powerful prophetic prayer times.

I remember Bryn as having very definite prophetic input, including the message: 'Three times you shall meet, and seven shall be your number.' This happened that year, but John Noble was invited as Lance had missed the initial meeting. The following year, we doubled in size to fourteen, and looking back at these gatherings I would suggest that these men represented the key leaders of the New Church Networks that emerged in Great Britain. Even when a division was perpetrated between us, primarily by Arthur and Bryn, I have retained friendship across the board and was glad to see so much ground recovered in later years. Bryn even asked me to come specially to minister to all his leaders. Sadly he died just before this happened; Linda and I were privileged to be at his funeral. Sociologist, Dr Andrew Walker has conferred with me twice on his erudite book *Restoring the Kingdom*[71] and I feel his presentation of these developments in New Church history is fairly reliable. One thing that has been clear to me is that the unique feature of all these developments has been the understanding that the Church must be relational, not institutional. We were friends who would eat together, play together and invest in each other's lives. I have not found much evidence of this in other countries to the same degree. Most of these men were my friends long before Arthur called us together.

As you will discover from the rest of this story, we had to leave Olveston, and much sooner than we had expected. It's easy to be wise after the event, but could we have done things differently? I believe we had a remarkable four years in Olveston, two-and-a-half in the Meeting House, and a year and a half in Hill House, before the amazing events

---

71. Andrew Walker, *Restoring the Kingdom* (Hodder & Stoughton, 1985)

that led us to New Zealand. We have faced all sorts of questions over this and had many more ourselves. We would have loved to purchase the Meeting House, and subsequently Hill House. These were early days in the life of the church and we didn't have the strong financial base that would come later.

The accounts I have given of how we came to Olveston, the Meeting House and subsequently Hill House, are all miraculous. They were all undergirded by significant prophecies. Shelagh McAlpine originally told me that I would be required to take many 'faith steps' and this has proved to be true. Now a new prophetic word to us was quite clear: 'God wants you to identify with Abraham. He wants you to sell your house and move out in faith in a new way.'

We even tried something of a compromise: the old cider mill, a wonderful stone building, looking out on orchards, and at the side of the property, with a separate entrance, would have made a lovely home. In addition, it had a garage joined to the front, and a potential flat above the garage. Sometime before we received this prophecy, I had asked my architect friend, Colin Wide, to draw up plans converting this to a four-bedroom home. We consulted with local authorities from the beginning and had a green light, right until the end. Then a frustrating series of events unfolded. Colin sought permission to join this part of our building to the main wastewater system in the village and it was declined. The explanation: the system is overloaded, and this can't be allowed. At the time, Monty Benson and other builders were managing to build rows of new houses in Olveston! Alright, we will install a septic tank. No, this is not permitted in the district. As a last resort, we lodged an appeal, which was also rejected.

Our plan was to have a home base in Olveston that we could rent out to others while we were away. This would have affected the value of the main house, but we could probably have sold it to someone in the church who could fulfil our vision. In the end, we had to let it go, and we sold the property to Brian Nathan[72] for £52,000, I believe. This allowed us to repay Nigel and Kirstie in full, clear the mortgage with the Halifax Building Society and return Andy and Ruth's gift as they were getting married.

We had just enough to settle everything, buy our return tickets to New Zealand, dispose of all we had, including giving a lot away. When we finally left on November 7th, we had just five suitcases and our duvets in canvas bags. That was us! Why did this happen? You must be the judge! A few weeks after our arrival in Auckland, we received a letter from the council. They had rescinded their previous judgement. Now we were free to join the sewage system! They had cost us thousands of pounds, but these things we leave in God's hands and refuse to harbour resentment.

Tony and Muriel made a great job of including the Meeting House in the life of the church. Later, they bought another house in the village, and John and Sally Birch took over. John became a local GP, and he and Sally ran the home well for many years until they joined a new church-plant

72. A strange little footnote: when Brian Nathan bought our house he said, 'You will see my family, the Nathans, fairly prominent in Auckland.' We did, and the family mansion became part of the University of Auckland where my daughter, Amanda, had her office for many years, working for Alumni development and responsible for major events in the grounds of that house.

with another of our leaders, Dr Nic Harding and his wife Jenny. They established Frontline in the heart of Liverpool. Whenever we returned from New Zealand during the period from 1977 until 1983, it was always to Olveston, often staying in different people's homes.

We loved these early years in Olveston, in spite of all the challenges. In retrospect, I would say that the steps of faith required of us during this time, established us as nothing else could for the journey ahead.

Chapter 17

New Zealand

Having nothing, yet possessing everything, was never more dramatically fulfilled than in the events that sent us to New Zealand. We had lived for four years from 1973 in Olveston, in two of the most prestigious houses in the community, the Old Quaker Meeting House and, subsequently, Hill House. As I have already said, we went into these homes with no personal finance at all, and in that process experienced unique training in the life of faith we were to pursue.

How did this come to pass? Our guidance came through the means that the Lord has used repeatedly over these last fifty years. Firstly, and perhaps primarily, he sent his word. At the start of 1977 I was impressed to meditate in the life of Abraham, mentioned throughout Scripture. This was in addition to my daily consecutive reading and meditation in the Bible, which, for me, as with the psalmist, is

A lamp to my feet and a light to my path.[73]

For almost two months I had been contemplating Abraham's life very carefully and speaking regularly about him, especially during a ministry trip to Norway. When addressing our Olveston community in the Old Meeting House on my return, I focused on the testimony to Abraham in the great faith chapter Hebrews 11:

---

73. Psalm 119:105 ESV

By faith Abraham, when called to go to a place
he would later receive as his inheritance, obeyed and went,
even though he did not know where he was going.[74]

The next day the drama unfolded! I received a phone call from a young woman called Gilly Bell, asking if she could come and see us. Such calls were not uncommon and I assumed she was seeking counsel over some issue. What was interesting was that I scarcely knew her as she lived in the neighbouring city of Bath and was a member of a church that I was helping to get established there. However, things moved very quickly. Gilly was working for Rolls Royce Aero Engines in Filton, just a fifteen-minute drive from our home. There was a sense of urgency in her voice, 'Could I come straight away during my lunch break?'

Soon after, there was a knock at our huge imposing door and there stood Gilly looking quite frail and anxious. I should also say that her hearing was impaired and she relied a lot on lip-reading. We didn't have time to sit down as she immediately blurted out the reason for her visit as we stood in the mahogany-panelled entrance hall. She immediately attracted my attention with, 'God wants you to identify with Abraham.'

All the bells began to ring at this point, as I had been constantly meditating on this for two months. Then she said, 'You will have to tell me if this is all wrong, but I believe you should sell your house and move out in faith in a new way.'

---

74. Hebrews 11:8 NIV

As she had just driven up the imposing drive to the front door of our classical English manor house, this was a very courageous thing to say. We encouraged Gilly to sit down and have a cup of tea with us before returning to work. What she hadn't told us was that she had been fasting and praying for us over the previous two days. We assured her that her obedience was very important in this matter and that we would weigh her words very carefully.

Gilly went back to work, and Linda and I spent the rest of the day until quite late in the evening giving due consideration to what she had said. One thing we felt sure about was that a prophet had spoken. Alongside the Lord speaking to us through his word, he has repeatedly sent his prophets to us. I remember our final discussion before we went to bed: 'If this is God, and I believe it is, there will be more!'

The very next day – and consider this carefully if you are among those who are sceptical of prophecy – a letter arrived in our mailbox. It was from a prominent solicitor in Bristol whom we had never met, and when I read it, I ran up the stairs to Linda, literally shaking as I gave it to her. The essence of the letter was this:

Dear Mr Lyne, is there any possibility of you selling your house in the near future? We have an important client who is interested in your historic home and think it might be mutually beneficial if you were disposed to consider this.

Apart from anything else, consider the logistics of this happening with such impeccable timing! I said to Linda,

'We must call the leaders together and get them to weigh all this with us.' They felt it was serious enough for the church to come together that weekend. In the meantime, I believe it was the Friday night as we were going to bed that we said, 'If the Lord has shown us so clearly to go, we can equally expect him to show us where we should go.'

That night, the drama unfolded, Linda awoke around 2am with a clear voice within saying, 'Go to New Zealand.'

Quite independently, I said to her, 'Love, are you awake? I believe God has shown me where we should go. New Zealand.'

Linda, who had been holding her breath, sighed with relief, thrilled that we were on the same page.

At this point I said, 'Let me go downstairs to pray and confirm if this is correct.'

I went to our farmhouse kitchen which had a comfortingly warm Aga range that I used to sit by. I picked up a book I was reading by the great missionary pioneer to India, Dr E. Stanley Jones. I opened to the next chapter of my reading and Dr Jones was speaking about the faith of Abraham. He then shared a very helpful principle of guidance:

> *If ever I have had uncertainty about a particular course of action, the words from Psalm 127 have been a great help to me: 'He gives to his beloved sleep.'*[75] *The margin says: 'He gives to his beloved in sleep'. When*

---

75. Psalm 127:2 ESV

244

I retire to bed for the night, I lay my problems before the Father, and go to sleep. Again and again, I have awakened knowing exactly what I should do!

My New International Version alternate reading says,

For while they sleep, he provides for those he loves.

This is literally what had happened to Linda and me!

Later that weekend, as we shared all these developments with the church, one of our elders, Mike Roberts, a reputable prophet, interrupted us and said, 'Just after Christmas, I had a vivid dream in which I saw you sell Hill House and move overseas. I have not known what to do with this but have been wandering up and down in the fields surrounding Hill House praying for the appropriate time to share it.' He then went on to prophesy very powerfully concerning our going forth, which included a promise that we would go out in abundance.

So, in addition to God's word, incredible circumstantial confirmation through the solicitor's letter and the counsel of our brothers and sisters who loved us, we were now convinced that we should set the wheels in motion with New Zealand as our destination.

In important matters of prophecy, Paul says:

Two or three prophets should speak,
and the others should weigh carefully what is said.[76]

---

76. 1 Corinthians 14:29 NIV

Here are two additional and important factors in guidance:

1. Agreement – especially between husband and wife.
2. The written or preached word from anointed men and women.

When we had discussed destination in the previous days, I had wondered if it should be Norway because of my frequent travel, teaching and preaching, and encouraging new churches, over several years. Strangely, New Zealand is very similar to Norway in many ways. Its population, its physical similarities with the fjords, its political independence, even harness-racing, which is both a Norwegian and New Zealand sport.

Now we were certain of our direction in the new faith journey. We set our sights to cover all the bases. We had nine people living with us and three children under five. We put the wheels in motion for the sale of the house. The initial enquiry didn't come to anything, and I put the house on the market with Knight, Frank and Rutley, England's premier property company at the time.

Here's an interesting aside: when our agent secured serious interest from Brian Nathan, his surveyor reported a serious disease in the wooden beams, particularly above our master bedroom. It was in danger of collapsing. The agent said to me on a Friday afternoon, 'Let's take it off the market temporarily and I will try to get another interested party and hope they don't get a serious survey done.'

My response was immediate, 'I'm sorry, but we don't do business like that. Anyone who purchases this house will know exactly what the situation is.'

The line went silent. The following Monday, I received another call from the agent, 'Mr Nathan wants to know how much he must pay to achieve this purchase.'

Today, when I read this account to Linda, she rightly pointed out that I had glossed over the immense, emotional challenges of this time. When we got to the day before we left the UK, we had insufficient funds to provide for us on the journey, let alone anything else! People often say things like, 'You must be so excited about this trip you are taking', not knowing how it feels to be on tenterhooks as to how it will work out. Fortunately, Tony Pullin interrupted the worship that night and gave us a cheque for £1,000, and everyone cheered as we breathed a sigh of relief. This generous gift paid for a two-day stopover in Los Angeles en route and our first nights on arrival in New Zealand on November 11th.

One very specific aspect of the word that we had received regarding Abraham was that we should go out *not knowing*. We were not to go through any pre-arranged contact. For example, two couples that had been my main mentors, Campbell and Shelagh McAlpine and Arthur Wallis, had fulfilled extensive periods of ministry there. Also, David and Dale Garratt of Scripture in Song had stayed with us in Olveston on their first tour of the UK.

It was only after we arrived from the long journey in Auckland that the penny fully dropped! We had come through what seemed to be a basic aircraft hangar – not the sophisticated international airport that is in place today – and we were sitting in the back of the taxi, driving into Auckland, when the thought came to me: 'What have I done?'

I needn't have worried. We collapsed onto our beds and Linda opened the *Daily Light*, which we regularly read at that time. The little book that has been such a blessing to us has a Scripture in bold type at the top of each page, followed by similar confirming verses. The reading for November 11th said,

He led them on safely.[77]

Behold, I send an Angel before you to keep you in the way and to bring you to the place which I have prepared.[78]

With that, we fell asleep!

---

77. Psalm 78:53 KJV
78. Exodus 23:20 NKJV

Chapter 18

Identify with Abraham!

Before pressing on with the narrative of our arrival in New Zealand, I want to take more time unfolding the life-changing prophecy from Gilly Bell. As a student of the New Testament, I have discovered that important doctrine is often scattered throughout the gospels and epistles, but is also focused in a particular passage that emphasises its importance. As an example, consider spiritual gifts. They pop up all over the place in both the Old and New Testaments, but Paul's exposition in 1 Corinthians 12 to 14 is of paramount importance. So it is with faith; Hebrews 11 is the great faith chapter in the New Testament, and although a galaxy of heroes is mentioned, and evidently the writer would have wished to include more,[79] Abraham is undoubtedly the central figure. This view is endorsed by Paul in his pivotal statement central to his Galatian epistle:

If you belong to Christ, then you are Abraham's seed, and heirs according to the promise.[80]

Subsequent to receiving this word from Gilly, I have seen this as the Abrahamic call which has shaped so much of our lives in the following years. When the Lord called Abraham to leave the security of his life in Ur of the Chaldees,

---

79. Hebrews 11:32
80. Galatians 3:29 NIV

followed by a staging post in Haran where his father died, he headed on towards the Land of Promise, homeless but carrying a seven-fold promise!

1. I will make you into a great nation and
2. *I will bless you*
3. *I will make your name great and*
4. *You will be a blessing*
5. *I will bless those who bless you and*
6. *Whoever curses you I will curse*
7. *And all the peoples on the earth will be blessed through you.*[81]

Here we see God's all-encompassing intention. He wants all the peoples on earth to be blessed by Abraham's obedience. The promises are massive, to Abraham personally, but they are not solely focused on him. A much greater purpose is in view.

At twenty-one years of age, when I finally capitulated to the Lordship of Christ, I began to soak myself in Scripture. At the same time, I pursued anointed Bible teachers wherever I could find them. One of these, Graham Perrins from South Wales, greatly helped me in my early understanding. During 1980–1983 I was leading the Valley Road Baptist Church in Mount Eden, Auckland, and invited Graham to speak at some special events in New Zealand. I will never forget his introductory message. Talking about Abraham

---

81. Genesis 12:2-3 NIV

and the extraordinary promises God had given to him, at the end of his life, what exactly did he possess? When his nephew Lot had finally separated from his uncle and had grabbed the most promising parts of the territory, the Lord told Abraham it all belonged to him anyway.[82] We are also told that although he was essentially a nomad, he was, perhaps, the richest man on the earth in terms of his flocks, herds and monetary wealth. But what did he possess?

Graham pointed out it was essentially two things: a child of promise – Isaac – and a burial plot – the cave of Machpelah – that he purchases in Genesis 23. It is literally *having nothing, yet possessing everything*. The postscript at the end of Hebrews chapter 11 says this,

These were all commended for their faith, yet none of them received what had been promised, since God had planned something better for us so that only together with us would they be made perfect.[83]

A humorous footnote to this is that a few months ago, Linda saved up and bought me a burial plot in a cemetery that overlooks Mangawhai in New Zealand. We may not have a house still, but we do have a grave suitable for two coffins and scattered ashes of others. I've always said I want to be buried, although Linda is indifferent to this. Now, even though we still don't have a house, we are prepared.

And as for the child of promise, we do have seed in New Zealand: ten grandchildren who are prayed for every day,

---

82. Genesis 13:14-17
83. Hebrews 11:39-40 NIV

and everywhere we go we encounter people impacted through our ministry. On a fairly regular basis we have had wonderful long lunches at Mark and Mieke Bond's beautiful Olive Grove, and some thirty former Bristol people now living in New Zealand, gather for this, usually with our old stalwarts who still live in Olveston, Angus and Fiona Macaskill on flying visits – literally!

Chapter 19

Upper Hutt

After our long journey to Auckland, I rose very early the next morning to find a newspaper pushed under the door. I scanned this and found a page devoted to property letting where something caught my eye. A couple were going overseas for three months and wished to let their home situated in a suburb called Mount Eden. I didn't know where that was but as soon as I felt it was an appropriate time, I made the call. Their immediate response was, 'We've had lots of interest in this, but you sound like just the right people. Can you come and see us?'

Of course! We had no other plans. They explained where we could get a bus and so we arrived at Ellerton Road, at a delightful home in a popular suburb close to the city. After a short tour, they explained how they were educational psychologists going on a study trip to the United States. They offered us a three-month rental, fully furnished at a very reasonable cost.

'What are you doing tonight? they said.

Nothing, of course!

'Can you come out for a barbecue?'

We were thrilled to comply, and it only got better. Over that great Kiwi tradition, the barbecue, they also offered us their fairly new Citroen car at a very basic rental. This is something we hadn't even thought about. Auckland didn't have a public transport system to equate with London, and it has one of the largest sprawls of any city in the world. Also, under the existing Muldoon Government, car finance was 28% and mortgage finance would have been 30%. Eyewatering figures! The car proved a fantastic asset.

They then said, 'We aren't leaving for two weeks, but our aunt has a bach at Waiwera up the Coast, would you like to go there?'

Apart from not being familiar with the term *bach*, or where Waiwera was, we were ready for anything. It turned out to be a classic Kiwi holiday cottage right on the beach at a resort famous for its hot springs nearby. A bus got us there in about one hour and we settled into a delightful twoweek holiday, recovering from all the pressure of our final wind-down in Olveston and the immensely long trip to the other side of the world. During our time at Waiwera, an Auckland lawyer and his wife befriended us, and when it came time to relocate to the house in Ellerton Road, they helped us transfer everything back to the city.

Yes, he did lead us on safely, and who could predict how this would unfold? We settled into Ellerton Road, got Amanda into the primary school nearby and began a very different existence. We had been right at the hub of a rapidly expanding community, managing our large extended family and fulfilling many ministry responsibilities with the growing House-church Movement in Britain.

In those first few weeks, the phone scarcely rang – usually for the absentee landlords – and there was no flow of people through our front door. It was a very important break for us. Having lived life at such a pressured level, we now had time for each other and the children. We made friends with a couple in the street with whom we played cards, and on our first Sunday, we visited the local Baptist church.

Little did we know when we discovered the Valley Road Baptist Church on the corner of the High Street in Mt Eden, the significance of this place, or, indeed, the part it would play in our future. They were meeting in a new building with perhaps 300 people and had been exposed to some influence from the Charismatic Movement circling the globe at that time.

At the end of a fairly mundane service, we shook hands with the pastor, David Jacobsen, at the door, who enquired where we had come from. When I mentioned the UK and some of our connections there, he was visibly excited. He said, 'Please wait here a moment, I want to introduce you to somebody.'

In our initial exchange, the names of my key mentors, Arthur Wallis and Campbell McAlpine came up. David returned with their senior elder, Blythe Harper. He said, 'Blythe and I were responsible for bringing Arthur Wallis out to New Zealand!'

I remembered walking in the country lanes around the village of Talaton in Devon, where Arthur and Eileen lived, and him telling me the story of how he came to go to New Zealand. One day, a letter had arrived in the post, inviting Arthur to speak on revival at a conference there. Arthur's iconic book *In the Day of Thy Power* had had quite a far-reaching impact and they were keen for him to come. It must be said that in the Sixties, international travel was not what it is today. The voyage by ship would take at least six weeks, and even plane travel was quite complicated. Arthur's response was a sustained chuckle! He had never received an invitation to go so far for three or four weeks of ministry. However, the first letter was followed up soon afterward with the inclusion of plane tickets. He began to make serious plans to pursue this.

The rest is history. Arthur's one-month visit turned into seventeen months! In the midst of it, arrangements were made for Eileen to join him, but with son Jonathon at home, she couldn't stay too long.

Overlapping with this, my other mentors, Campbell and Shelagh McAlpine, were in New Zealand for four years during this time. Both Arthur and Campbell were at the forefront of bringing the message of the Charismatic Movement particularly, to the evangelical churches including the Open Brethren in New Zealand. Great things happened and considerable opposition was stirred up.

Shortly after Campbell and Shelagh returned from New Zealand in 1964, I became a close friend and was deeply impacted by their ministry. When they had first arrived in New Zealand, they had experienced great acceptance and particular encouragement from the vibrant Open Brethren churches. A significant figure in this was Sir Robert Laidlaw who founded the Farmers Trading Company, still a very successful retail organisation today. Campbell told me that Robert and a group of his colleagues had met with him not long after their arrival and said, 'Campbell, we want to provide you with a house, furnish it and put a car in the garage.' A fantastic offer, but as Campbell was praying, he felt the Lord say to him:

Let no one say I have made Abram rich.[84]

He turned it down! Later, when Campbell and Arthur were excommunicated by the Brethren because of their teaching on the Holy Spirit, he realised how important this was. The trouble was that Robert could not accept the charismatic emphasis, but when they left New Zealand on a ship to return to England, he came on board before they departed and wept over them and their lost friendship. Letters had been sent all over New Zealand declaring Arthur and Campbell to have 'unclean spirits' because of their teaching on spiritual gifts and speaking in tongues. These were two of the most holy men I have ever known. I believe in that moment, the Brethren Movement had cursed itself!

I realise that Linda and I owe a great debt to Campbell and Shelagh for the life of faith that their example encouraged in us. Let me mention two other examples.

During their four years in New Zealand, they faced a major challenge through a health issue with their daughter, Patricia. She developed an undiagnosed disease where one of her legs was wasting away. All hospital visits proved to no avail. It seemed that treatment involved lying on a plank for long periods of time, and, despite persistent prayer, things were getting worse. One night, Campbell

---

84. See Genesis 14:23

and Shelagh, in desperation, faced the crunch. The Lord confronted them with a question: 'Are you willing that I should take your child?' After excruciating prayer, they reached a place of total surrender and offered her up to the Lord if this should be his will. With that, the burden suddenly lifted. They anointed Patricia with oil and prayed before they went to sleep. The next morning, she ran into their bedroom with her leg completely restored!

I can't resist sharing another story. During a later relocation to the United States to be teacher-in-residence at a big church in San Jose, Campbell was on a preliminary visit prior to their move. On the way in, the airline had lost his bags, so he proceeded to the church and taught the Sunday morning congregation. He preached on the 'open cheque' God gave to Solomon:

'Ask! What shall I give you?'[85]

At the end of the service, the pastor told Campbell that his bags were at the airport and that a member of the congregation would drive him there to collect them. On the journey, the man driving the car passed Campbell a cheque. He said, 'You may use this for anything you need – new house, car, whatever! I won't know until I see the money gone from my account.'

Campbell internally began to make plans, then the Lord spoke to him. He handed the cheque back to the man and said, 'The Lord wants you to know you've passed your test. Incidentally, I've passed one too!'

---

85. 2 Chronicles 1:7 NKJV

While we were enjoying being together as a family in this new country, the emotional struggles and logistical elements of what we were doing were never easy! We missed home and the dynamic of the community that we had established. We dutifully went along to the Valley Road Church, but we were now spectators of a religious set-up that was in the early stages of its death throes. Many times we vowed never to return there.

The relational dynamics that were so important to us in England were never very evident in New Zealand and still are much the same. The churches have tended to pursue American models that the Australians also embrace, revolving around programmes and success, rather than a New Testament expression of the Body of Christ. There are exceptions, but I have yet to see any major change in this. People become pew-sitters with various forms of authoritarian leadership whose motto seems to be 'My way or the highway'.

We had a monthly support cheque from our Bristol church, which enabled us to survive financially. We learned to live on a very tight budget having previously managed a huge household with constant hospitality. Treats involved a walk down to Potters Park or an occasional visit to the beach, but we couldn't afford to go very far, and I don't recall any restaurant visits. There were many moments when we felt like throwing in the towel and using our return ticket to come home. Some friendships we made helped alleviate this, but I remember Senior Pastor David Jacobsen visiting us just before we left to relocate to Upper Hutt. He came to our house and said that he felt 'impoverished' that he hadn't drawn us into a relationship with the church. His words, not mine! I really don't think he knew how to do that and, after a relationship with New Zealand spanning more than forty years, I still don't think most leaders know how to do this either.

One respite in terms of the ministry at Valley Road at this time came in the form of two talks by veteran missionary, Ivor Davies, of the Worldwide Evangelisation Crusade. He shared his own remarkable experience of revival in the Congo. It was fantastic stuff but had a sad sting in the tail! The majority of the missionaries there who had prayed earnestly for revival for years, couldn't accept it when it happened! All too messy for them. Sounds like a familiar story.

As Christmas approached, we got to make more new friends, and the associate pastor David McBride and his wife and family took us under their wing. When Linda and I had been preparing to leave for New Zealand, a very clear sense of direction had been given to us. We were not to simply engage in itinerant ministry as it opened up, we were going to come into a place prepared for us. As it turned out, these weeks in Mt Eden were a preparation for this.

Just prior to Christmas, we met a couple who were on the leadership team of a Baptist church in Petone, a suburb of the capital city Wellington. They enquired if we would be willing to drive the 400 miles down to Wellington for a weekend of ministry. We had a sense that it was important for us to go even though very little provision was made for the journey. We took an inadequate tent and stayed the night on the shores of Lake Taupo. I slept in the car! Then we had an overnight visit to Palmerston North, staying with a key apostolic figure, Ken Wright. I think he was quite unsure as to why we were in New Zealand. The next day we arrived in Petone and were housed in the home of a couple who were away on holiday.

As we had been driving towards Wellington the previous days, Linda and I had a growing sense that this was where we were supposed to be. We took our meetings at the church and were warmly received by the people but didn't feel that this was the place where we were supposed to be. The final day, feeling somewhat reluctant to pack up, we received a phone call. It was the wife of the elder who had invited us down to the church. She said, 'I have just been talking to my uncle who lives further up the Hutt Valley from here and he is keen to meet you. I wonder if you would mind giving him a call.'

When I called Hudson Salisbury, he asked if we could come to lunch at their home in Silverstream, halfway up the Hutt Valley. Upper Hutt is a small city that is a suburb of Wellington. Of course, we were free, we had no plans, so we set out, not knowing what was in store for us!

Hudson and Joan received us on their lovely patio with a swimming pool and surrounded by grapevines. He was a builder of luxury homes and had been an elder of the Brethren assembly. He and his brother-in-law, Jack, had physically built the local Brethren Assembly together. The Charismatic Movement had a powerful impact in churches across the valley and Hudson and Joan had opened their substantial rumpus room for a series of Life in the Spirit seminars. Doing this, he and Jack had fallen foul of the Brethren eldership. Steeped as they were in dispensationalism, they had no place for speaking in tongues and spiritual gifts.

So Hudson and Joan decided to launch out on their own, gathering some new contacts to form a small house-church which had just begun to meet. Over the lunch, we really warmed to each other. There was something special about our meeting. Then 'Hud', as we called him, dropped the bombshell. He said, 'I have been praying for over six months for God to send me a man to help establish the church here. I believe you are the answer to my prayers. Will you come?'

I looked at Linda, who was equally overwhelmed by this turn of events, and we both knew this was it, the place prepared! The logistics were possible. Our three-month lease was almost at an end. It's important to say that we must always be sensitive to the promptings of the Holy Spirit. Prior to this, as the end of our lease approached, our card-playing friends in Ellerton Road were off overseas and had offered us their home. We had agreed as it seemed such a timely provision, but that night Linda hadn't been able to sleep, and in the morning felt strongly that we should turn it down!

To ratify all this, Hudson asked us to move into their home for a week, so we went back to Petone, said our goodbyes, and loaded our meagre belongings into the car. This first week was important as Hudson wanted me to meet city leaders and then the members of his fledgling church who seemed to come from every denomination in the valley. The leaders evidently approved of us. We met Tom Marshall, the gifted Bible teacher and leader of the church at Raumati; Eric Chambers, pastor of Miramar Baptist Church near Wellington Airport (formerly pastor of the Amersham Baptist Church in the UK and he already knew of me); Gordon Langrell, a key Anglican priest also in the Hutt Valley; and Frank Garrett, who had a powerful deliverance ministry. All of these leaders became friends, and we ministered freely among them.

When we met with the church group, they wanted us to come as soon as possible, so we made plans to drive back to Auckland, sort out everything to do with the house and car and friends and church. Then we took the overnight Silver Star train and embarked on our adventure to Wellington. We now had nine months to run on our tourist visa before we had to leave the country, and incredibly, these would prove to be some of the most dramatic and fulfilling months of all our ministry.

Hud got us into a big, rented house round the corner with a tennis court and lots of children's toys, which the family left for our children – very helpful, as they had had to leave nearly all their toys in England. If this sounds glamorous, and on the surface it appeared so, it had its drawbacks. The rental house was immediately sold the day after we moved in, so our tenure would be less than three months. Also, it was a 'troubled' house. Looking at the bookshelves, we discovered the people were connected with the occult Siam Society and strange things happened there! We needed a lot of prayer for this. Later, we had to have another temporary rental house, and all these upheavals were not easy on us as a family.

Immediately a lot of people began to gather, and I realised straight away that my priority was to establish a clear foundation of commitment to this mixed multitude. For several weeks, I ran a commitment course on very basic foundational truths for church life. Much of this was to establish a relational foundation, not a religious structure. I presented the material in this way: 'The teaching I am providing will require a response and at the end of this series, I will be looking for a definite level of commitment. However, if you feel your roots are really in the church you have come from, or somewhere else, then these principles we have shared will help you make a wholesome commitment there. We have to build with people who know that this is where they are meant to be set in the Body of Christ.'

At the same time, I prepared our emerging leadership to take responsibility for those who were coming: answering questions, praying for their needs, and helping them to make a response that would best suit them.

Meanwhile, at the Sunday Gatherings, faith levels were rising, and new people were coming. We began to relate to a lot of students from a nearby training college. Every week, people were coming to the Lord and being baptised in Hudson's pool in the back garden, and there were miracles of deliverance and healing. At the same time some opposition arose and these incidents I well recall, as they resulted in significant signs. When John Wesley sent out his apprentice preachers, he would ask them two questions when they returned: Did anyone get converted? Did anyone get mad?

If the answer was negative to both questions, he would say that he thought the person was not called to this kind of ministry.

One Sunday night, at the end of a busy and fulfilling day, there was an urgent banging at our front door. I found Hudson outside looking very anxious. 'There's trouble and we need to meet with the leaders straight away,' he said.

We drove up to Trevor's house and sat around in a group in the lounge. There was obviously an awkward atmosphere, but I couldn't discern what it was. After some initial to-ing and fro-ing, Hudson said, 'I think we should pray.'

I responded, 'I don't want to pray; I want to get to the bottom of what's happening here.'

So we sat in silence. After some time, our youngest leader, Paul Jackson, brought a very powerful prophecy. With this, Trevor crumpled to his knees and began to weep as the truth came out. Early on in our meetings he had been leading worship on the piano but he was not skilled enough and everyone was on the edge of their seat waiting for him to hit another wrong note. I had said it would be better for us to sing unaccompanied and it seems he took offence. Subsequently, a young married woman with a baby began to cause trouble and although Hudson and I sought to bring counsel and discipline to her, she would have none of it. She actually abandoned her husband and the baby, but before she left, she found Trevor's ear and filled him with her offence against me.

At this point Trevor said, 'I felt the Lord showed me that the devil had sent you to New Zealand to destroy the Church.'

There was much brokenness over this and a thorough repentance; he became one of our closest friends. But just imagine if we had not brought this to the light and tried to soldier on with such a problem at the heart of our fragile leadership. In my experience, leadership teams have often had critical issues that have been swept under the carpet and not been thoroughly dealt with.

The second opposition came from an unexpected quarter and could have proved even more damaging. We had another very positive weekend of ministry, but the following morning, I took the children down to school and kindergarten and returned home to find Linda in a state of agitation in the kitchen.

'What's wrong?'

'I've just had the devil on the phone, and it was terrible!'

I quickly tried to defuse this unlikely event, and then the phone rang again, and yes, it was a heavily demonic voice!

'Who are you?' I said.

'You know who I am. I was the only one wearing a hat in the meeting yesterday morning.'

This was all in guttural screech, but I was beginning to put a face to the voice.

'Look,' I said, 'I'll come straight down to see you!'

'You haven't got the guts to come here,' she yelled, accompanied by a flood of abuse.

'I'll come straight away,' I said, and put the phone down.

Again, there was a hammering on our door, and sure enough, it was Hudson, looking very flustered.

'Have you had a phone call?'

'Yes, and I want you to take me straight there.'

'I'm not sure it's wise for you to go there right now,' he said, but I insisted and, full of apprehension, he drove me to the home of his father and mother–in-law!

We walked into a house full of tension. On the one side sat father-in-law, a saintly man with a shock of white hair, who had been an elder in the Brethren assembly. Sitting away from him, glowering at me, sat his elderly wife, in a very aggressive stance. What was I to do?

I began by saying, 'Before I address anything else, I must say that in all my time of ministry I have never had anyone address me in such an abusive way as you just did.'

'I didn't,' she said with a snarl.

I replied, 'So now, in addition to everything else, you are calling me a liar!' Inside I was thinking rapidly: 'Wow, this is great. My first real act of discipline. I'm going to have to put Hud's mother-in-law out of the church!'

Then came 'the word of wisdom'! I turned to her saintly husband and said, 'You've been listening to me teach and have got to know me a little. Can I ask you, is what I just said true?'

He hung his head in shame and said, 'I know it's true because that's just how she speaks to me.'

I breathed a great sigh of relief! 'Now,' I said, 'I know what we're dealing with. That hat on your head is a complete charade. You're not in submission to your husband or anyone else. This is a powerful religious spirit!'

Suddenly she broke and began to whimper. A tiny voice cried out from her, 'I know I'm wrong. Please help me!' And so began her deliverance, and her other son-in-law, Jack, who had a powerful ministry of deliverance, helped clean the house.

I will never forget the next Sunday morning meeting. On her own initiative she got up, testified, and was completely set free! Imagine all those years going to the Lord's Table, hat firmly jammed on her head, and yet she was in rebellion to everyone and especially the Lord. God was favouring us with signs.

When we wrapped up the commitment series, so many made it clear that this was their church that we had to hire the first of a number of school halls as the congregation grew. Underpinning this new expression of church were the house-groups, where discipleship was taking place, and I focused on my next primary initiative. Having established clear commitment from the members of the church, I realised I had about four months left before we were going to have to leave the country. I focused on our fledgling leaders. They became our house-group, and I was determined to get them into shape. Almost every denomination was represented among them, except the Pentecostals; they had Frank Houston's Bridge Church down the valley, from which his son's Hillsong Australia eventually emerged.

Initially I wasn't sure if any of these guys was an elder, so I sought to explain to them the issues at stake. Hudson was obviously a leader, but not in the traditional mould. He found public communication quite difficult but was a great shepherd of the sheep, and Joan was a wonderfully hospitable person. They commanded respect.

I was watching the clock tick and not sure when we could return. I knew I had to do something before I left and planned ahead for a large gathering with citywide leaders who would join us to recognise the leadership before the church. I must admit, I was very apprehensive and even the night before, I was unsure what to do. As has so often been the case, the Lord spoke to me through Scripture and confirmed it by his Spirit. It came in a passage in the first letter to the Corinthians. Paul is contrasting the wisdom of this world with the wisdom of God and a verse in chapter 1 grabbed hold of me:

> But God chose the foolish things of the world
> to shame the wise;
> God chose the weak things of the world
> to shame the strong . . . [86]

Simply put, the Lord said to me, 'You must work with that you've got.' So we had a great night with the leaders, laying hands on them. I asked everyone to recognise Hudson as an 'elder of double honour'[87] and I'm sure they were all pleased to do that. You can't have all chiefs and no Indians!

86. 1 Corinthians 1:27-29 NIV
87. 1 Timothy 5:17 ESV

Prior to that, at a meeting of Wellington church leaders, Eric Chambers prayed for, then prophesied to me, words to this effect: 'A wandering Aramean was my father...[88]' – a statement from Jewish history, said to be more ancient than the Bible itself. 'I don't know how to say this to you, Peter, with your wife and young family, but it is always going to be like this! Right now, I feel you should change your ticket, and go home by a different route.'

We obeyed this word and went first to a missionary family in the YWAM base in Kailua Kona, Hawaii; then on to Vancouver for a very important time with our dear friend, the late Barney Coombs, at that time leading the West Coast Fellowship and the emerging Salt and Light Ministries. Our journey from Honolulu to Vancouver was significant. We boarded the flight with only $2 and there was a charge for the in-flight headphones, which we couldn't purchase. We arrived in Vancouver at the beginning of the Canadian winter in our summer clothes, which were all we had. The church put us in a lovely motel, stocked with food and drinks and took us out for fantastic meals. In Hawaii, we passed McDonalds every day, but had no money to take the children in. The man with the glass bottom boat approached us every day, to no avail.

Barney said, 'You must go and buy suitable clothes for all the family.' He pushed a lot of money into our hands and sent us to the mall, which was novel for us, as it was entirely underground.

We had the privilege of ministering to this vibrant church, the first of many such visits. When we finally made it home

---

88. Deuteronomy 26:5 ESV

to the warm welcome of our Bristol church, we had been so blessed and even able to enjoy the in-flight entertainment on our transatlantic flight! Having nothing, yet possessing everything!

We went back to Bristol, back to the Olveston Community, expecting to return in a couple of months. We had been negotiating with the authorities for a special visa. Apparently, a special two-year visa was available for ministers in certain circumstances. In fact, it took until the following Easter to get it. However, that gave us an important time at home with our family and the church and my links into the national leadership forum of the emerging House-church Movement.

God was preparing us for a new thrust.

Chapter 20

Back to Base

Imagine this picture if you can. We return to our village of Olveston for an English winter and the dynamic of community life. When we had left the previous year, we had owned the beautiful old manor house at the far end of the village and the local school fete had been held in our grounds. Now we were to live at the other end of the village, in a cottage just below the pub and opposite the church. Over the years of pioneering in New Zealand, we always returned to our Bristol church, never quite sure where we would be living. On this occasion, Iain and Cora McDonald, who I had married, moved out of their wee cottage and lived with other friends so we could be together as a family.[89]

When I say 'a wee cottage', I really mean 'wee', a good Scottish word. It would be hard to imagine anything smaller as five people could scarcely fit in the lounge! But what a sacrifice for them. We had been loaned an old car. Fortunately, the cottage was at the top of a hill, and we could park in a rolling-down direction to jumpstart the battery. The ground was visible through holes in the floor

---

89. Incidentally, just two weeks ago, as I write, Iain and Cora flew down to London from Scotland to spend the day with us and Richard and Sharon Burt. Richard, Iain and Cora were all foundation members of the church and lifelong friends. We were staying at Richard and Sharon's apartment close to London Bridge and their business, and we went out for lunch just a few hundred yards from the latest terrorist atrocity which interrupted the meal we were enjoying together.

and the windscreen wipers had to be operated by two pieces of string held by the driver and front seat passenger! That winter we had an unusual amount of snow, and boy, it was cold. The dislocations were not easy for our children, but they made good friends. Only in later life have we fully realised the price they paid for our Abrahamic call.

We had an exciting time with the church as we had so much to share of God's blessing in New Zealand. To renew contacts with our national leaders was very important to us as well, as the House-church Movement had developed into the New Church Networks. It was an exciting time to be around, in the light of all that God was doing!

As I have said, we were expecting to return quickly to Upper Hutt. In the event, it took nearly six months to get the new visa. Our return was marked by a significant event. I received a call from the Valley Road Church in Auckland. They were planning a big Easter Convention in association with YWAM on my favourite theme, the Kingdom of God. Would I be able to orchestrate our return in conjunction with this? Yes, we were delighted to accept this important opportunity, and what a special event it proved to be.

YWAM had provided a guest speaker, an Australian called Tony Fitzgerald who became a firm friend. The conference was packed to capacity, and I delivered four sessions on the Kingdom, which I still see as a benchmark in terms of my ministry. I believe what I taught then even more strongly today. The tragedy is that so many Christians have a gospel of the church not a gospel of the Kingdom. An important question for me when I meet with leadership teams is: How much of your time, energy and resources, goes into the production of a Sunday meeting for just one or two hours?

The titles of the sessions as I recall them were:

- The Gospel of the Kingdom
- The Parables of the Kingdom
- The Signs of the Kingdom
- The Consummation of the Kingdom

This platform at the start of our next term in Upper Hutt, began to open all sorts of doors. For the next five years I was 'flavour of the year' – a bit of an exaggeration perhaps – but doors were opened to me. Also, I had further opportunities overseas even though we were now back in New Zealand. I took a young man I was discipling, Paul Jackson from Upper Hutt, on an international itinerary that included a big church conference in Vancouver and the South and West Bible Week on the Royal Agricultural Show Ground in Wadebridge, Cornwall.

When we arrived back in Upper Hutt after the Valley Road conference, we were excited to see what was happening. The leadership we had put in place was flourishing and the church was prospering. Having used various school halls, Upper Hutt Christian Fellowship took on the Town Hall and eventually became the largest congregation in the Wellington area, all of it undergirded by house-groups. Linda and I had a house-group made up predominantly of surfers, many of whom were new Christians. This was always exciting and unpredictable. She developed a creative arts team using dance and drama, which we took out to other churches.

I was invited to speak at national conferences such as Youth for Christ and Women's Aglow Fellowship. We encouraged Iain and Cora McDonald to come down to New Zealand and put on their *Lovesong in Harvest*[90] musical in the St James Theatre in Wellington. This event is etched in our memory as one night during rehearsal the news came through of the terrible Mount Erebus plane crash near the South Pole. Our friends, Mark and Mieke Bond, who spent a strategic time in our Olveston community, lost Mark's parents on that flight. Even Iain and Cora had contemplated going on that flight, but mercifully didn't.

The church saw dramatic conversions and growth. Bruce Billington, who owned a garage in Upper Hutt, was just one example. When his wife was converted and he started showing interest as well, his father came to Hudson and warned him. He said, 'If you interfere with my son's marriage, I'll bring my shotgun and blow your head off!' He meant it! Bruce subsequently became one of the leading teachers in the church. Part of his repentance on turning to Christ was to confess incidents of insurance fraud with cars he had personally totalled.

Living as we did, put us somewhat at the mercy of other people when it came to housing. Hudson and Joan were always very kind and took us in more than once when we met a stalemate, never easy with three small children! Two incidents stand out in my memory.

---

90. https://iainandcora.co.uk/video-recording/ and https://iainandcora.co.uk/resources/peter-lyne/

Hudson had just finished a beautiful new home in a lovely, wooded setting, not far from their house. He took us round to the property as he felt that living there would suit us for our next phase. It was magnificent, and, of course, we loved it, but someone in the leadership dissuaded him as they thought it was too good a look for us!

Then a perfect house became available, just five minutes' walk from school. It was $65 per week, $5 too much some leaders said. So we hunkered down at Hudson and Joan's. When we secured a nice home further up Ferguson Drive, it suited us, but often involved the children in a long walk, even crossing the railway when the barriers were up and walking up the busy main road. A conveniently placed dairy halfway up sweetened the pill.

I mentioned the successful house-group Linda and I led. At its core, we had quite a community of surfers. What really connected us together was one weekend when we all skipped the Sunday services. They weren't big on Sunday meetings that interfered with their surfing plans, so we agreed to a weekend with them. Their favourite spot was Castle Point, a dramatic beach on the coast beyond Masterton. Linda and I went with them, booking a cabin on the campground and armed with a lot of bacon and eggs for the hungry tribe. All was well until they tried to get me up on a board. I dutifully put on a wet suit and strode confidently into the water with them, but nearly drowned in my valiant efforts to stand up in the massive swell. However, this weekend really cemented our friendship, and they became an important part of our lives, some even agreeing to wear underwear, which had evidently been lacking. They rarely missed a gathering of the church after that.

Our group was not without its challenges though. Our friends, Bruce and Tui McKenzie were part of the group. Bruce was a typically white, Anglo-Saxon male, whereas Tui was like a Maori Princess, very cultured and refined. Tui mentioned to us that she had been feeling a bit uncomfortable in the group as her Maori culture was being criticised. I asked for her permission to open this out publicly in the group if she could trust my leadership in dealing with it appropriately. She was a brave lady, and one night I encouraged her to share frankly with everyone. It immediately brought an animated response: some felt she wasn't Maori enough, too Westernised! Others felt she was too Maori! As we got to grips with this, a spirit of repentance and acceptance came, and I'm glad to say that love prevailed.

During our three years in the Hutt Valley, two special friendships developed. We had made lots of friends and worked closely with our leaders, but we needed the support of people not involved in the leadership with whom we could be ourselves and develop strong life links. Bruce and Tui were such a couple. Soon after one of our first meetings, Tui invited us to dinner. From that time on, we were frequently together. I got on well with Bruce, who was struggling with Christian commitment and needed someone to talk to. Tui had exceptional gifts of hospitality and we were never happier than sitting around a fire, enjoying one of her special meals. She had a way of preparing everything so that she was never buried in the kitchen, and our conversations were always lively and challenging. Being used to hospitality, it was good to reciprocate, and Linda and I formed special bonds with them both.

I must recount a breakthrough with Bruce that occurred quite a long time after we first met him. Tui was frustrated because there was a kind of barrier with Bruce that not even she, as his wife, could break through. We were acutely aware of it as well, and no amount of counselling or dialogue seemed to make any difference. One day, the dam broke!

We were in the house at Ferguson Drive when Bruce rang me early one morning. He was weeping on the phone, desperate to see me, so I encouraged him to come straight away. This is the story he told me. His mother had died when he was quite young, and if that wasn't bad enough, his father married again, a woman who was very unkind to him. It turned out she was a closet alcoholic. Bruce had earned money faithfully doing a paper round and small jobs, which he entrusted to her as he was saving for a bike. The day came when he planned to buy his bike, only to discover she had drunk the lot! She was often mean to him. Bruce suffered from travel sickness sitting in the back of the car. He purchased some sickness pills which he kept in his pocket. On a journey once, when he reached for his handkerchief, the packet of pills fell out and his stepmother grabbed these and threw them out of the window. As Bruce shared all this with me, the tears came like a flood and he said, between sobs, 'I vowed never to trust another human being again!'

The release and healing that came was wonderful to behold.

Another friendship was established early on which has stood the test of time. At a meeting of Women's Aglow in central Wellington, a very distinguished, tall lady with blonde hair came to speak to me after my talk. She said, 'I wish you could talk to my husband'. I said that I would be happy to, and we exchanged phone details, but before I could do anything about this, matters were taken out of my hands. We had been invited by Pastor Eric Chambers to speak at the Miramar Baptist Church one Sunday. Miramar, famous for the *Wētā* Workshop,[91] is on a peninsula at the head of Wellington Harbour. At the end of the morning service, Eric introduced me to our hosts for lunch and it happened to be Judi Bagust, who I had just met at Women's Aglow. Home we went for a delightful lunch with Danny and Judi and their children, Petra and Justin. We gained very special friends that afternoon, and Amanda found a dear friend in Petra, who is still her closest friend to this day. Danny had a Christian background that he had wandered from, which was why Judi was keen for me to talk to him. Having another firm friendship like we had with Bruce and Tui was a great encouragement to us.

When developments meant we would be moving to Auckland after three years in the Hutt Valley, Danny walked with me in Trentham Park one day and said a surprising thing, 'Jesus said *Follow Me* to his disciples, and I believe I should follow you.'

And they did! To Auckland, then later, when we moved back to England for four years, they came too. Judi is very creative and artistic and Danny, I have often said, was the most resourceful man I have ever known. He has all the practical skills I don't have.

---

91. Wētā Workshop is a special effects and prop company based in Miramar, Wellington, in New Zealand, that produces effects for television and film. Wikipedia

Chapter 21

Valley Road

Towards the end of our third year in Upper Hutt a fresh direction for us was coming into focus. The Upper Hutt Christian Fellowship was now meeting in the Town Hall. I met regularly with the leadership team, and they were clearly finding their feet. The house-group structure was strong and there was evident growth on all fronts. Linda and I felt it was time for us to make a strategic move to Auckland. Wellington is the capital and the seat of parliament, but Auckland was fast becoming an international city with probably a third of the population in its environs.

We had shared with Hudson the new sense of direction, and an opportunity came for us to test this practically. Te Atatu is a northern suburb of Auckland and both the Baptists, and the Open Brethren had thriving congregations there. Brian Hathaway was a significant Christian leader among the Brethren and respected by a much wider caucus. He had approached me to come and work with his leadership team and invited me as the guest speaker for the Te Atatu Family Camp at Eastern Beach. I asked Hudson to travel with me on this weekend so we could carefully weigh this up.

One of the legacies of the Open Brethren in New Zealand was the development of great Family Camp Centres all across the country. The local Education Authorities use them extensively as well, and Hudson had been one of the businessmen in the Wellington area who had developed the magnificent Waikanae facility. What foresight these great Christian leaders had, buying up valuable land, then setting up shower and toilet blocks, camp sites, bunk rooms and motel units.

We arrived at the Eastern Beach camp on a Friday evening in time for dinner, and as we queued at the serving hatch got our first surprise. Tacked to the wall as we stood in line was a set of camp rules. Two of the forbidden items generated a lot of chuckles:

- No Speaking in Tongues
- No Dancing

Being thoroughly charismatic in our leadership, Hudson and I wondered what was to come! We need not have worried as when we approached the first session, there was lively dancing, singing and yes, a lot of tongues in evidence. These Open Brethren were more 'open' than I had imagined!

That first evening was excellent, and the Saturday sessions exceeded my expectations! Then came Sunday morning. Being Brethren, a communion service was planned with the emblems of bread and wine shrouded by a white cloth! Suddenly, this exuberant group became very sombre. A strange thing happened to me – for the first and only time, a speech was quickened to me, not from the Bible, but Shakespeare! I used to perform this speech

– Mark Anthony over the dead body of Caesar – with my schoolfriend, Fred Ward, lying under a white sheet. This morning I declared: 'Friends, Romans and Countrymen, lend me your ears, I come to bury Jesus (Caesar), not to praise him!' I explained that Jesus is not dead anymore. He's alive! To me, this little ceremony, practised by so many churches, is so far removed from the *breaking bread from house to house*[92] where it was an essential part of the meal. People can't help themselves. They come over all religious at such moments.

As Hudson and I flew back to Wellington on Sunday afternoon, I felt clear enough to confirm to Hudson two things:

- We were to move to Auckland
- It would not be to join Brian's Team at Te Atatu

I felt that we were again to take a step of faith and go out *not knowing!*[93]

That evening, a remarkable thing happened. Hudson and I met with our leadership team in his rumpus room. There was an additional person with us that night: Marcus Ardern, a reputable prophet that we loved to include if he was in town. At the beginning of the meeting, Hudson said, 'Peter has something to share with us tonight.'

Marcus, immediately jumped in and said, 'Can I say something before Peter speaks?'

---

92. Acts 2:46 NKJV
93. Hebrews 11:8 NKJV

He then went on to prophesy that we were to move to Auckland and that God had anointed us for this task. There was also a warning that I would come up against opposition and be labelled 'a false prophet'. I was overwhelmed by this. Marcus said much more, and subsequently, everything he said came to pass!

So we swiftly prepared for our move. On our final night, everything was packed up, not that we had a lot of stuff, but we still didn't know where we were going! Later that evening, I received a call from Wyn Fountain whom I had met at the Kingdom Conference. He said, 'I understand you are moving to Auckland. Where are you going to go?'

I replied that at that moment we had nowhere to go. In response to this, Wyn said that he had a large house on Kohimarama Road, and his son Warren and his wife Margaret had the cottage next door. They were willing to move out into Wyn and Shirley's basement flat to allow us their cottage at this time!

And so we arrived in Auckland, initially for about two months before we had to return to our family and the Bristol church. Shortly after arriving at Wyn's home, I received a call from David Jacobsen, pastor of the Valley Road Baptist Church. This large, charismatic Baptist church was in some difficulty, with serious conflict among the leadership. David asked me if I would consider coming and taking the Sunday services and the mid-week Bible studies for the foreseeable future. I felt an immediate check in my spirit against doing this. I did, however, agree to meet with him and some of the leaders privately to see if I could help them. The way I saw it, if I started taking all their public meetings it would be like giving aspirin to a terminally ill patient.

We returned to the UK as planned and settled into Olveston. Not long after this, I received a call from the church leadership. They had all resigned, including the pastor, and would we consider moving back to unravel this conflict and move the church forward. This time, we felt some clarity to take it up. Initially, I gave the leadership four conditions for our coming there:

1. I did not want to be paid for the first year. Instead, I wished them to continue supporting David and his family. Our Bristol church continued to support us.

2. I required David to totally remove himself from the church.

3. After a year, when the dust had settled, I wanted to bring the Jacobsens back and publicly honour them for all their years of faithful service.

4. They must give me the authority to do the job, otherwise I would be wasting my time.

Although David struggled with this, as he wanted to be some kind of Pastor Emeritus, he was in conflict with even his closest friends, and he eventually bowed out gracefully. The point that met the most resistance was number 3, honouring the Jacobsens. One of David's closest friends did not want us to do this. My response was: 'If you don't do this, I'm out of that door. You will end up cursing yourselves!'

I suggested that we would be with them for two years. It turned out to be three. And so began some of the most enjoyable and challenging years of our ministry. Healing flowed and the church took off! The first Sunday that I was 'in charge', so to speak, a strange thing happened.

Quite a crowd gathered to see the 'new kid on the block'. Most of the people I didn't know and they didn't know us at that stage. The service was still quite formal, so I announced the first hymn. As the music started, two ladies I didn't know were seated on the front row, and they immediately began an odd sort of dance right across the front of the church! Back and forth they went, mimicking each other. I can still remember the dominant partner as she was taller and had bright red lipstick.

I breathed a sigh of relief as the song ended, and announced another one. No holds barred! They were off again, and by now, the heads of the congregation were moving from side to side, rather like watching a final at Wimbledon! Then, when a pause came in the music, red lips turned and started to prophesy in a stentorian voice: 'Thus says the Lord, this is my servant and I have anointed him . . .' at which point I stepped in.

'Please, please stop! I don't entirely disagree with what you're saying, but do you realise how you are dominating this meeting. Please could you sit quietly and join everyone else in the worship?'

Two things happened. The congregation let out an audible sigh of relief. (Some people actually thought that I had brought these women in to spice up the worship!)

Irene and her friend accepted my admonition. We were eventually able to help them as they had been kicked out of every going concern in the city. Now the congregation knew I wasn't going to allow any nonsense.

We rapidly grew. There were so many creative talents. I drew in my friends David and Dale Garratt of *Scripture in Song* to help with the worship. We had the whole Pink family whose music had won *Opportunity Knocks* on television. At least ten pianists had letters after their name. As things mushroomed so quickly, I eventually got Dave and Rhian Day from our Bristol church to come and help us. Linda and Rhian worked with David Garratt on a creative group, perhaps seventy strong, which really influenced what we did. One Sunday, TVNZ came to Valley Road and filmed our whole service live on TV1. A similar thing happened in Bristol when the BBC filmed us as we met in Bristol Grammar School.

There are so many outstanding memories. One Sunday we took the whole church onto the Auckland waterfront and did *Air Waves*, which included a Breaking of Bread with the crowd. I was approached by a young couple, both studying music in Auckland University. They wanted me to marry them and a thought struck me. Would they allow me to marry them as part of our Sunday morning service? It meant that I could do some live teaching on marriage and some special music could be included as well. They were happy to do this and the outcome was very special. Virtually all their group, including the professor and his wife, came to the Sunday-morning wedding. It seemed such a natural thing to do, and afterwards, we helped with a big reception in our old church hall.

The night before the wedding, I did a rehearsal with the couple, the bridal party and their parents. All went well until the end of the rehearsal when I suggested we pray together. One of the fathers aggressively remonstrated with me. He was an atheist and there was no way he was going to pray! Amazingly, subsequent to the wedding, the atheist father and his wife were regularly members of our Sunday congregation, always sitting near the front!

Eventually, I drew in another couple, Dennis and Noelene Grennell, and they joined Linda and myself, plus David and Dale Garratt and Dave and Rhian Day in steering the ship. Our main auditorium, the platform and most of the large foyer were packed out. David and Dale were unique in their generous hospitality and creative gifts. Dave and Rhian provided a lot of pastoral care, as did Dennis and Noelene. I could always rely on Dave's wisdom and Rhian's spiritual gifts.

In the early days of our ministry, Dr Iain McDonald gave Linda and me a prophecy that we have seen outworked over the years. He addressed us both with these words: 'The work of a master builder is often stark and inhospitable, but Linda, you will provide the soft furnishings and colour that will make this acceptable' – or words to that effect. How true this has been throughout our lives. People love Linda, but the truth is that many are a bit scared of me! She has time for people, always going the second mile in care and hospitality. To illustrate this, I can tell you that at a London meeting of Pioneer leaders in a pub in Putney, the guest speaker was an American prophet called Dale Gentry; he scarcely knew me, but gave me some direct words: 'The John Wayne of the Church, always looking for a fight, always putting things right.' The other leaders fell about laughing but I had to admit it was true. Thank goodness that Linda is at my side!

Here's another example. Being a city church, near a lot of halfway houses and the like, we had more than our fair share of unusual people turn up. One Sunday morning in a packed church, as I was speaking, a guy took a dive on the floor near the back of the auditorium and caused quite a commotion. Some of our leaders got him out, and when the meeting was over, I walked across the foyer to my private office and here was this guy sitting comfortably in a chair, shoes off, feet on a cushion, being plied with tea and biscuits. I was surprised to see him in my inner sanctum! I immediately said to him, 'Get your shoes on!' He kind of started and I continued: 'If you really want to get right with God and turn your life around, we'll be here for you. But if you've come to create a spectacle and draw attention to yourself, please don't.'

With that, he got up and said, 'Right. I'll never darken the door again,' and shambled out.

Some days later, we heard that he had taken his life. Some of the leaders felt concerned about how I had treated him. However, he was our first 'resurrection', as some weeks later, he appeared again.

Another Sunday morning, we had a different, troubling scenario. I got up to speak and sensed unrest but was not sure what it was. As a teenager, I was injured in a soccer accident and was virtually blind in my left eye. I managed to get through my talk, then discovered what the disturbance was. As usual, our platform was packed with people. On the front row was a wild young man, almost naked. He had on a tatty pair of denim shorts that were half undone. Through my talk, he was giving people the 'evil eye', pointing at folk, putting his hands around a girl's neck! Not one of my elders had moved to get him out. I think they thought, 'Peter has seen him,' and left him to it. This led to an important talk with my team.

The following week another strange man shouted out in the service: 'Beelzebub was here!' He surely was! I am much swifter to deal with such events, and often, the Lord pre-warns me to be on the lookout for inappropriate activity.

One Sunday morning, Linda and I were standing at the front, surrounded by a group who wanted to pray for us and our children as we were leaving that evening on an important trip to the UK. Once more, a strange guy attached himself to the group and began to prophesy in a loud voice, 'I see you all going down in flames of fire . . .'

Not one of the leaders moved, so I had to step in again with direct confrontation, silencing him and refuting his words, as well as encouraging him to get right with God. Poor Linda! After that terrible prophecy, she had to lead her dance group in the song *You shall go out with joy!*

My own prophetic / teaching gifts came into their own in this environment. Coming from a background of pioneering the House-church Movement in the UK, and then developing New Church Networks, I was keen to tackle religiosity in all its forms and get us on a healthy foundation. Once again, I challenged people's understanding of communion at a Baptist-style communion at Valley Road. It was tacked on to the morning or evening service. The deacons filed onto the stage, very sombre in their formal suits. There were tiny plastic cups with juice in them (not wine – the Bible obviously got that wrong!) and miniscule squares of bread, and everybody screwing up their eyes to think of the cross. Now in charge, I did my first and last communion by holding up one of these little cups, I said, 'Please, if you invite me to your home, don't give me a glass like this!' When the laughter died down, I said, 'This is what we are going to do. Biblically, it was obviously a Jewish family meal. I do encourage you to *break bread from house to house*[94] with family and friends, but next week, on Sunday evening, I want you to bake nice loaves of bread and bring them along, and we will have flagons of wine and spend the whole evening sharing this communion together.'

It was a great success. However, I did make a mistake when I said, 'If you have anything against your brother or sister, this will be a time to put it right.'[95] David Garratt and Linda had a big laugh about this, as long lines formed in front of me and Dale!

We made sure that church business meetings were handled well, issues talked out, finances transparent. So when the issue of abolishing the constitution, which was like the Bible for some people but bore little relevance to what we were doing, we had important discussions and even asked Dr Edgar, the General Secretary of the Baptist Union to come and address us. (I must add here that I was not instrumental in taking the church out of the Baptist Union.)

94. Acts 2:46 NKJV
95. Matthew 5:22-24

The whole issue of alcohol was a conflict, and we needed to face it head on. In our wider leadership group we had 'total abstainers' and one deacon who said that he enjoyed a couple of cognacs when he came home from work! I said to the group, 'Let me handle this. I will deal with it on a Sunday morning when, as far as possible, everyone is present.'

The Sunday came and word had got out. We were packed out and the tension in the atmosphere was electric. I opened my talk with the following introduction: 'Today, I am going to speak about the "privileges and responsibility of sonship". My particular emphasis will be on our attitude as Christians to alcohol, and in preparation, I have considered carefully every reference in the Bible to wine and strong drink. I want to give you an overview.'

I then went on to point out that the Bible had as much to say about eating as drinking, or we could have talked about sex in the Bible! As in all these subjects, there seemed to be conflicting statements: for example,

> *Wine is a mocker, strong drink a brawler,*
> *and whoever is led astray by it is not wise.*[96]

> *Wine to gladden the heart of man.*[97]

The New Testament doesn't say 'Don't drink', but 'Don't be *given to much wine'.*[98] The call is to sonship and responsible living. I confessed to enjoying a drink, but not drunkenness.

---

96. Proverbs 20:1 ESV
97. Psalm 104:15 ESV
98. 1 Timothy 3:8 and Titus 2:3 NKJV

A trump card had been placed in my hands only that morning. Someone, without asking our permission, had brought a huge pile of temperance magazines and put them on a table in the foyer. I held one of these aloft and said, 'Just look at this. On the back cover is a picture of a very beautiful girl, the current Miss New Zealand. She neither smokes nor drinks! But what doesn't it tell you? Well, actually she is a Mormon, and she doesn't drink tea or coffee either!'

We must be honest in our appraisal of what the Bible really teaches. As I left the auditorium that day, a man who was formerly the President of the Baptist Union approached me. He said, 'Peter, that was the finest talk I have ever heard on that subject.' Also, as I crossed the foyer, I noticed that the pile of temperance magazines had mysteriously disappeared.

Let me add a postscript on this sensitive issue. Most of the Holiness movements have their roots in an unusual group of people in the Old Testament: the Nazarenes. There is even a denomination called The Church of the Nazarene. Samson was instructed by his parents that this was to be his lifestyle. So yes, this meant that alcohol was forbidden. Again, what they don't tell you is that grapes and their juice is also forbidden, as is the owning of property.

But what about the alcoholics? We must always be sensitive to people who have problems in this area. However, I like what my friend Bob Love, leader of a church in Exeter, told me. He had been an alcoholic and was powerfully converted. The British evangelist, Don Double, asked Bob to give his testimony in an evangelistic mission in a Cornish town hall. Bob shocked Don with his opening remarks when he said, 'I was an alcoholic, but you know, I had a drink before I came into this meeting tonight. I really have been set free by Jesus!'

When we moved into Valley Road, we declined the church manse as a home because we wanted to live near to friends and a school in the Kohimarama area that Wyn Fountain originally introduced us to. We rented a house at first in Sprott Road, and when Dave and Rhi joined us, they also took a house a few doors down from us. Our friends from Wellington, Danny and Judi Bagust, bought a home opposite us and we became close to an older friend, Pat Metcalfe, who had a state house nearby.

This area of Auckland suited us well, with St Thomas's School and the nearby Madills Sports Grounds, plus the beautiful beach waterfront including Mission Bay and along to St Heliers. It's been the main area where we lived until recently, and our son, Richard, with Anna and our two youngest grandchildren, still live there. Richard has a real estate company just off Kohimarama Beach. Jesse and Stella are still at St Thomas's School. The main secondary school, Selwyn College, where I did relief teaching from 2000 to 2017, is close by. After renting for nearly a year, the church sold their manse and bought us a home nearby, in Godfrey Place.

Our little community flourished from the start. Many of the church members lived nearby. On a Sunday, we would stop at a lovely baker's on the way home and have great ad hoc lunches, often outside in the warmer weather. It was great having the school so close. When our youngest,

Simon, started, he insisted on going barefoot – very Kiwi! – and within days would walk to and from school with Amanda and Richard, unattended. This was 1980 when New Zealand seemed back in a time warp – such a secure place to live. After the turn of the millennium when I was back school-teaching, I used to say if we had one murder a year in the early Seventies it was a huge media event. Now, we have murders every day, gang fights, shootings and ram-raiding of shops in broad daylight, with children as young as ten years old participating!

I had an excellent study at home and a more formal office with secretaries at the church. I have always been an early riser and try to give myself to study and prayer first thing. As much as possible, I would endeavour to be home after school to get the children down to Madills for soccer and cricket and to the waterfront. Often, Linda and I would be tied up at night with special meetings, counselling and other responsibilities, so late afternoon and meal times were very important to us.

We hadn't been in the Godfrey Place house six weeks when tragedy struck! One night, a young man arrived on our doorstep unannounced. He had come from Upper Hutt where our first church was and someone had given him our address. He was in a terrible state and we took him in. His marriage had broken up and he was coming north to try to find his wife and seek reconciliation. We fed him, counselled him all evening and gave him a bed for the night. In the morning we were in a rush, getting children to school and my first appointment was at 9am at the office. Linda was coming with me to paint rooms for the children's work and we were cutting it fine. We still managed to give further counsel and pray with him; then we had to hurry out. We had a fire in the grate and Linda ran her hand through the ash, then put the detritus into a clean sack. This we left in the laundry. As we left the front door, Linda said, 'I can smell smoke. Can you go and check before we leave?'

I ran to the laundry, opened the door and, unusually, there was thick fog. I thought I smelt woodsmoke in the air. Someone had a fire. I locked the laundry door, rushed back to the car and sped over to Mt Eden. Soon after I was settled in the office, a phone call came for me. It was the fire brigade. Our house had burned down! They checked for our children. One of the officers had crawled into a back bedroom in breathing apparatus. He felt a body in the bed, but it was Richard's life-sized toy chimpanzee. For the first time Linda had left a bedroom window open and our precious Siamese cat, Ba Ba, was found trembling in a basement at the back of the house. It's still difficult to describe how we felt!

When Linda said how she had run her fingers through the ash and put it in the clean sack, the fire officer said it could have been responsible as a latent spark can ignite. Danny, our friend who had checked the house before we moved in, said that in his view there was a lot of faulty wiring. Amanda, our oldest, has always remembered being told at school about the fire and that she should go home to Danny and Judi's. Quite something for a seven-year-old!

We all returned to the Bagusts' house and camped down for the next few nights. We lost virtually everything in the fire, although some crockery was retrieved. The church only had a verbal commitment to the insurance, nothing in writing. Then the miracles began to happen. The insurance company stood by their word and later, Danny got a whole team together to build a new home. People were so kind to us. Gifts started to pour in from around the world. Our lovely Pat Metcalfe moved out of her bungalow so we had a temporary home. Then the church agreed we should return to England to the church in Bristol as part of our recovery.

But the most important thing to me was the word God gave me during that first fitful night. I couldn't sleep so I crept out to the kitchen and sat down with my Bible. Linda and I have always read consecutively through the Bible, and still do, so this is not a game of chance. My reading during those early hours was from Nehemiah 13:1-3. It tells how the Ammonites and Moabites had hired Balaam, a powerful occultist, to put a curse on Israel. In parenthesis it says,

Our God, however, turned the curse into a blessing.[99]

That night the Lord visited me and showed me how he can turn every curse into a blessing. The burden rolled off me, and I can't begin to tell you how many people we have brought to healing through this word. I wasn't out of the woods yet! I backed a Bagust vehicle down their steep drive into my own parked car across the road. Soon after, a man phoned me in the middle of the night and threatened to kill me! Soon after this, a letter was pushed under the outside door of my church office saying that he wished my family and I had perished in the fire!

---

99. Nehemiah 13:3 NIV

When we returned from the UK, Danny and the team were working on the renovation so we rented a home nearby until it was finished. They did a wonderful job, much better than the house had been before. With gifts we had received we could purchase a lot of new furniture. We didn't know that we wouldn't live there for a long time.

Over the years at Valley Road, we enjoyed so much blessing. To be honest, Linda never wanted to leave. We had so many friends and dynamic things were happening. Visiting ministries enriched us in many ways. The first was Graham Perrins, who I felt was the greatest prophetic teacher we had in the UK; Steve Hepden, our beloved friend and a great healer of the broken; Barney Coombs with his wonderful wisdom and counsel. The list goes on!

We had some remarkable encounters during this time. On the city front we met with a diverse group of leaders. We were asked to host a special day conference for leaders with David Pawson, the great British Bible teacher. Our facility was packed for this, and my friend, the organiser Ian Grant of Youth for Christ, involved us in great events in the town hall and the Alexander Park Raceway. I don't think any of us will ever forget David's town hall message: *Samson's Hair is Growing Again!*

We greatly appreciated nights of worship and prayer hosted by Bruce McGrail of the Queen Street Assembly of God. Many years later, we would lead a house-group with Bruce and Christine who have been special friends to us. Our church had a number of families who had lovely homes on the 'posh' side of Mt Eden, opposite the Mercy Hospital. One couple, Bruce and Jan Conyngham, became firm friends. Bruce was a consultant gynaecologist at Mercy, and Jan had special gifts of hospitality. Later, they had a lovely home at Coatesville, north of the city, where we hosted many leaders' conferences, even weddings. What a remarkable spiritual gift hospitality is!

We had an unusual encounter because of Jan's foresight and hospitality. A cancer specialist attached to Auckland University had a lovely home opposite the Mercy Hospital. We had never met before but the Conynghams lived nearby. His name was John Collins and he was from the UK and a Manchester United supporter – all points in his favour! Jan had become friendly with an emerging landscape artist, Da'Vella Gore.[100] John kindly allowed them to use his own house for a display of her work, and Linda and I were fortunate enough to get an invitation to this event. Two remarkable things happened. Outside, Jan and Da'Vella met us and said, 'When you have seen the exhibition we would like you to choose one of the paintings as a gift from us!'

This came as a complete surprise and we chose Da'Vella's extraordinary painting of Lake Hayes on the South Island, not far from Queenstown. Then two things happened to this. The publisher Collins asked to borrow the work as they were publishing a compilation book of Da'Vella's paintings. As a result, Da'Vella received a lot of publicity as she set up a centre for her work on the edge of Lake Hayes. There is a story that she used stones from two derelict churches and moved them onto her land to build the art gallery.

---

100. http://www.davellagore.co.nz

When we finally left the home, John Collins was standing on the steps and greeted us. He asked who we were and I explained that I led the Valley Road Church on the other side of Mt Eden. John's reply to this was, 'Oh, you're with the happy clappies.'

I said, 'Well, I guess we're both happy and clappy.'

We ended up having a great conversation with him. But that was not the end!

Bruce and Jan had a *bach* (a Kiwi holiday home which can be anything from a shed to a very grand house). They had offered Linda and me to take the children there for a break, and we were due to go for three days. The bach was at Whananaki, just north of Whangarei on the coast. Our journey there was one of the most difficult we have ever had. First, our exhaust pipe needed repair in Whangarei. When we turned off the main road, we met with catastrophe on the long, winding dirt road to the beach. Rounding a corner, a grader used to fill in the potholes, had thrown up a large stone which damaged our exhaust again. Fortunately, there was a garage on the main road. They took our car in for repair and loaned us a vehicle. We drove cautiously back along the winding beach road and arrived at a delightful bay, with a row of holiday homes right on the water's edge. It seemed deserted as it was out of season. Gratefully we got out of the car, but another disappointment faced us. We had left the key to the bach in the front pocket of our car that was being repaired! The bach was locked and shuttered, and no one else was there. I burst into tears. Leaving Linda and the children, I drove back to the main road to get our key, wishing that I could be going home.

We crashed out early that night, but with the new day a remarkable chain of events occurred. There was another person at the beach! We saw this man walking with his young son past our bach. It was none other than John Collins whom we had met on the steps of his house just recently. He had a bach at Whananaki. His son was pleased to find our children there. I invited John for coffee; he stayed for lunch; then we had dinner together. It was one of those divine appointments that brought him to a vigorous faith in Christ that to my knowledge has never waned! Later, he moved to Melbourne, Australia, for a prominent role in the medical school there.

During our Valley Road years, 1980–1983, another life-changing event occurred. Our team was always praying for people who sought our help. Linda and I became aware of a recurring theme with many of these people. Rejection! I am sure this is still common. A root of rejection is at the heart of so many people's problems, even from childhood, or broken relationships in later years. For us this issue had a very personal application. Linda has shared (in chapter 14) something of her amazing story. The birth of her twins, Tanya and David, was a major watershed for her. When she faced the fact that it was impossible for her to keep them, with a colossal personal struggle she gave them up for adoption. Formerly in the UK, it was not possible to find the whereabouts of these children. However, the law changed and we determined to try to find them. The reason for this was motivated by the desire to tell Tanya and David that they had never been rejected. Linda loved them dearly and wept for them for months when they had gone.

On one of our visits back to Bristol, we advertised in national newspapers and wrote to social services. We didn't have our own home in Olveston, but we stayed in a variety of friends' homes. One night, when at a friend's house where we had stayed on a previous visit, Linda was told, with a measure of surprise, 'Linda, there's a letter come for you, addressed to this house.'

It was from the social services in Slough, a city not far from Windsor on the edge of London. The message was that Tanya had come forward in an effort to find her mother. The authorities wanted Linda to come to Slough to meet with them to see if it would be beneficial for her to meet the twins. In the letter, they said that Tanya had suffered significantly from rejection, which was why they were proceeding with caution.

As soon as we could, we left for Slough. We met the social services representative in a pub for lunch. Afterwards, she was keen for Tanya and David to meet Linda at their office, but I was not allowed to be present for this meeting. Having not seen the twins for nearly nineteen years, you can imagine the pathos of this first meeting! That night we took them for a meal in a restaurant opposite Windsor Castle. When the waitress came to the table to take our order, Tanya said, 'I want you to meet my mum. I haven't seen her for nineteen years!'

That was the beginning of a friendship that has continued to this day. They have lived on the Isle of Wight for many years, and this is always an important visit for us when we visit the UK. Early on, we met their adoptive parents, Michael and Dilys, and the rest of the family at their home in Slough. I remember a very special occasion when Tanya and David came to our home in Olveston along with Linda's mum, Elsa. At church at the Ark on Sunday morning, we had a whole row to ourselves, along with our children, which I think quite startled everybody!

During my time at Valley Road, we had a special relationship with Tony and Janet Cann from Te Atatu. We had some input into a big house-group they had out there. Tony, who had a very responsible role in business in the city, always had time to pop in and see me. It was like having a personal motivator, as well as a friend. He taught me a great deal about handling people and situations, for which I will always be grateful. Leading a big congregation, you can't please everybody and some will fall out with you. This included the former pastor, David Jacobsen, who had originally written in his final newsletter to the church that he 'welcomed the apostle Peter whom the Lord has sent to us'.

However, sometime later I was at a big leaders' gathering at the church, and David rushed out to speak to me on the pavement, with this complaint: 'My cousin Balfour had been to your Bristol Christian Fellowship and was told that he had to sell his home and put the proceeds into church funds if he wished to join!'

I was flabbergasted. I said, 'David, that is an absolute lie, and I have never heard of anybody who had such demands made of them. I have never even heard of your cousin Balfour and I must warn you not to spread false rumours. They will damage you more than they damage me.' (I must confess that from that time, 'Cousin Balfour' was like a personal joke. I don't think any of us ever met him.)

As our final year progressed, several things happened. I had promised to serve for two years and it was now approaching three. I was convinced that we should move to Melbourne, Australia, and go in faith just as we had originally come to New Zealand. Dave and Rhi and their family had to go back to Bristol, and we would follow them for a time before returning en route to Australia. A special event had been planned to coincide with our return to Britain. Linda had been working with David and Dale Garratt on a new album. In the creative team they had organised a number of congregational dances to involve as many people as possible. The album was called *A Sound of Joy!*

In our last months I was looking at who should succeed me in the leadership role. I felt this should be Dennis Grennell, who seemed to have a lot of support in the congregation, and he would be a safe pair of hands. We had all of our household goods packed and stored with a shipping company with instructions that they would eventually go to Melbourne.

Before we left, I encouraged Dennis and Noelene to move into our newly restored home that belonged to the church. We also gave them our new car, which is another story. One morning, when we were worshipping as a congregation, I felt the Lord speak a word into my heart from 2 Samuel 24:24:

I will not offer to the Lord that which costs me nothing.

I thought, 'What have I got to give that will really cost me something?' Immediately, the thought came back: 'Your car.' I took Linda and the children out for lunch and broke the news over the table. It was a brand-new car which was a first for us. A metallic silver station wagon with sheepskin covers on the seats. If we had sold it, we would have had sufficient to buy a replacement in England, but instead, we ended up with a rusty old Fiat! So Dennis and Noelene got the car, and I never regretted that.

Going back to the UK, we immediately prepared the *Sound of Joy* tour. This stretched from main centres such as Edinburgh in Scotland down to Plymouth. The Garratt family came with their key musicians, and our Bristol church sent about fifty very creative people who also travelled with us. At each venue, we laid on creative teaching and workshops with a big celebration in the evening, and some Sunday church meetings as well. It was a great experience for us all, as well as the local Christians who got inspired. Les Moir, of Kingsway Music, where he was responsible for the 'Big Five', the UK's top worship leaders, told me that coming to our tour at a south coast venue had greatly influenced his life and future direction.

When I left Valley Road, it was with good grace, and a prescient comment from Dennis: 'We can't do this without you!'

Chapter 22

Redirection

When our *Sound of Joy* tour was complete and the Garratt team had returned to Auckland, we spent some time with family and friends and our Bristol church. At the same time, we were preparing for our next faith step. The plan was to return to Auckland briefly and see how Dennis and the church were doing, but our focus was now to be Melbourne, Australia. After all, our furniture and other items were already packed and with the shipping company. We moved temporarily into a house next to the Garratts in Omahu Road, and then things began to unravel!

Almost at once, tragic news reached us. My brother Alan's lovely wife, Pauline, had suddenly died. They were full-time officers with the Salvation Army in Southampton. In recent times, Pauline had had some unexplained bouts of feeling unwell. Everyone loved Pauline, an only child, and she and her mum were like sisters. Only a week before we left the UK, we had all gone for a family picnic at Portishead. Linda remembered Pauline saying to her, 'I've never felt better.'

However, the boys had gone out to a movie on a Saturday afternoon, and when they returned home, they found Mum lying on the floor! Pauline had been out collecting with the *War Cry* newspapers. Alan called an ambulance which didn't arrive until 7pm, by which time Pauline had died with an undiscovered tumour on the brain. Everyone was devastated, especially us, feeling helpless 12,000 miles away!

In that week, we received more bad news. It was thought that my mother was going blind! If this wasn't enough, our return to Valley Road was even more unsettling. Dennis had dismissed the Garratts from their worship-leading, and it was almost like they didn't want us there either. Although we had taught the church faithfully over three years, it was as though they didn't even want us to bring a report of the UK tour. We had meetings behind the scenes to seek both understanding and reconciliation, but I suspect Dennis and Noelene felt very insecure. Who knows! Anyway, it all left us feeling uncertain about moving on to Melbourne. Hudson came from Upper Hutt to see us and also had a lot of negative things to say.

We had rented a home in the Glen, not far from Newmarket. It became something of a refuge during this troubled time. I remember my old friend Lance Lambert was speaking at the Racecourse to the Green Lane Christian Fellowship. He came for lunch with us, which in fact was the last time we would see him. He moved from Richmond to live in Jerusalem, not far from Derek Prince. They became friends and prayer partners, and our only regret was that we didn't take up Lance's offer to go and stay at his home in Jerusalem. We were to visit Jerusalem more recently, but by that time Lance had died.

While we were in this unsettled state, we became more and more convinced that we should get back to Bristol. Dave and Rhi Day came out to Auckland to catch up with the many friends they had made there, and also to spend time with us. They confirmed that a return to England was the best solution and, again, something truly remarkable happened. The reality was that this would be the third set of international flights within twelve months! After praying with us, they were due to leave for their flight home the next day.

On the way to the airport, Rhian received a clear word from God for us. She had been gripped by the words: *Peter said* in the gospels. What had he said?

> *'We have left everything and followed You.' So Jesus answered and said, 'Assuredly, I say to you, there is no one who has left house or brothers or sisters or father or mother or wife or children or lands, for My sake and the gospel's, who shall not receive a hundredfold now in this time – houses and brothers and sisters and mothers and children and lands, with persecutions – and in the age to come, eternal life.'[101]*

What had Jesus said? Well, in the midst of all the sacrifices and persecutions, there was a promise of receiving a hundredfold! Rhian said, 'I believe you will receive the hundredfold.'

The day after they left, we called in to see some close friends nearby for coffee while the children were at school. This couple had been a great encouragement to us, and we felt they should be among the first to know that we were not going to Melbourne, but back to Bristol. They said, 'We don't mind where you go, but we have this for you to help

---

101. Mark 10:28-30 NKJV

in the coming days.' They passed us an envelope and inside was a cheque for $50,000! We were overwhelmed.

When we returned to Olveston, Dave and Rhian were seeking to sell their house in the village to join our special friends, Steve and Chris Hepden, in a joint venture purchasing a large house with land that looked out over the Severn Valley. It is called 'Severn Ridge'. For many years it became a centre of activity, including the church's International Training School for two months each summer. We purchased their house in Denys Court to help to release funds for this project. Soon after this, Danny and Judi Bagust, with Petra and Justin, moved to join us from Auckland. At one time they rented the house opposite us in Denys Court.

Young Peter in Black – the Preacher!

It was good that we returned home during this time as a number of things happened. Mum didn't go blind, although her sight was impaired, but during this time, my dad died. I had gone with friends across the Severn Bridge to the Welsh national rugby ground, which was then called Cardiff Arms Park and has since been replaced by the Millennium Stadium. It was to see the All Blacks play one of our hapless British teams! As I arrived home, Linda came out to the car and said, 'Your dad had a stroke while shopping with Mum in the city centre. He is in hospital, but it doesn't look good.'

When we reached the hospital, we found Dad had been paralysed and lost his power of speech. He had been such a vigorous man, so full of life.

Some days later, we sat with Mum on a seat in the rose garden outside the hospital. I asked Mum what she wanted to happen, and she answered very clearly, 'I hate to see Dad like this. I wish the Lord would take him.' So Linda and I took her hands and asked the Lord to do this. Within a couple of weeks he was gone. I believe it was Linda and Steve Hepden who ushered him into the Kingdom. What a faithful man he had been! He could have played soccer for England, but he chose to serve the Lord with his unique gifts while staying in business for more than fifty years. People loved him and he was very special to Linda and me and our three children. He was still tapping a soccer ball around with them even in his retirement!

In the Bristol Fellowship things had steadily grown. Linda and I were finding leadership particularly fulfilling at this time.

Our team tried to meet every week for at least a day together. We had six couples plus Raewyn, our Kiwi superstar. She functioned as our secretary and also as a great worship leader from her keyboard. Three couples focused more on the outward development of the church, and the others on its internal strength. Eventually, what was originally made up of three house-churches grew to be about a thousand people strong.

One of the things that I helped promote at this time was the Spring Bank Holiday celebration. On that long weekend, we pitched a circus tent on the fields of a local farmer, Mike Spratt. He had a farm on land between Olveston and our market town of Thornbury. People camped. Many shared hospitality in their homes. A children's programme with Ishmael and his team was simply fantastic. We had many seminars, great worship and probably about 1,500 in the main marquee at night. The first year we had great weather. The second year can best be summed up by our friend John Perry, a professional musician. He and Jean, with their family, were travelling down the M4 when it started to rain! John declared prophetically, 'There must be a Bible Week somewhere!'

John was a member of the Cliff Richard band, come to help us in worship. How right he was! Our friends Danny and Judi had painted a great backdrop for the main stage. The people who had leased us the big top, assured us that it was waterproof. It wasn't! That first night, the heavens opened, and water started splashing onto the stage. Dave Day, opening the meeting, gesticulated with his right hand and water splashed on it. So he withdrew his hand, stretched out his left arm and water splashed on that. Judi's beautifully painted wave was literally becoming one! Our main sound expert was threatening to take down a serious sound system. He had just lost a rig at Spring Harvest. By now, Danny was lying up the outside seams of the marquee, accomplishing a temporary fix. Later, he would get railway sleepers and lay them across the walkways.

The rain did stop eventually, and even Judi managed to repaint her backdrop. What I do know is, we couldn't have done it without Danny! When he had a company called Gold Coast Removals in Wellington, New Zealand, their T-shirts announced on the front: *We can move anything.* On the back it said, *When you're the best, it's hard to be modest.*

Just to illustrate this, a large insurance company in the centre of Bristol needed help moving a huge statue, near the roundabout where the main A38 road from Gloucester joined the Broadmead shopping centre. Danny did it. He got the police to close the main road on a Sunday night and brought in a huge crane! The company thanked him profusely. Like so many Kiwis, Danny epitomised resourcefulness. The first day he went up to Severn Ridge to help with some repairs there, he put on his extraordinary leather tool belt and was wearing shorts. I don't think our Brit builders had ever seen anything like it!

For the three years we were back in Bristol, we had excellent Spring Bank Holiday conferences. One was especially memorable. There had been a move in the church to set up a Christian school. An excellent property became available at a reasonable price. This was in the days when there was no government support for Christian schools. The word went out that an offering for the school would be taken, and special preparation was made. One of our leadership couples, Dr Nic and Jenny Harding, downsized their house to help accomplish this. The night I received the offering, it came to nearly £50,000. That was in the mid-Eighties. The new facility was purchased and Oak Hill School established.

Linda had written a great musical inspired by the life of Nehemiah. It was agreed with the school that we would train the children to perform it, so over a few months, we went in regularly to get it off the ground. I'm sure it exceeded all expectations – amazing when you think Linda is not a musician but she set up the dialogue, libretto and the music. One of her songs was eventually recorded in the States by Danniebelle.

During a teachers' conference that included an overview of Oakhill School and a performance of Nehemiah, the representatives of the Local Education Authority were impressed, and especially with Linda's musical. At that time, it was sent to Scripture Union and received a national award. Later on, when we were in Sidcup during the Nineties, we put it on at The Worx with great success. We will never forget the performances of three of our older young people, as the 'baddies' Sanballat, Tobiah and Geshem, that was worthy of a West End stage! I wish we had published it more widely. Perhaps we still could!

'Nehemiah, Nehemiah,
Don't you listen to the voice of that liar!'

Linda

During our last year based in Bristol, we moved once again, and this was probably due to being overstretched financially. I have often thought, a leader's strength can be their weakness! King David loved and was seemingly not the hard man that Saul was, but his passion almost destroyed him. I have never been a great money manager, which is why others in the life of our churches handle the finance. Personal budgeting, for example, is not easy when you have lived the life of faith that we have. A budget-minded person with no personal finance whatsoever would not have offered £45,000 to buy Hill House. This is not to excuse any personal failure, but we have always been very generous and had remarkable faith for finance.

In Denys Court, we overspent on renovation, and it put pressure on us. So we sold the house and moved as a family next door to Dave and Rhi in Severn Ridge. Steve and Chris had purchased a more modern home on the Bradley Stoke housing estate, which was more suitable for them because of her advancing multiple sclerosis. Also, this housing development, I believe the biggest in Europe at the time, was particularly strategic.

Our side of the house was pretty cramped, and the large lounge was still used for leaders' gatherings and other meetings, but we enjoyed being with Dave and Rhi and the family, and the arrangement was going to be short-lived anyway. I also sold my BMW car that our friends in a garage near Salisbury had got us. It was the cheapest car bought for our team, but when it went into the workshop it could be so expensive. So we paid more for a reliable Japanese Toyota, and it proved much cheaper to run. I have to say that in later life, Linda has managed our finances very well, and it was a great triumph for her when she cut up my American Express card!

During this last year in Bristol, we were meeting in Thornbury with our local congregation. As a church, we embraced David Pawson's concept of 'Cell, Congregation and Celebration'. In our meeting, the use of spiritual gifts was encouraged, even with the children. In one Sunday morning church meeting, a young boy, possibly eight or nine years old, said he saw a jigsaw puzzle with one piece missing, but now all the pieces were in place. He prophesied to us, 'You're free to go now.'

My father had died, and my mum had sold their mobile home and moved into a council bungalow in a sheltered cul-de-sac at Winterbourne, on the edge of Bristol. We always felt Mum was the least healthy member of our family, but she outlived Dad by eighteen years and right to the end was wonderfully cared for in her little bungalow. We had been sensing for some time that we should return to New Zealand. Calls had come from some leaders that we were needed back there, and so, after careful discussions with Dave and Rhi and our team, we made the decision to go.

Alan's Wedding to his second wife, Barbara

The Lyne family from left to right:
Eric and Christine with Elizabeth, Robert and Suzanne
Alan and Pauline's two sons Andrew and Martin are in the back row
Mr and Mrs Lyne Senior flank the bride and groom
Peter and Linda with Amanda, Richard and Simon are far right

Chapter 23

Upheaval

The next five years proved very challenging on a number of fronts. We initially joined David and Dale in their house-church, which centred around their home in Omahu Road. Some of our former Valley Road people were there as well. We arranged a retreat together at a campground south of the city, and I invited John Noble, one of our prominent UK leaders, to join us. He had been planning to visit Australia and would come on to us. Sadly, he had to withdraw at the last minute, and I regretted this. We were encountering some conflict of vision with David and Dale. They wanted to retain their close-knit community, whereas we felt an urgent need to reach out on a wider front. We parted company amicably, but now planned to develop Bridge Ministries on a broader platform.

During this time, a new development took place. I had to return to Bristol for a few weeks, and one of our American friends, David Baumstark, whom we met through the Garratts, asked if I would consider coming back through California and visiting the Vineyard church. They were about to celebrate their fifth anniversary. They invited me to come as guest speaker for this special weekend.

Bakersfield is to the north-east of Los Angeles at the southern end of the San Joaquin Valley, the breadbasket of America. We had an excellent weekend with this vibrant

Vineyard church, part of John Wimber's New Church Network. I stayed with Ron and Susan Ford and enjoyed being with them. It was the start of a friendship that continued over several years, and some important relationships developed.

The Vineyard was always big on praying for people. When I had finished speaking on Sunday morning, a tall, distinguished redhead came forward for prayer. She told me she was standing in for her husband who was terminally sick with AIDS. I asked if anyone had prepared him for death and she said no.

'Can I come and see him with you?' I asked.

Vicki was very pleased about this, and soon I was sitting in their home with Charles. They had a lovely house with a pool outside. Charles had a good job and I believe he was a Christian, but he had a secret life as a homosexual. I found him thoroughly repentant and very sorrowful, especially as he had put his wife and two children at risk. We had a very fruitful time of fellowship and prayer. He was finally hospitalised, as he was dying, and the staff in the hospital spoke fondly of him. He had found a place of grace and, mercifully, the family was not infected.

The story didn't end there. We invited Vicki to come down to us in Auckland as part of her recovery. At that time, we had a close friend, Jeff Howie, who worked for TVNZ. Jeff often took us out to dinner and plied us with lovely things. He was the epitome of generosity. This particular night he called us and invited us to a nice restaurant. We said we would love to come but we must bring an extra guest who was staying with us. We thought at the time that Jeffrey accepted this grudgingly. However, over the dinner table, things went surprisingly well. Jeff and Vicki had a lot to talk about, more than we imagined!

After her time with us, Vicki went over to our Bristol church and spent a year with Dave and Rhi and the team. What we didn't know was that Vicki and Jeff had begun regular communication, exchanging cassette tapes with each other. So a year later, when Vicki had returned, Jeff stepped off a plane in Los Angeles and, in three days, they were married! We were invited to go to the wedding, but it was impossible to arrange at such short notice.

Over the years, we have retained a special relationship. Jeffrey always engages in the most interesting correspondence with me. For many years, they have been involved in the big YWAM school at Tyler in Texas. We have stayed with them several times and I have spoken at their week-long school for mature Christians called 'Crossroads', which Jeff has run for several years. He is now the pastor of this base. A few years ago, I joined him on a mission trip to Mongolia. We led two Missions Training weeks, in different parts of the country, and spoke at various other events, including a Prostitutes' Collective. For a moment, I must stray from my main theme here.

In Ulan Bator I stayed with my friends, Rick, Jill and Ronan Donovan, as Rick was now special assistant to the US ambassador. I even cooked for the ambassador and his daughter one night. Linda first met Jill at a gym, and we became friends, often eating together at one another's homes. It was sad news for us when we learned of their new posting overseas. Visiting their lovely home opposite the Rose Garden in Parnell, they showed us many of their personal things that they couldn't take with them. I took a special interest in Jill's four-door Smart car in the garage. I thought it would suit us, so I asked her to get a quote for a realistic price. As the weeks counted down, I prompted her on this matter. Finally, Jill arrived at our home with the car, and said, 'I've managed to get a price. It's $240!' That proved to be the cost of registering what was virtually a new vehicle! Thank you, Jill! You and Rick and Ronan were such special friends to us. We have now lost touch with them, and our emails are returned. The government used to move them around a lot, but we wish that we could find them.

The next time I was in Bakersfield, I stayed with a very special family, John and Carol Gombos. This was the beginning of a wonderful friendship that has persisted over the years. When you see Linda and Carol together, they look like sisters, and, in a way, they are! I, at times, have been an advisor to John, and have been involved in his business. Covid put a stop to our travel, but twice in the previous two years, they had got us up to their new home in Santa Barbara. We hope to be there again in 2023 as part of my eightieth-birthday celebrations.

One of the things that Ron and his team got me to do in Bakersfield was an evaluation of a ministry group named 'The Kansas City Prophets'. The Vineyard had been impacted by this group led by Mike Bickle, and Ron gave me a series of tapes and written material to carefully consider. Also, they took me to a 'Gathering of Prophets' in the University of Southern California. During this conference, Mike did a lot of the teaching and Paul Cain spoke, but I noticed that John

Wimber, the founding leader of Vineyard, sat off to one side with Bishop Pytches of the Chorleywood Anglican church in London. I felt the conference was quite a mixed bag, but Paul Cain's testimony was amazing, and Mike's teaching very solid.

When I finally gave my report to the Vineyard, Bakersfield, I tried to summarise all that I had seen and heard. My main concern was the emphasis on prophecy without the balancing gift of an apostle. The Church in the New Testament is *built upon the foundation of apostles and prophets.*[102] But John Wimber was sitting off-side, as it were, and to my mind, he was an apostle! John himself would never accept this title, but that's evidently what he was. In the end, a lot of chaos ensued but there were good things as well. I know that Paul Cain later came in for a lot of flak because of personal issues, but he operated at a different level to most ministries that I have seen.

Ron went with me on one occasion to a conference at the University of Michigan in Ann Arbor. Paul Cain spoke one night and then functioned in his unique gift. There was a crowd of over 2,000 there, but he called out the name of my friend Ron Ford, who stood up beside me. Paul gave him a great word of encouragement. He said that he had briefly met Ron on the way into the meeting, but then gave specific words, naming Ron's leadership team that he had never met! For example, he said, 'Cathy is good value, but look out for Catherine, she is of special importance to you.'

I couldn't wait for the conference to end, and when I got back to Ron's house, I shot across to see Al and Cathy, part

---

102. Ephesians 2:19-21 NIV

of the leadership team, who lived just across the road. There were two women called Cathy on the team, so I said to this Cathy, 'What is your name?'

She said, 'People call me Cathy, but I am really Catherine, which I prefer. Take a look at my cheque book.'

There on the cheques, the name Catherine was written! I said to her, 'You will be pleased to know that the Holy Spirit knows your name!'

When we last visited Bakersfield, pre-Covid, Al and Cathy were still leading the church there. Another word of Paul's that night I was able to verify personally. He pointed down into the audience and asked a man to stand, then said words like this: 'The Lord has seen and knows about the trauma you experienced when you were at the lake that day. He wants you to know that your son is safe with him, and all will be well for you and your family.'

The next day, I happened to meet the man who was a doctor, and I enquired about Paul's word. He told me that they had been on holiday at a lake, and his son went fishing. He had on big waders and stepped into the water, but soon got into difficulty. His waders filled with water, and he drowned before they could save him. This dear man said to me, 'I can't begin to tell you what a healing word that was for me and my family!'

Back in Auckland, change was taking place at a fairly swift pace. The house we had rented in St Mark's Road was about to be demolished, so we had to find something else. Richard and Simon were both in Auckland Grammar School. The

Bagusts also had returned to New Zealand, so Amanda and Petra Bagust went to Epsom Girls for their final two years before university. The rule in Auckland was that you had to live in the Grammar zone to attend the school, so this narrowed the field of where we could live. I answered an advert for a house in Parnell which was nearby.

On the morning I viewed the house, a man called Roy arrived in a builder's truck and a not particularly flash suit. The house was on a hill, with a very steep drive and was unsuitable for us. Roy said, 'Would you like to see something else?'

I agreed, and he took me back down the hill into a side street where there was a cul-de-sac with a handful of smart townhouses, perched over the Orakei Basin, the inner harbour looking out to the ocean. It was a delightful place, and we swiftly reached an agreement. It was in fact Roy and Ali's city home, but they had just bought a country estate out in Coatesville that they wanted to develop. They became good friends and were to figure in our lives for some years.

Roy asked me back to his office to sign a contract. As he laid it out on his desk, he asked me what my occupation was. I explained, 'Well actually, I'm in Christian ministry.'

I could get no further as he immediately said, 'Well, I'm an atheist!'

To this I replied that I rarely met genuine atheists, who really believe in nothing, that there is no hand of design in the universe! We went straight in at the deep end, and after an hour, I still had not put pen to paper.

We met Ali back at the house, and some of the spectacular furniture was left which we could buy later if we were interested. We still have the big wrought-iron bedstead. The huge pine dining table, we had to sell as part of our house sale in 1992 when we left the country. None of us wanted to let it go. We were into hospitality, and so many people dined with us around that table. I don't think Amanda ever forgave me for selling it!

You will know from earlier chapters that part of our purpose in life was to have the unchurched around our table. We always ended up with Linda's hairdressers, and now, Roy and Ali became firm friends. They used to get us up to Coatesville and remarkable developments took place there. They built a copy of Monet's famous waterlily garden with its white bridge, behind their sprawling farmhouse, that eventually the public came to view. I'll say this for atheist Roy, when we sat down at his table with their friends, he never failed to ask me to pray over the proceedings.

Ali did something very special for me. She was an excellent chef, trained in the *Cordon Bleu* tradition. She knew that cooking was my special interest, so she invited me to attend their school. We met regularly in her farmhouse kitchen, and I was probably the only man present. She and an assistant would work through specially prepared notes for about two hours, perhaps for a midwinter dinner party with three courses. Early on, she taught us a foundation of *Cordon Bleu* cooking – the preparation of stock. I have a reputation for producing great soups. A leek and potato soup is sitting in the fridge as I write. I will never forget the first soup Ali prepared for us – curried parsnip – beginning with the sweating of vegetables in the saucepan with butter and seasoning underneath greaseproof paper! After the demonstration, we would sit around a huge farmhouse table with a glass of wine, and eat everything, accompanied by very animated conversation.

Roy, in his builder's truck, was in fact the owner of the Location Group that developed luxury accommodation across Auckland. Sadly, as the years wore on, cracks appeared in their marriage, and they subsequently split up. It's a long time since we last saw Ali, but we have occasionally met up with Roy and his companion Margaret, who was a very gifted gardener. One day, we dropped in unannounced at Coatesville for a cup of tea when Roy and Ali were still together. They asked if we would go to dinner with them in a local pub. Ali drove Linda, Roy asked me to go with him in his new Porsche. As we swung out of the drive, he startled me by making a profound statement. He said, 'Peter, I can tell you one thing: money can't buy happiness!'

We were in the townhouse for less than a year when we felt we should move to a cheaper property just below us on Shore Road. At this time, several developments took place. A good friend, John Muys, had an office block in Parnell, not far from where we lived, and he gave me a very nice office on the first floor. We had asked leaders from our church in Bristol, Neil and Zoe Edbrooke, to join us in the work. Zoe was very homesick for a time, but they made friends, home-schooled their boys, and worked alongside us. Zoe helped lead worship, and Neil was a wise counsellor and gifted teacher. He shared the Parnell office with me. On days off, they loved to take the boys swimming on the beautiful beaches, where the water was invariably cold! They were rewarded with 'swimming chocolate', which seemed to be a successful bribe.

We met at times in various school halls, not the most uplifting venues, but then for a while we struck gold in a great venue in the heart of the city at the Wynyard Cafe. It was right next to the university in Symonds Street and across the road from the old Anglican church, St Paul's, where some years later, we would engage with Mike and Bex Norris and their team from London – but that's another story!

We loved being in the Wynyard Cafe because the venue epitomised 'non-religious' Christianity. We even had a dog as a member that came faithfully and sat in the front on Sunday mornings. We wanted to buy the cafe and the accommodation upstairs and use it as a going enterprise, but the Christian owners wouldn't sell, perhaps wisely as it was in such an excellent location. Certain memories stand out. Eric Delve, the famous British evangelist, came and spoke one Sunday morning. I believe his children attended our Oak Hill Christian School in Bristol for a time. I do remember how he had talked to a Brethren youth group with the title *All the Swear Words in the Bible*. One of the young men who was powerfully converted joined the Brethren Assembly on the Sunday morning and Eric asked him within earshot of many of the saints: 'How is it?'

In a loud voice the boy replied: 'Bloody marvellous!'

And of course, it is! The cross of Christ is both bloody and marvellous!

From our office in Parnell, we managed all sorts of things such as Patrick Dixon's tour, visits from Gerald Coates and Noel Richards three times, a special South Auckland project that we helped, a lot of counselling appointments and even training sessions. I remember doing one entitled *How to Preach the Word of God*.

When Dr Patrick Dixon came, he had just released one of his books, *The Truth About AIDS*.[103] As a doctor and member of a Pioneer church in London, he founded ACET, which is 'AIDS Care Education and Training'. We saw him speak at Gerald Coates' memorial service in Westminster just a few weeks ago, and he's still going strong. He mentioned at least twenty nations where ACET is still helping the acute AIDS problem. He is now a futures consultant for many major companies around the world. Patrick and Sheila have been good friends of ours, and it was a privilege to set up his tour. I took him down to the Beehive to the Ministry of Health in Wellington, New Zealand's seat of government. He also gave a memorable lecture in Auckland University, crowded with medical students and people from the medical profession. Linda and I were asked to help some acutely ill AIDS patients, which we did with a mix of success and failure.

Two other doors that John Muys opened to me during this season were significant. He had been responsible for a lot of special events in Auckland for the business community. He brought in the finest motivators from overseas – largely, the USA – for day seminars, usually at the Logan Campbell Centre. He would have all the real estate agents

---

103. Dr Patrick Dixon, *The Truth about AIDS* (Acet International Alliance; 4th edition, 2004)

in Auckland, for example, to hear Denis Waitely or the incomparable Zig Ziglar. Denis Waitley did the best talk that I have heard on small, accountable groups for mentoring. It was he who prepared the first astronauts for the moon landing. John always provided tickets for me, and I learned so much from these masters. Zig had a huge crowd, who had paid hundreds of dollars for tickets and book packages, eating out of his hand. Then, right in the middle, he would say unashamedly, 'What you guys really need is the Lord!'

Another thing John did was to involve me with a Christian fellowship in Hastings that met in the Old Fire Station, and needed help, so I was flown down every month to get alongside the leaders and the church there. John had helped with the Garratts' worldwide distribution of *Scripture in Song* materials. David Garratt was facing a crisis in the UK with an underperforming company and asked if he might fly John and me over for a week to try and sort it out. Being with John, was like watching a master operate! We met up in Los Angeles at Chuck Smith's Calvary Chapel, then flew on to London. Arriving at Heathrow on a wet, miserable morning, we immediately drove to Basingstoke to the offices of this defaulting company. They took us out to lunch, but I don't think I got to eat anything! As John confronted them about their poor performance in the light of promises made, they said it wasn't too bad and what were our expectations anyway? With that, John dived into his briefcase and produced a pile of printouts with copies of all their communications, highlighting the promises they had made. They collapsed like a house of cards.

I managed to get John around to churches like our Bristol Fellowship and John Noble's at Romford, and also to alternative publishers. I believe we settled on Kingsway in the end, but I'm not sure of this. The biggest surprise to me was a final meeting at Olveston where John asked if I would take on the UK responsibility and move back there! Something I wasn't prepared to do, but nice of him to ask anyway. It was no surprise to me when in later times, Selwyn Hughes asked John to help him run his operation out of the UK. We saw quite a lot of John and Rosemary, in and around Waverley Abbey!

Gerald and Noel's tours, with the help of Richard Burt, our old friend, on sound desk, went extraordinarily well, in spite of mishandling of his prophecy about the earthquake by people who should have known better. I have written about that elsewhere.

During these years, and several homes later, it was felt that we should purchase a home. Our beloved friend, Bruce Bremner, who is now with the Lord, had gone into real estate. He was one of the finest pianists I have ever worked with, and, among other things, travelled with us on the *Sound of Joy* tour in the UK. He approached Linda and me with a proposition for a nice villa in Acorn Street, near the Royal Oak shops and in walking distance of Cornwall Park. The thing about this property was that its renovation was unfinished, and this drastically affected the price. We were not afraid of this kind of work. Linda is quite an expert at it!

The bank was helpful, and many friends contributed gifts towards it. Bruce and Jan's son, Ali, was an excellent builder, and we eventually employed him in the construction work. I even got the bank manager to come to lunch one day, to see the property and the value of his investment in us. Linda spent a huge amount of time polishing the remarkable wooden doors. A very skilled guy restored the unique floors with special French-polishing techniques, and others lent a hand.

During this time, lots of things happened and I'm not sure that I can record this chronologically or accurately. The house was used for a lot of hospitality. I remember it packed for Gary Phipps' fiftieth birthday. When Ron Ford came down for, among other things, our Bridge Church conference, my friend John Gombos came with him and stayed in our unfinished house. Later on, Carol came too. John did an amazing thing! On his return to California, he sent us a very generous gift so that the necessary work on the house could be completed. Our bank manager was so surprised when we said we no longer needed his loan. Later, he was to say that we were one of his best customers!

There were baptisms in our pop-up pool in the back garden, including our psychiatrist friend, Patte Randall; many meetings in our delightful lounge; my weeks of prayer and fasting there; countless people around our long table in the kitchen. Our children were with us, although Amanda's room was unfinished, and Richard was in the basement. Simon had his own room where he could practise his saxophone. He later toured the West Coast of America with the Grammar band, and this included Disneyland.

It was during this time that Richard started to push the boundaries. I saw so much of myself in him! Amanda and Simon probably took after Linda more, but one incident with Richard I must record. I had been out late at some meeting, and when I got home, Linda was in tears. He also had come in quite late, was very off-hand with his mum, and decided he would drive down to Parnell to see his friends. Linda summed it up, 'Richard is using us like a hotel and lacking in respect towards us.'

I decided to go after him although it was very late. When I got to Parnell, I wasn't sure where he had gone. So I scoured the neighbourhood.

Finally, I saw a familiar car parked outside a block of flats, so I went inside the front door. There was a stairwell, so I began to walk up the stairs, very much in prayer. It was getting on for midnight! I went to a door midway up the block and apprehensively pushed the buzzer. Guess what! Richard answered the door, very surprised to see me! I asked him to step outside for a moment and shared my concerns with him. I reassured him of our love and Linda's concern at the way he was treating us. I drove home, but within minutes he was there and gave his mum a heartfelt apology and a big hug!

During this time, Raewyn, our Kiwi administrator and musician, came out from Bristol with her new husband. She had been living with Dave and Rhi for some time, and during conversation with Rhi about how she would like a husband, Rhi jokingly said, 'I'm sure there's a Mr Winnie for you somewhere.' (We all used to call Raewyn 'Winnie'!)

Not long after this, she met Steve Whinny, and they married. What are the odds on this story! We were in Sidcup, just on the edge of London, for most of the Nineties. Later, when we were back in New Zealand, we heard that she had motor neurone disease. What a tragedy for one so young, but when we saw her, now in a special chair, she was hanging on valiantly to the end. She was such an important part of our lives when she lived with us in Olveston. I'm sure Dave and Rhi and Steve and Chris, members of our team that she lived with, would say the same thing about her.

During our time in Bridge Church, there were various ups and downs. Quite a number of disaffected Baptists came to us from a church where they had been in conflict with the pastor. I'm not sure that it helped us much, as some of these folks had serious problems. It would also be true to say, that a group within our church seemed to get disaffected with us. To this day, I'm not sure what this was all about, but it certainly caused an unpleasant undercurrent. I can describe it best by telling you Linda's reaction to all this. A leaders' gathering was arranged at our house, along with outside advisors that we didn't approve of. As the meeting got more and more difficult, Linda got up and left the house. It was several hours before I found her, as she had been walking in Cornwall Park on a beautiful sunny afternoon. She summed it up like this: 'Families in the park seem so happy! Why does the church make us so sad?'

Of course, not all the families in the park were happy, but we went through a phase with our group that made me sadder than I had ever been! I'm not going to name names or try to attempt a post-mortem, but twice I came home to Linda feeling completely broken after meetings I had had with disgruntled leaders. We went to our last family camp, but I didn't speak in any sessions. I think we mostly did the washing up! When our decision was reached to return to the UK, they suggested the church would give us a send-off. This we declined. In fact, when we left, I thought that we would never return to New Zealand again!

We shouldn't be surprised at all this. We were given a lot of warning. Just prior to our leaving Upper Hutt to move to Auckland, my old friend, Marcus Ardern, gave us the initial prophecy to come to Auckland, recorded earlier in this book. He had no knowledge that this was already being planned. He spoke so positively of our impact there, saying we were uniquely anointed for this task, but then he added a serious warning that I would be spoken against and called a false prophet!

The second warning was from Steve Hampton, who at the time was leading a Vineyard church in Hawaii. He knew me through visits to Honolulu and California. He phoned us in New Zealand in the middle of the night as he had received a disturbing vision, which he felt an urgency to share with me, 'I saw in a vision that you were confronted by a Maori warrior doing the traditional Haka', (which the All Blacks famously perform before their international rugby fixtures), 'and saying, "Get off my land."'

He went on to say, 'A major principality has been raised up against you . . .' and he included details that I can't fully remember. He said it would be an important matter of prayer for him. What I do know is that this certainly came to pass in terms of my public ministry.

Even a small, failing Baptist church managed to accommodate a couple who did an 'investigation' on us and, among other things, said we were on a list of false prophets! When a friend searched for this list, they found a name similar to ours, but spelt differently.

The clincher for me happened on New Year's Eve 1991. I was again in Bakersfield, staying in Ron and Susan Ford's house. Jet lag meant that I was often awake during the night, so I turned to my Old Testament reading for that day.

> *Go back to the land of your fathers and to your relatives, and I will be with you.*[104]

It could not have been clearer to me if the Lord himself had stood in the room and spoken to me! At the time, the phrase 'and to your relatives' did not have the significance it would later have. However, my main concern was Linda! When I finished my itinerary in the USA, I was stopping off in Hawaii and she would join me there for a few days. The difference between Linda and me was that from the first day we sat on the beach in Mission Bay, Auckland, in 1977, she said to me, 'I feel that I have come home!' And so it has been for her!

Me, I'm an Englishman to the core and love my country, and for me to live here and not there has always been a sacrifice. What would she think when I shared this word with her? I needn't have worried. The Lord had already prepared her so that when we met in Honolulu, we were clearly of one mind.

So we returned from New Zealand, and our friends David and Dale Garratt with their group gave us a delightful send off. We also received a great prophecy from the leader of the Apostolic Churches in New Zealand. The years ahead, based in Sidcup, and also working with the Pioneer

104. Genesis 31:3 NIV

Network, proved to be some of the most fruitful we have ever experienced. However, I must share one experience that happened quite early on. It concerns Gerald Coates, who died during my writing of these chapters, as did Christine Noble, our great women's pioneer, almost on the same day.

Gerald asked me to come to a Leader's Day conference at Fairmile Court in Cobham. Early on in the day, he asked me to pray for all the leaders there, a most significant group from the wider London area. Before I prayed, I made a personal request. I said, 'As you know, I love to pray and prophesy. However, for some time now, when I start to minister like this, a tight band, almost like an iron ring, forms around my head and is very uncomfortable.'

With that, Derek Brown, leader of the big Aldershot church came over. I didn't know him well, and I'm sure he knew very little about us. He asked the group to stand and then laid hands on me, saying, 'This band represents a resisted anointing from the nation of New Zealand, and I want you to break it now, Lord, in Jesus' name!'

Wow! The result was immediate and I had a great time of prayer and prophecy with the group!

Just before we left New Zealand, we were miraculously protected! We had sold the house and I called in to the Mt Eden office of Barfoot & Thompson to enquire about our equity on the sale. Their office was close to the Valley Road Church. This in fact was the only time I had been in their office. The guy I spoke to said, 'We have the equity, and I will forward it to your solicitor.'

I replied, 'Don't do that. We are leaving the country this week. Put it straight into our account.'

The next day, my Christian solicitor was discovered as having misused clients' funds! He went to prison for four years, and lots of good people lost their money.

Dennis Grennell once said to me, 'If ever there was a man I would trust with my wife and my wallet, it would have been him!'

Chapter 24

New Generation

When we left New Zealand in 1992, I thought we might never return. A remarkable series of events had unfolded during the year that meant we were returning to the UK with a specific purpose. When my old friend, Gerald Coates, got wind of our plan to come back to the UK, he phoned me with a request. By this time, he was leading the successful network of new churches called Pioneer. His enquiry was two-fold: a struggling church in the London suburb of Sidcup had recently joined Pioneer and was desperately in need of leadership. Would Linda and I consider taking up this role? Also, would I be prepared to work with him in the national forum?

I had felt a sense that this would be an important step for us, and I took a trip to the UK, primarily to meet with the Sidcup church and to engage with Gerald and a forum of national leaders that included representation from our Bristol team, Barney Coombs (head of the Salt and Light Ministries network) and John Noble (chairman of the Charismatic Leaders Conference), along with others. On all fronts we received a very definite 'green light'. On the family front, Amanda and Simon agreed to come. Richard was not sure until nearer the time that he should, but we were thrilled that he finally did.

When I met with the leaders and the Sidcup church on that visit, they were very frank with me. They were a group of about thirty-five adults with some children and a few young people. They were based in a former Brethren Assembly building, now called the Acorn Centre, in Birkbeck Road, which was a pedestrian thoroughfare to the train station ferrying commuters to Central London in about half an hour. It was very much a commuter town with quite a depressing High Street, in the London Borough of Bexley, London's largest borough. One thing you couldn't fault about these people, they were very committed and had been doing church together for about seventeen years. Their reaching out to Gerald and Pioneer was almost a 'last ditch stand'. They felt for some time they hadn't been making progress.

A leading figure in the church at this time was Mike West, who had a successful company in the computer games industry. His was probably the most important business in the area and he employed several people in the church. Mike and Kay and the other leaders were exemplary in welcoming us in this important transition, and we were showered with kindness.

In the Autumn of 1992, Linda and I travelled back to the UK ahead of our children who planned to arrive nearer to Christmas. We wanted to be settled in, and hopefully secure a house before they came. I will never forget what happened right at the start! Mike and Kay opened their home to us and provided us with a nice bedroom. We were tired from our journey and went early to bed. Linda had never been to Sidcup, so the next morning, which was quite wet and dismal, I determined to show her around the town – not that there was much to show. Mike had given me the key to the Acorn Centre, and after breakfast, I decided that we would start there.

It was a short walk, and soon we were outside this narrow building, sandwiched between residential homes. There was a glass front to the external door, but as I engaged the key in the lock, I realised it wasn't the right fit. At that moment, I looked down at the mat inside the front door and saw an envelope lying there addressed to us. Now we were curious but couldn't get in. We tried back doors and found one that eventually yielded after at least twenty minutes of frustration.

We walked through the front meeting room to the porch where the envelope lay. I immediately opened it and inside was an anonymous letter with a Building Society cheque for £5,000! The letter welcomed us to Sidcup! Whoever they were, and I still do not know after all these years, it assured us that they were not members of the Acorn Church, but felt excited at the prospect of our being there and hoped their gift would help us in the transition. To say we were overwhelmed is an understatement. We just worshipped in that moment and felt that the Lord had put his seal of approval on our being there.

In the two months before our children arrived, we were able to sort out a lot of things. The church gave me a generous salary and suggested that I see my role as two-thirds local and one-third in the wider network and my international ministry. Mike also offered to sell me two of his company vehicles, a Ford Granada and a Ford Sierra, at a very reasonable cost. The Sierra saw us through another 100,000 miles and I wished I had the Granada as well, once Richard got his hands on my Sierra!

We began to meet regularly with the existing leadership and the Pioneer London leaders' team. Gerald and Steve Clifford (then General Director of the Evangelical Alliance, UK) gave me a lot of encouragement. I remember going to the Swanwick Convention Centre with about 500 of Barney Coombs' leaders. I was a keynote speaker with George Verwer of Operation Mobilisation, still a good friend to this day. He and Drena live not far from Sidcup. This amazing couple have just celebrated their sixtieth wedding anniversary and 2020 was the fiftieth year of the ship ministry. I would say if you have any money to spare, give it to them! They are well worth it.

I can still remember my opening remarks at Barney's conference, which were actually setting our own future direction. They met with some resistance at the time. I asked, 'How many of you here are under thirty years of age?'

If I say there were ten, I think that would be generous. Soon after that I was invited to meet with Tony Moreton and the Cornerstone leaders. Tony shared a fantastic testimony as to how he got started as a student in his twenties. My own testimony was the same; but what had happened? Why had we lost our edge of young radical leadership and why were we now playing safe? I remember casting out demons when I was twenty-two and I didn't know much about any of that! All of this was preparing me for the main thrust of our Sidcup ministry, eventually recorded in my second book: *Baton Change – Releasing the Next Generation*.[105] I believe this has been my most important book to date. Also, one of the reasons I was with Pioneer was because

---

105. Peter Lyne, *Baton Change – Releasing the Next Generation* (Sovereign World Ltd, 2000)

they were encouraging women in leadership. A lot of new church networks were stuck in a rut on this one. Some still are!

I was now teaching and preaching at Sidcup, preparing the church for a new direction. At the same time, we were looking for a suitable house to cope with our family and our ministry of hospitality. We found a place in Carlton Road that really suited us. A three-storey, semi-detached house with five bedrooms and two bathrooms, a nice garden inhabited by foxes, in walking distance of Sidcup High Street and our Acorn Centre, as well as Sidcup Place – an extensive park area, which would become very important in our future. Completion was due early in the year, but I found a great solution for us and the children to celebrate Christmas.

We owned an exchangeable timeshare in Spain and I managed to get a fantastic apartment jutting out over the Thames right opposite the huge Docklands development at Canary Wharf; this coped with us and our children's friends as well. It was a short hop into the City. So, Christmas shopping at Harrods and Selfridges, and the magic of the lights at night reflected on the Thames, were sensational, and our family began their great connection with the Kensington Temple Performing Arts group. In the following years, many of our London leaders' events were held at Holy Trinity Brompton (HTB, famous for launching the incredible Alpha Course), and we have always valued the interaction with their leadership. The vicar, Sandy Millar, was a guest speaker at one of our big conferences on the showground in Exeter.

I'm sure the stay down by the Thames eased the pain for my daughter Amanda. I remember the first day she arrived and was trailing behind us as we walked up Sidcup High Street. It was raining, as it frequently is, and Linda turned and saw tears streaming down Amanda's face. 'I didn't think it would be as bad as this,' she said.

Readers must understand that Mission Bay and St Heliers waterfront beach communities were quite different from Sidcup High Street with its Pound shop, charity shops and boarded-up premises, along with the greasy spoon café we had just passed. However, a redeeming feature was the plethora of Indian restaurants and our friends who ran them.

Number 15, Carlton Road would soon have five other people living there. The first was Charlene Muys from New Zealand. After a few days she said, 'My best friend is coming to London. Can she come out and visit us?' The best friend turned out to be two best friends, Katie Hawkesby and Joe Mcleod, who stayed for more than a year. Then came Chrissie who was escaping a difficult religious set-up in Auckland. To cap it all, François arrived from South Africa. Our son, Richard, met him at Performing Arts in the City and brought him home. Frankie, as we called him, had come over to France to play Rugby, then moved to a Bible school in London. He had given all his money away in an offering, and couldn't work because of his visa. So, he was ours for more than a year and kept us all entertained. In addition, my assistant, Penny Leighton, had an office in the house. Now it was full, but a very happy place!

In this first year, we sought to set the pace. Two things stand out in my memory. We began to do special Guest Nights on Sunday evenings. It was like the currently popular Café Church. Small tables were set up in the rooms, with nice nibbles, wine and soft drinks. People sat in groups with friends they had brought along, and I introduced a special guest, often with musical gifts or unusual testimony. To give some examples, one night we had John Perry, who had been a backing singer for many years with Cliff Richard's band and was also a great singer/songwriter in his own right. Another time we had Dave Marquee, plucked out of the Royal College of Music by Eric Clapton, with whom he toured for several years. These guys were great communicators and very accomplished musicians.

To demonstrate the problems we were confronting, just prior to the first of these events, one of our leadership team said to Linda, 'No one will come. *Ichabod* is written over the front door'! (Ichabod means 'the glory has departed'.) He wasn't trying to be difficult. He really meant it, but I'm glad we proved him wrong.

Christmas was special. Along with special music and other contributions, I hired a donkey from the local donkey sanctuary. Two of our members, John Arundel and Nicky McKenna, did a fantastic impromptu dialogue between Joseph and Mary with the donkey, the best I've ever seen. A tarpaulin was carefully placed across the front to cope with any accidents! The place was packed and there was a great response. We really wanted to turn the church inside out.

However, we do not wrestle against flesh and blood, but principalities and powers, according to Paul in Ephesians 6. Linda and I were conscious that there were things unseen challenging our growth and we planned a specific week of prayer, punctuated by two planned events: Wednesday was a day of prayer and fasting and we arranged to meet that evening for specific prayer. Then, on Sunday night, I invited a special guest, Norman Barnes, to come and share with the church. To 'Stormin' Norman' as we called him, my brief was clear. For many years, he was Director of Links International, an excellent mission support network. However, I wasn't looking for a missions talk or even necessarily that he should preach. I wanted him to prophesy to us as a church and in this regard, I didn't want us, in any sense, to 'prime the prophet'. We wanted him to bring something from the Lord, tailor-made for us at this time.

There was an important prelude to the Wednesday night prayer. Linda had been at a gathering, when Faith Forster (wife of Roger, who had a powerful ministry in her own right) came and sat beside her. In reference to our Sidcup situation, she saw a picture of someone knitting, but there had been a dropped stitch. It was necessary to go back and fix this if the work was to be continued satisfactorily. Faith's sensitivity in prayer has always been important.

Now as we all sat in the back room at the Acorn Centre, we were encouraged to get to our feet and begin marching all over the building. There were shouts and praise leading to positive declarations. During this, Linda received a specific revelation. She shouted out, 'I can see what this is. It's a spirit of passivity and it comes from the Brethren roots in the history of this church!' After a lot of powerful intercession surrounding this word, we went home.

Then came Sunday night. Norman and Grace arrived and took their place in our midst. We had some worship, then I introduced Norman according to my brief and just let him loose. He did not disappoint! He began to prophesy; then, as the tempo rose, he suddenly blurted out these words, 'I can see what this is. It's a spirit of passivity from the Brethren roots of this congregation!'

Now, Norman was not there on the Wednesday evening when Linda had exactly the same word. No one had briefed him. People who struggle with the reality of spiritual gifts need to take note of this remarkable sequence. The prayer of faith is always the same; it carries the promise of Hebrews 11:

> Faith is the assurance of things hoped for,
> the conviction of things not seen.[106]

With such assurance, we were able to stand with Norman and in the authority of Jesus's name break the effects of this passivity. I had never heard of a 'spirit of passivity' before, but I could immediately see how it affected all of us. It is subtle – not obvious – opposition, but deadening in its effect, making faith responses virtually impossible. That night, God set us free, and I knew we had a divine mandate to forge ahead.

Norman also said during his discourse that I should buy a tuxedo, as we would become a church of significant influence. This may have been symbolic, but when, in later years, I was seen in a photograph wearing a tux (albeit a

---

106. Hebrews 11:1 ESV

Marks and Spencer suit with a special shirt and bow tie), it brought some significant verbal opposition. What I do know, as the years have passed, Paul and Paula Weston and their team have taken the church into increasing areas of national influence. Knowing Paul, it's unlikely that he has worn a tuxedo, but they carry a God-given authority that people in high places respond to.

As the year unfolded, we received a very clear idea of what we should do. All this time, Pioneer was developing TIE teams (Training In Evangelism). Young people were giving a year of their time to receive excellent training under Pete Gilbert's leadership. All sorts of gifted people inside and outside Pioneer were lending their assistance to this project. They developed something called the 'Hit Squad' where a team was released for a period of time in a specific evangelistic project. A germ of an idea was growing in us that we felt would help push the church out into the community in a dynamic way.

I remember the night when I first shared what was now germinating in our leadership team. Our plan went something like this: 'We want to set apart two weeks in the summer to engage the church, with help from TIE teams, to saturate Sidcup with the gospel. I suggest we engage Peter Gilbert and some of his experts to come and train us for this on a regular basis. We want to lay our plans and push the green button as soon as possible.'

The response was less than enthusiastic:

'The time isn't right.'

'It is too soon.'

'We don't have sufficient resources.'

Etc., etc.

However, Linda and I were clear in our resolve. There would never be a 'right time'. We had been brought here to do a job and we needed to go ahead and make it happen. We selected a two-week period in the summer of 1993 and asked if people in the congregation could sacrifice some of their summer holidays for this purpose. There was an enthusiastic response from the church.

We secured Pete Gilbert to come each month to train us. He enlisted two gifted teachers to join him in the project: Steve Lee, an outstanding evangelist, skilled in all sorts of engaging performance arts, and Andy Reid who took primary responsibility for ministry in the pubs.

We began planning a programme together that would be underscored by prayer. Each Sunday afternoon, we gathered to pray-walk the perimeter of Sidcup in small groups, stopping at strategic points. Usually, this lasted from 2-4pm each week. We divided the two weeks in our thinking. The first week focused on street work, schools, free car-washing in our car park, social events in some strategic houses, pubs, retirement homes, etc.

The second week, we would erect a large circus tent for bigger events, including a children's holiday club in the daytime and everything at night from a circus to a fantastic gospel choir. I wanted Sidcup Place for our circus tent but the council refused to allow it. They gave us a field down by the railway. Now, after twenty years of Lark in the Park under Paul and Paula's leadership, the council can't do enough for us! A few years ago, when the mayor opened Lark in the Park he said, 'This is the biggest event in the London Borough of Bexley!' However, our initial event was simply a prelude to what would come later, and we didn't have a groovy name like Lark in the Park. It sounds dated now, but we called it Design for Life.

A master stroke happened near to the opening of our event. I had wanted to find premises to host a 'Drop In' for teenagers. Sidcup High Street had a lot of empty shops advertising potential leases. I contacted them all – seven, I think – and the last one (which, in fact, was the most suitable) agreed we could have it. It was right next to the notorious Black Horse pub, which is now closed. We set up a dance floor with a DJ, and some games and a refreshment bar in the Drop In.

As the day approached, everything fell into place. The church had devoted their time and resources, and excitement was in the air. We had a cracking TIE team with their outstanding leaders, and a lot of extra talent as well. Teams were at the bus stops as young people were going to school. They were on the streets talking to shoppers, business people and anyone they could find. They took school assemblies and classes, and there was a clean-up task force for the neighbourhood.

To get a flavour of what happened, let me describe a particular Friday night that I experienced.

I was at the Drop In, which was a huge success, packed with young people every night. Someone told me, 'There's a journalist out on the street.' So I went outside to speak with him. He was a senior reporter with the *Kentish Times*. After an initial chat, he went inside to interview some of the young people. When he had finished, I asked him if he would like to see some more. He was very keen, so a short walk took us down Craybrooke Road where a special event was happening. Mike and Kay West and Brian and Val Marriott, who had been such important figures in getting us to Sidcup, had adjoining gardens behind their houses. There must have been about seventy people there, mostly neighbours and friends, and as we walked through the gate, Steve Lee was sawing my wife in half on a raised platform. Steve was such a great communicator. Then a choice barbecue was happening. I asked my reporter friend if he would like to see something else after he finished his hot dog.

By now, he was very keen. So we retraced our steps to the infamous Black Horse pub. I should explain that we were not allowed to preach in the pubs, but Andy had done a fantastic job visiting all the landlords and getting their permission to have a team and entertainment in the public bar. As we walked in, the pub was jammed, one of our great singers was performing and a lot of team members were spread through the bar talking to the customers. The pub landlord called me over. The journalist was right at my side. He said, 'Peter, this is fantastic. Your team is doing a wonderful job.'

He had gone forward at one of Billy Graham's London crusades, but he went on to say that he had never seen 'church' like this, and he was hungry for more. Later on, we did a number of special events in a big music room above the pub, with Australian musicians, Steve and Rebecca

Bennett. Needless to say, the *Kentish Times* reporter was hugely impressed. He gave a wonderful write-up in the next edition of the paper. One thing that can be said for the impact of Design for Life, it brought us, as a church, out of the back street into the High Street.

As I look back, I have so many memories, but I want to share one or two that stand out. My friends Tony and Jo Davies had a beautiful, detached home in one of Sidcup's premiere streets. They gladly loaned it to us for an event. It was a fabulous summer's evening; the garden looked beautiful; the drinks and canapes were great; we had an award-winning singer/songwriter, Caroline Bennett, performing, and a couple of Charlton's First Team soccer players were mingling with the crowd. I gave a brief but pertinent address, and afterwards engaged at tables for at least two hours with people hungry to know more. One lady, who gave her life to the Lord, joined another church in the town, but I didn't mind that.

Another memory comes from the circus tent, as I saw our intrepid leader in a straitjacket, suspended from a rope which caught fire. The extent that some people will go to in their pursuit of sharing the gospel! Not long ago, I was chaplain at Lark in the Park when I visited from New Zealand. On one of the last nights, in a much bigger circus tent, the visiting evangelist was Peter Gilbert who now lives in Scotland. He did a fantastic job of bringing the message of the gospel once again, and I was thrilled to see that the fire has never gone out!

When we sadly had to leave our Drop In premises, the search was on for a new venue. It took quite a while but out of this setback, a new phase was born. The story of The Worx has been told before, in my book *Baton Change – The Next Generation*, but it bears repeating. This faith step, again, shaped our future.

Just prior to Design for Life, there had been an important sequence of events. We were known as the Acorn Church, meeting in the Acorn Centre. Who doesn't love acorns? They have such a unique shape and smooth exterior, but for us, the name carried a stigma. Acorns are only ever embryonic but in the right circumstance can grow into a powerful oak tree. We wanted to aspire to a future of growth and maturity! Linda and I, along with the young people in our homegroup, wanted to change the name before Design for Life. Understandably this met with some resistance from some of the more long-standing members of the church. Two significant things happened.

We were invited to a United Churches prayer meeting, hosted by the nearby New Frontiers church. Dave Holden was Terry Virgo's second-in-command, and Terry had, and still has, the most successful New Church network in the country. Dave's church was having great success, and to join them in prayer can be intimidating. They had impressive facilities, good leaders, great music, and we were struggling not far away! As I waited for the meeting to start, an unusual dialogue ran through my head: 'Why don't you close down and join them? They've got it together, and look at the numbers...'

At that moment, I felt a specific word from the Lord drop into my heart: 'I have given you a unique niche in the marketplace, to reach the kids that others don't attract.'

With that, my heart was at rest. Great worship followed and in the midst of it my daughter, Amanda, brought the meeting to a pause with a powerful word about the new generation. It was so clear that Dave Holden stepped in and redirected the focus of the meeting around this.

Not long afterwards, a group of the young people were at our house and we shared with them the reluctance of our leaders to change the name of the church. Linda and I didn't feel that this was right, especially as we were about to go very public with our summer events and the young folk present were very disappointed. We brainstormed together and agreed that it just had to happen. As we dialogued together, the word from Amanda's prophecy dropped into place. New Generation was born. I had no hesitation in telling our leadership that this was what we were going to do. I'm not one for autocratic leadership, but sometimes leaders just have to lead!

By now, Paul and Paula Weston had come more into the picture, something that really excited Linda and me. I had felt for some time that they were important, and at a time when they were unsure, they received a specific sign that encouraged them to throw their lot in with us. They became the driving force behind The Worx.

One day, after a lot of further searches, one of our guys drew our attention to a printing works that had shut down, right behind Sidcup High Street. There were drawbacks! The lease being offered was too high; it was short-term – a big supermarket development was planned behind the town. The buildings were in a dilapidated state. As usual, a prayer team got involved and the building was surrounded by people fervently laying their hands on it. As a result, we secured it at a quarter of the stated price, but in a very fragile month-by-month arrangement. When we finally got inside, it was worse than we thought, very industrial and the floor had printer's ink in the concrete, which would prove troublesome. Undeterred, our creative team got to work and with the smell of an oily rag (symbolically and literally), The Worx was born.

The team stayed with the industrial theme, blacked it all out and featured the pillars. Even the drinks bar was the front of an old truck with headlights that went on and off. Next came the music system, dance floor, games tables and machines and new toilets, all of it overseen by a small room up a stairway that was our prayer room. There were rumblings about the cost. 'Why would you spend so much on something that won't last because of the proposed development?' I was confident that the God who had taken us in there would keep us there as long as was necessary to fulfil our purpose. Two major companies engaged in a supermarket war that kept us in there for at least eight years!

At first, the plan was to open for teenagers on a Friday night. A trial was run, without advertising, and about seventy turned up, along with some serious teething problems. Some louts got in who tried to undo our hard work – damaging the toilets and pulling hand basins off the walls. This almost made us feel like throwing in the towel, but when there is opposition or difficulty it's so often a sign that God is at work! Paula Weston was manning a desk at the door, and she noticed a guy with something in the sleeve of his jacket. It was an iron bar!

We quickly realised we had to set up a computer system and register the details of people coming in. In just a few months, there were a thousand names on our database. The second week, twice as many came and the third week, there were more outside than in. Some rampaged down Sidcup High Street and the police had to have extra help and arrested quite a few. I have to say, the police were always helpful and encouraging. Later, a young woman from the force who they used up front in difficult situations, trained us in security measures. We had a great security team outside, and a regular team working among the youth inside.

Some in the local council tried to shut us down, and the local press had a field day. I remember one front page headline that screamed: *Worx Branded A Nuisance!* The chairman of the council called me and said, 'Peter, can you come up to the council meeting Monday night? I happen to know that we have a councillor who is going to move a motion in "Any Other Business" to shut you down!'

So up we went to a packed council chamber and waited, apprehensively, until the chairman called for AOB. Sure enough, a guy sitting close by me, launched into a tirade, wanting to close us down. The chairman let him speak and then said, 'Peter, who is in charge of this project, is here tonight. Why don't we hear from him?'

I thanked him and said, 'Well, you can shut us down, but let me ask, where are these young people going to go? I have a team of dedicated people seriously trying to do something for the youth of our community and frankly, we need your help, not your censure!'

There was such a change in the atmosphere. I must have fielded questions for at least an hour, and even my opponent apologised. I invited the journalist who wrote the lurid headlines in our paper, and she came to meet me. Typically, she had never been to The Worx.

Eventually, Bexley Council called us in. I remember going to the council chamber and taking some of our new young people, only to find we were the focus of attention. Everyone was there – Neighbourhood Watch, police, youth workers, councillors. There was one question that night: 'How do you do it? We spend thousands of pounds on creating youth centres and the like, but they are very poorly attended. Yet you have all these young people engaged.'

It was significant that we received nothing at all from public funding. All our workers were volunteers. Since then, certain significant things have happened. The council has often used our facilities. The police developed an ongoing relationship with us. The Chief Commissioner of Police in Bexley got Paul into planning meetings with his officers and gave him a private number to call anytime. The scope of The Worx broadened and significantly took us into the public arena.

One night, when we were closing up, one of the skinheads saw us going up the steps to the prayer room and said to Ben, ''Ere, what are they doing in there?'

'Praying,' Ben said.

'Can I come up?' he asked.

Next minute, he joined in a team prayer meeting. Soon after, he gave his life to Jesus, and then he surprised us by saying, 'Can I be baptised?'

This sparked a major transition in our church life. Our Acorn Centre had a baptistry built into the floor, so a Sunday night was appointed to baptise him during the meeting. He came with about thirty of his friends and relatives. Pete and Jan had arranged refreshments out the back, and this guy changed into his togs in an anteroom out there. When we baptised him, his mates all gathered around. There was a lot of whooping and shouting, then we prayed for him, but when he went out to get changed, his supporters went with him! I did a very stupid thing. I tried to carry on the meeting, while out the back, the crowd fell upon the refreshments and had a good time. Paul came up to me as we concluded and said, 'Never again.'

We had about thirty of the lost that we were trying to reach, but like good Christians, we persisted with our meeting!

The next baptism was different. We had lots of friends running the curry houses in Sidcup. I think it was Ben again who got Oliver to loan us one of the big wheelie bins they use for the restaurant rubbish. They valiantly tried to hose it out, then we had it in the centre of The Worx with a set of steps. Everyone could crowd around. We all escorted the bin outside and we tipped the individual and the water out into the car park.

There was a time when some of the more traditional people wanted a service to suit them; so we obliged the older folk at the centre, and the more radical at The Worx. It didn't last long. Our folks soon recognised where the anointing was, and we gladly came back together.

All sorts of transitions happened in these years. There was an important prayer phase where a prayer tent was established in a corner of The Worx. People met in there most nights of the week from 10pm. It was a hallowed place. If the police saw some of our young people wandering down the High Street after midnight, they got used to being told, 'We've been at the prayer meeting'.

Weddings happened in The Worx, and it wasn't unusual for some of the alcoholics who slept in our garage out back to slip in, and even participate! We had a great cast for Linda's children's musical, *Nehemiah*. We won't forget that in a hurry! There were some great jazz nights with the cream of Christian jazz musicians.

It wasn't always easy. Sometimes we had to separate gangs and defuse fights. One memorable night at The Worx we were warned of a potential gang conflict. A group had arrived from another part of the borough and the temperature was rising with some of the Travellers. I went outside to Ray, heading up security, and said, 'We must get these guys off site. Help me as I reverse my car up to the back door. Then we'll get these guys out to my Ford Sierra.'

All went well until the last moment. I had crammed the guys into my car and revved the engine, but at that moment the other group pressed out of the front door and one of them lay on my bonnet clinging to the windshield. Down the lane from The Worx was a left-hand bend. As I swung round the corner my unwelcome passenger flew off. I managed to take the other guys well out of harm's way. They were impressed. It felt like Starsky and Hutch! A Seventies flashback! Fortunately, the guy was not badly hurt and he came up to The Worx the following week to apologise. A lot of the Traveller community in Sidcup came to us. Even to this day, they come to Lark in the Park and bridges of friendship have been built.

These days, if you visit Sidcup, you'll find an excellent Morrisons supermarket on the car park and territory that housed The Worx. The church has met on Sundays in the Bexley multiplex cinema for many years, and often in the ancient St Stephen's Anglican Church on Sunday nights. Now we have Hope School just off the bottom of Sidcup Hill, and Paula Weston and her team have transformed the Blackfen library; they picked up this failing enterprise and now have 5,000 members there. If you're lucky enough to be in Sidcup at the end of July/beginning of August, walk up into the tent city that is Lark in the Park. Last time I was there, at least 32,000 people had visited the site!

Before I leave The Worx, two incidents are prominent in my memory. One night, Chilean evangelist, Miguel Escobar, was at The Worx. He was dog-tired from international travel, and after a powerful message with a lot of people responding, he passed Paul the microphone, apologised that he needed to go straight to bed and asked him if he'd mind handling the ministry time. An interesting sequence followed. Paul asked a young woman called Mary if she would help him in praying for people. A stage whisper came from Chris Lowth, 'She's our babysitter, here for the first time. We're not sure if she's a Christian!'

Paul pressed on regardless. The first person prayed for was overwhelmed by the Spirit, fell to the floor and began speaking in tongues. Now Mary interjected, 'Is that speaking in tongues?' she said. 'I've just written a philosophy paper for my school A level, but I've never encountered it before!'

Later, Mary was to receive the second highest marks in her A level paper in the whole of the United Kingdom. She went on to shine at Cambridge University and returned to be an important part of our team. She is now married to John, one of our leaders, and although having young children, she has been a driving force in the development of Hope School, Sidcup, and a new school in Southampton.

Another incident involved me and Pete Austen, who sadly passed away as I was writing this chapter. I had been at a London leaders' meeting in a golf clubhouse in Ewell. The room was packed and that afternoon, an unexpected guest joined us: Mike Bickle, from Kansas City and now leading IHOP – the International House of Prayer. I had met him once at a conference in southern California but doubted that he would remember me. After a brief introduction, he singled me out and began to prophesy powerfully over me. It must have gone on for 10-15 minutes, and I was prostrate on the floor, overwhelmed by the power of the Holy Spirit.

On Sunday, I was at The Worx and I shared about the powerful experience I had through Mike's ministry. I said, 'Tonight, I want to do something different. This anointing is for you as well, so instead of me laying hands on you, I want you to come and lay hands on me.'

Peter Austen immediately came forward, not usually a first-up responder, but as he put his hands on me, the power of God fell upon him, and he was down on the floor, receiving a special healing. My last memories of Pete were seeing him in his accustomed seat by the security entrance for our team at Lark in the Park. A faithful man who, with his wife Jan, was with us from the beginning at the Acorn Centre.

Sometimes, things would happen outside as well as inside. Walking across the open land in front of The Worx, I noticed a commotion with a group of young people at the edge of the property. When I got to them, there was a young girl on the ground pretty much the worse for wear. When I asked the girls trying to help her what was happening, they said, 'She's got boyfriend trouble, and she's just sculled half a bottle of vodka.'

I sent a messenger quickly to our registration team with her name. They had her mother's phone number and sent it to me. Mercifully, the mother drove up quickly and I said, 'We must get your daughter straight away to A&E at the nearby hospital.'

I helped lift the girl onto the back seat of her mother's car and I jumped in the front seat. Mum was quite hostile – but then, she was very shocked. When I told her what the girl's friends had said: 'Boyfriend trouble,' Mum snarled and said, 'she doesn't have a boyfriend!'

I mentioned the vodka, and she was even more incredulous, 'Where would she get that?'

I mentioned that sometimes it was stolen or purchased on their behalf by an older teenager. Fortunately, we arrived swiftly at the hospital, and she was taken in immediately and her stomach pumped. The next day, her mother called me, very apologetic, and thanked us for our care and swift action in a situation which could have gone terribly wrong.

Often parents are totally unaware of where their young people are! The Worx proved to be a fast learning curve for us all.

Chapter 25

Back to the Future

1999 proved to be a very significant year for us. On leaving New Zealand in 1992, I had said we would never return, that is, permanently, at any rate. I was wrong. Events unfolded that were somewhat outside our control.

When we lived at Carlton Road in Sidcup, we had several boarders on their OE (Overseas Experience), especially from New Zealand. Our son Richard fell in love with one of the girls, Kate Hawkesby, and after a preliminary visit to meet her parents in New Zealand, he didn't return to live in the UK again. Later, we all went back for the wedding, and at this time, Simon and Amanda eventually decided they would rather live in New Zealand.

We were left rattling around in a big house, missing our family, and becoming increasingly aware that we had some important decisions to make. We sold the house and moved in with our friend, John Arundel, for a while. He had a nice apartment just around the corner. He is used to rescuing us! Friends all over the church agreed to take our stuff, and a great couple called Richard and Linda, who had recently joined us, received the final delivery. I can still see the look of surprise on their faces as they looked at the truck and asked, 'What's for us?' Our belongings completely filled their garage and a bedroom as well!

Before I continue, I must mention the night we baptised Richard and Linda. They had recently come to faith and he was keen to be baptised, but she was very apprehensive. We discovered that the reason for this was a poor relationship with her father. On one occasion, he had decided to teach her to swim, and simply threw her into deep water. From then on, she was gripped by a fear of water. One Sunday night, Richard proceeded with his baptism – full immersion in a special baptistry in the floor of our meeting hall. Linda stood by, fully clothed, watching her husband as we dunked him in the water and then prayed for him. A crowd was standing around the pool. Suddenly, Linda tore off her skirt and jumped into the water in her knickers, freed from her fear. We were overjoyed to baptise her.

My Linda was very unwell for some time with pneumonia and pleurisy, but we had a chance to rest and recover in John's apartment. Then a beautiful cottage in the Kent village of Farningham came available to rent. Farningham House Cottage was picture-perfect and only fifteen minutes' drive from Sidcup. It was not available for sale, being joined to the manor house. Had we been able to buy it, we could never have left it!

The first night after we moved in, Paul Weston's face appeared at our window with a group of our young people. Lots of visitors came to stay with us, including one more permanently: Stuart Stock, from the Upper Hutt church in New Zealand, came to live with us. It was not long before he met our former PA, Penny Leighton, whom he married and whisked off to live in Wellington.

Our cottage was opposite the pub which had a folk club on the back. One of our visitors was Fletch Wiley, a famous

American musician, who had played trumpet and flute for the Andrae Crouch band. We arranged a night with our church and friends that packed out the club. I asked Fletch to share his testimony and play for us. What a night! I doubt if that club has ever witnessed a musician of his calibre before or since. Next door to our cottage was the antique furniture business of Polish Prince Peter who also became a friend. We had a great catch up with him three years ago on our last visit to the UK.

When we could no longer stay in Farningham, we purchased an apartment right next door to John's except he was on the top floor and we were on the ground floor. We loved it there and frequently played croquet on the lawn out back with our neighbours. The day we moved in, special friends from the USA visited us. I had been working a lot with Bill and Melinda Fish in Pittsburgh, Pennsylvania. Melinda was a well-known author and editor of the *Toronto Magazine* for years during the Toronto Blessing. Melinda has a huge voice with an amazing Texan drawl. She had never met Linda, but when I ushered her in to our block, she called out in a voice that everyone in the street would probably have heard: 'WILL LINDA LIKE ME?'

We loved them. Sadly, our time was overshadowed by the death of Princess Diana. When Linda and I walked through Central London the next day, the whole city was subdued, with huge floral tributes outside Buckingham Palace and people talking in hushed tones. The only time we have seen anything like this was at the death of our Queen, which I have recorded at the end of this book.

We have had many international guests in our homes and churches over the years. It was always a privilege to welcome Wayne and June Drain of the Fellowship of Christians in Russellville, Arkansas. Wayne is a gifted singer, songwriter and prophet, and his beautiful wife, June, is such a hospitable Southern lady. For many years I was the Pioneer link person with their church and Wayne has toured New Zealand and Australia with us and the Garratts. The churches have loved his unique gifts. I remember him saying that when he encountered Pioneer in the UK, he felt he had come home. The feeling is mutual! Two other special friends who live just off Manhattan Island in New York are Drew and Lyn Lynch. Drew was a journalist and Lyn, after bringing up eight children, went back to college and did a Masters. Theirs was one of the best run homes we have ever been in. They are still prayer-walking much of the British Isles every year and Drew has done important work on the inter-testament period. We always look forward to being with them.

As more and more responsibility for leading our Sidcup team was passing to Paul and Paula Weston, we recognised an important baton change was going to be needed in the not-too-distant future, and when the news reached us that our first grandchild was expected in May 1999, we had to make definite plans. I was feeling concerned, and I shared this with Linda just before Christmas 1998. I was very conscious that throughout our lives together, we had moved with clear direction from the Holy Spirit, not simply because of circumstances. Around this time, I was due to go to the annual Charismatic Leaders' Conference. As I was about to leave, Linda said, 'We really need a clear confirming word from the Lord – as clear as when we first went.'

When I arrived at the conference, our first session was led by Faith Forster who encouraged us to get into prayer with someone near to us. I found myself standing by Peter Butt, whom I scarcely knew. He was part of the Cornerstone team based in Southampton. Before we prayed, Peter immediately caught my attention with his opening remark: 'I understand you're going back to New Zealand.'

I asked him how he could possibly know this as only Linda and myself had discussed this. He then said something like this, 'I had a dream the other night and I saw you making this decision.' But then, the kicker was: 'Your son is Simon, but he will be Peter, and this decision will be especially important for him.'

I was gobsmacked. Simon was indeed Simon Peter, and he was in some difficulty with the circumstances that he was living in, which we did not know the full extent of at that time. I thanked Peter for his faithfulness. As you will know, the importance of spiritual gifts is a regular theme in this book, and I couldn't wait to get on the phone to tell Linda how apt her admonition had been to me. Mind you, I'm quite sure her thinking was already running on more pragmatic lines: 'My first grandchild with you, Peter, is on the way, and I want to be there.' So our plans began to take shape.

During the previous few years, I had been given a role with Pioneer as Chairman of Major Events. The History Makers event had been a big success on the Royal Norfolk Showground, with some 5,000 people in attendance over the May Spring Bank Holiday weekend. I was already engaged in planning our Event for Revival the following May.

The baby was due to arrive in May! Linda made plans and would go to New Zealand ahead of me in April. I would follow immediately after the event finished. I also needed to ensure that we had thoroughly commissioned Paul and Paula and their team. The church recently had a twenty-one-year anniversary celebration as a surprise for them in January and I sent a message to the church for them:

The time seems to have flown by, but you have accomplished so much – in fact, much more than we could ever have achieved. We knew from the beginning that your place was with us at New Generation, and we have never had more confidence about laying hands on anyone than we had about you!

Some years before, I was commissioned by the Pioneer team to write a book on apostolic ministry, which was first released at our 1999 event. It's called *First Apostles, Last Apostles*.[107] One thing I am sure is central to the nature of apostolic leadership is this: the recognition and release of leaders. Think of Jesus with the Twelve. More important than all the miracles and the wonderful teaching was the recognition and release of these gifts to the Body of Christ – more than anything else in the church today. I believe we have so many leaders who have a stranglehold on succession, which makes it impossible to pass the baton and release the gifts that will take us into the future.

As our final session of the Event concluded, I took off to London, ready to board a plane to Auckland the next day. Grandson Jackson was delayed arriving, but I came very

---

107. Please contact me if you would like a copy: peter@peterlyne.com

close to missing that important threshold. Soon after my arrival, Linda and I moved into a house right in the heart of Old Remuera, leased from a friend who had gone to Australia to train for some triathlons. He also included his excellent Honda CRV, which was a great asset to our mobility. We began renewing friendships and made ourselves available for an important role that had been brewing before we left England.

We had become aware of the sad demise of a Christian leader of what was probably the largest Christian church in the country at the time. I should say that over the years, we had been consultants to church and business situations in different places. A fine musician, who had worked with us over the years and was a key member of the music team in this church, had been communicating with us. He felt we had gifts that could help the church in its time of need. Sadly, the prominent leader had been living a double life for many years, and new crushing evidence had come to light. Also, it was significant that an old friend, David Shearman, of the Nottingham Christian Centre, had been on the spot, staying in the pastor's house when the balloon went up. David had proceeded with an itinerary in Australia. He shared with the church what had transpired, and they sent for him to come back from Australia to help sort out the mess, so he returned for some days before he had to go back to the UK.

Now we were invited to meet with the elders and their wives. After our first meeting, they asked if we would take on a consultancy, initially for two months, in which we were asked to meet with the individual couples and regularly with the eldership team. We attended the church but remained 'under wraps' – a policy which somewhat surprised me.

At this point, I must mention a meeting that I had with a friend who had just resigned from the eldership. The offices of his company were just a stone's throw from where we lived. He said to me, 'You won't be able to help them, and this is why: one of the team desperately wants to step into the shoes of the former leader and this will prevent you from doing what you need to do.' How right his assessment proved to be! I thought I might be able to overcome this but, in the end, it proved to be a frustrating and insurmountable barrier.

For two months, Linda and I faithfully fulfilled our brief. It was a painful experience, but we sought to bring comfort and healing, and in some way to encourage a way forward for this damaged congregation. Right at the end, we were asked to visit the elders on a retreat they were due to have on Auckland's north shore and specifically to bring a report summarising our insights. We carefully prepared our report with some apprehension as we knew it would confront a sensitive issue which may not prove acceptable to some of the group.

Before we left for the retreat, I had popped into the church administration centre and just as I was leaving, the senior PA reached into a drawer and produced a document, saying, 'You might like to read this.' It was a copy of the report to the leadership that David Shearman had given them after his second visit to them in the wake of all that had happened. Amazingly, it included a passage that was virtually identical to the conclusion we had reached. Before

I opened up our report with the leaders, I asked them what they felt about David's comments. One of them said to us, 'We've moved on from there.'

My response was, 'I don't think you have and the issue you are facing is this: are you looking for apostolic endorsement or apostolic foundations?'

They had been considering the need for apostolic help for some time and had frequently used this term. The issue we confronted that day was that of the four leaders present, two of whom had more prominent ministry in the church, none of them was suitable to take on the overall leadership role.

I explained it like this: one leader had what I described as a circumstantial limitation. His lovely wife had a major illness and he had become her main carer. I felt he was the most spiritually gifted of the team and popular with the congregation, but his primary commitment made it difficult for him to fulfil such a demanding role. The other leader was a delightful man who had fulfilled a number of roles in the church and was now eager to take on this position. After careful consideration, we knew it was beyond his gift and could not honestly endorse him in this role, so our report caused quite a reaction.

I read the section of David Shearman's report, which was particularly relevant, and this is my paraphrasing of it:

As a leadership, you must not assume that the congregation who have afforded you such grace as you tackle the aftermath of this tragedy will continue to do so. I believe that none of you is in a position to take the overall leadership that the church desperately needs at this time, and you need to rectify this as soon as possible.

It seemed they afforded my report a similar response to David's original paper. I added, 'I don't want to blow my own trumpet, but if you would allow me to, I'll look for someone suitable to fulfil this role. I have contacts with churches in different parts of the world and would make it a priority to find a suitable candidate.'

We left the meeting soon after this, and I thought this would be the end of our consultation, but I was wrong. The leaders contacted us almost immediately and asked if we would continue for another two months but add personal interviews with all the full-time staff to our brief. At the time, the church had seventeen staff! We fulfilled the brief faithfully and even had a night of prophetic ministry with them all, which was well received.

Towards the end of this time, they asked us to join them for the national conference of their denomination in Christchurch. There were positive things about this. The main speaker was Joyce Meyers' pastor from the States, and he gave some great talks. Several of the national leaders took time to chat to us, but we had a difficult time with our own leader who was still desperate for the job.

When we returned to Auckland, he asked me to meet with him for coffee. He was struggling that we hadn't changed our judgement in the situation and admitted how hurt he was by our intransigence. After a while, I brought this to a conclusion. I said, 'Look, I'm not your enemy, and I don't want to become your enemy, but if we continue like this it will become very unpleasant. We will just withdraw, and you must do what you intend to do.'

With that, I left the café, then he followed me out into the street. Surprisingly, he wanted us to carry on trying to help them but I just had to put my foot down.

In retrospect, I must say this: should we have hung on in spite of everything? That is something I know Linda has thought we should have done. But notice, never once was I invited to address the church in the Sunday meetings, which to me is a salient point. Here is another surprising point. About three years ago, we were sitting in a café in Mangawhai with the other principal leader (who was now fulfilling a major international prophetic ministry. His wife whom he cared for in an exemplary manner, had passed away. Sometime later, he met a young widow who was also very gifted, and they make an excellent team). Out of the blue, he said to me, 'What we really wanted was to hand over the church to you and let you lead us.' Not one of those leaders ever suggested this to us at the time. Sadly, they probably lost at least 800 members of the congregation in a short time. How do we explain this?

In my book on apostolic ministry called *First Apostles, Last Apostles*, I have a chapter entitled 'Apostles in Conflict'. I use the conflict between Paul and Barnabas recorded in Acts, which resulted in their separation, as an example, and I also include my seven recommendations for handling confrontation. In my experience, you cannot be an effective leader without handling confrontation. This is where so much breaks down in a leadership team, not just in churches, but businesses and other institutions as well.

Chapter 26

Silence is Golden

I am just celebrating sixty years in public ministry. More than anything, I have loved to teach and preach the gospel, but in these last twenty-one years, a strange silence has been imposed on me much of the time, especially in New Zealand.

This latter period of our life and ministry has been something of a roller coaster ride with its ups and downs. On the family front, we soon witnessed the happy occasion of our son Simon's marriage to Bella Jane Hardy, the cousin of Richard's first wife, Kate Hawkesby. On the one hand, Simon married into a family of Presbyterian ministers, and Richard into a high-profile media family. I shall never forget coming down for Richard's wedding and seeing billboards all over the city with John Hawkesby's photograph and the caption *John tells it like it is!* At the time, he was a very successful news presenter and Kate was soon to follow in his footsteps.

Following our sons' marriages, grandchildren soon arrived and, to date, we have ten of them here between the ages of twenty-three and ten. These represent the delightful highs of the roller coaster. We have spent a lot of time with them all, especially in their earlier years. The lows have contrasted sorrowfully with the joys. Some of this is inexplicable. Simon and Bella Jane's loss of two babies in the womb, and the premature loss to cancer of Brian, Bella Jane's dad – such a gentle, spiritual man. He and Sylvia had devoted many years to the Presbyterian ministry, and she is still maintaining her role in the church at Takapuna, Auckland, where we farewelled him.

As Christians we have no slick answers for these sorrowful experiences, but in the gospels, Jesus gives us glimpses of our future hope. I love what he says in Matthew 18:10 about children:

> See that you do not despise one of these little ones. For I tell you that their angels in heaven always see the face of my Father in heaven.[108]

Another low was the devastating divorce of our daughter-in-law Kate from our son Richard. Having never experienced divorce in my family, this was a difficult new path to tread, and I am so glad we were on hand when Richard passed through the depths of this trauma. One thing you learn about divorce, and it catches you unawares, is that you all get divorced! Sides are taken and important relationships are sadly lost through no fault of your own.

The next high was experienced when Richard met the lovely Anna, and it was my joy to marry them in the crypt of St Paul's, Symonds Street, with most of the family present. I still remember Graeme and Robyn Hart coming forward to embrace Linda and me at the end of the service and saying how thrilled they were that Richard had found such a soul mate! We, too, are thrilled, and grandchildren

108. NIV

Jesse and Stella are the icing on the cake, as anyone who has met this remarkable duo will know.

When it came to work that might sustain us during this new NZ phase, it was quite a challenge to say the least. No longer having the support of a local congregation, I needed to do some 'tent making', as the great apostle Paul did in his leaner times. One thing that Linda and I often did together was clean people's houses, look after their children and, sometimes, older relatives. This has happened on and off over the years, and in Linda, people discover a cleaner and a carer second to none. She gives extraordinary attention to detail, great at ironing too. I'm not so good at this, but 'Grandad Treats', as I am fondly known, has other tricks up his sleeve when it comes to children. We have enjoyed such special relationships with family and friends as a result.

In this regard it would be remiss of me not to mention Kevin and Nikki Denholm and their beautiful children, who were part of our lives for so long. Kevin ran a very successful film production company, 'Exposure', entertaining us with his creative advertisements on television, one of which Linda featured in. He also made short films on mental health, and filmed in different prisons around the world for Chuck Colson's Prison Fellowship International.

Nikki's book on female genital mutilation is required reading for healthcare workers. She and Kevin are such creative people with demanding schedules, so for nine years, Linda oversaw their house and we spent a lot of time with their daughters, Isobella and Lucia, who were a joy to be with. Conveniently, the grounds at the back of their property ran over to the school. I regularly entertained them with my stories of the Puggly Wugglies and their special friend, Dragon Dago. Later, a beautiful third daughter came along, but by then Linda was working for Yvonne Milne, a very gracious society lady at the end of her life. Her father was George Court, who founded the Department Store and was a prominent figure in New Zealand's history. Proudly displayed on her wall, she had a photo of our Queen Elizabeth's parents when they were on a state visit to New Zealand. The future King George had gone fishing with her father, and the Queen Mother was missing her daughter Elizabeth so much that she asked if she might hold baby Yvonne for a time. We had three joyous years with this lovely lady before she passed into the presence of the Lord.

Another special Remuera lady had us cleaning her apartment and enjoying her company. Joyce also had a royal photograph on her bedside table. It was of her handsome brother during the Second World War. He and several other Anzac soldiers had been invited to tea with the Queen Mother. Sadly, he never made it home from the war. Seeing this photo saddened us to think of a life lost so young.

For some years we assisted Petra Bagust, Amanda's best friend, and her husband Hamish Wilson, as their family was growing and they both had very busy schedules. I had married them on the edge of the lake in Queenstown and this was recorded live on TV3. She was one of the most recognisable personalities in the media, and Hamish was, and still is, a great cameraman. As the marriage service concluded, a white helicopter flew in and collected the bridal party for an exclusive photo-shoot up in the

Remarkables.[109] Amanda was the maid of honour for this event, which actually stretched out over three days. Petra's parents, Danny and Judi, are our close friends, and I also had the privilege of marrying Justin, their son, to Michelle.

On a more structured work front, Linda has done two extended periods as front-of-house Clinic Clerk at two doctors' surgeries, the Maungakiekie Clinic, just off Greenlane in Auckland, and latterly, the Balmoral Doctors on Dominion Road. Sometimes I have just marvelled at Linda's tenacity. At the latter job, when she still commuted three days a week from our home in Mangawhai, nearly two hours from her work, it was nothing for her to leave at five in the morning and drive through all weathers and traffic congestion, arriving at 7am. She would then prepare the surgery for opening at 8am and, apart from a 30-minute lunch break when she was often serving lunches to staff, be at her desk until 6pm. Regularly, when she was not staying down in the city, she would drive home! In all of this, she always looked beautifully presented and had a winning smile for all who came. Did I marry Superwoman? I think I did.

You may be surprised to know that Linda became a TV star! For a long time, her advertisement for a collagen product was constantly aired. On the mornings that I was teaching at Selwyn College, just before I left, I watched the news on television. Without fail, my darling wife appeared on the screen before the headlines. I used to get frequent comments on this in the staff room. One day Linda was on the front desk at Balmoral Doctors when the husband

---

109. The Remarkables are a spectacular mountain range in New Zealand's South Island.

of Prime Minister Helen Clarke came in and said, 'Don't I know you?'

Linda replied, 'It's me that should be saying that to you!'

During these twenty-one years I have still travelled extensively overseas, in my ministry and some other projects, leaving Linda and the family often for six weeks at a time. This has not been so much, more recently, and on a number of occasions, Linda has been able to travel with me.

To help fund us at home, I revisited my teaching career from 2000 on until the Ministry of Education managed to side-line us about three years ago. I sent out my qualifications to three local schools and offered to be a 'relief teacher'. The first school to respond was St Kentigern's, a Presbyterian Foundation private school in the heart of Remuera. I had a phone call from the principal's secretary asking if I would come to meet him as soon as possible as they needed to appoint a new chaplain. When we met, he said that I looked the ideal person for the job, but I raised a query: surely the Board will require an ordained Presbyterian minister, and in response he assured me it would not be a problem. Sadly, he later told me the Board had insisted on this and he appointed a lady chaplain who turned out to be an atheist! Mercifully, not too long after this, they appointed Simon's brother-in-law, Reuben, who has done a fantastic job there.

After this hiccup, the nearest school to where we lived, Selwyn College, warmly responded, and for some seventeen years, I was one of their principal relief teachers. For many years we owned a delightful cottage on leasehold land just a few hundred yards from the school. I could be in school at a moment's notice, and I thoroughly enjoyed my time there both in the staffroom and the classroom. It gave me great opportunities to influence the new generation and I seemed to succeed at what I did. The school appreciated me and were equally gutted when the Ministry made it virtually impossible for us to continue in this important role.

Another spin-off was that St Thomas's Primary School was even closer to our home, and we had a regular succession of our precious grandchildren coming for afternoon tea and fun and games. I have never regretted these times, and it made a lot more sense of our being based in Auckland instead of back in the UK.

During this period of time, we have had three important church involvements where we have not had major leadership responsibilities but participated as members of the congregation. We have seen the church in New Zealand, not as visiting ministries, or to put it more crassly, not from the pulpit side, but from the pew side. This has, at times, proved very challenging! First of all, for me personally, I had to seriously examine my own motives. By the time I was twenty years old, I was regularly teaching and preaching. I was thoroughly disciplined in this, giving myself to the daily study of Scripture and prayer, wanting to be always on the ball spiritually, ready to fulfil what I felt to be the call of God on my life. Now, I had to face a serious question: did I simply do this because I was a 'professional'? Now that in New Zealand my opportunities to share in public ministry were increasingly spasmodic, would my prayer and study equally diminish? I'm happy to report it didn't and I'm as much devoted to seeking God and his purpose as I have ever been.

I can't tell you the many vibrant messages I have received over the years that I have never had the opportunity to share anywhere, except, perhaps, in one of our house-groups, or when I get on the road overseas in Britain and elsewhere. Why is this? I wish I had a simple explanation, but I don't. I know I received two warnings of this from reputable prophets (both described in chapter 23 on page 335).

For the many years of our travelling from Bristol to New Zealand and back, we have had a secure home in Bristol Christian Fellowship. Our wonderful team and the church supported us so faithfully. We feel indebted to you all for your love and care for our family during all these upheavals. Through the Nineties, New Generation Sidcup provided a secure foundation for our ministry in the UK. In the last twenty-two years I have returned so many times, sometimes with Linda, and have stayed with Paul and Paula, Charlie and Zac, and more recently Chris and Jane as well, and this coming year will be no different. We also look forward to seeing all our friends in Ramsgate, especially Mike and Stella, Hope and Jesse, and Pat Cook, who from the beginning have always been such an inspiration to us.

I want to identify some of the positive experiences that we have had in the three very different churches that we joined during these last twenty years. Our first was with the Anglican church, St Paul's in Symonds Street, close to the university in the city of Auckland. We joined the congregation just as a young priest in charge, Mike Norris, arrived with his wife and family and a team of a dozen volunteers from St Peter's, Bryanston Square in London. The way this had come about was that the buzzing, charismatic church in London had been a magnet for many Kiwis on their OE or extended jobs and study courses. Many would say, 'Why can't we have a church like this in Auckland?' It would seem St Peter's decided on a bold church-planting initiative. There were consultations with the Bishop of London and his counterpart in Auckland. As the plan unfolded, St Paul's seemed a good option for several reasons. It had a significant charismatic history, being a key gateway in the early years of the movement. It was uniquely positioned, right in the middle of the student population. It had fallen on hard times and was a shadow of its former self with a rapidly diminishing congregation.

From day one, Linda and I liked the flavour and Mike and Bex's unique leadership, along with their team. We threw our hat into the ring with many others and greatly appreciated the opportunity to be involved. This unfolded on two main fronts. Firstly, they ran Life Courses – their version of Alpha – that proved to be a great tool in evangelism. They tried to have three of these a year, beginning with an introductory banquet, then weekly events which began with a meal served at tables, followed by a talk. Then interactive Q&A in groups. Regularly we saw up to 120 people come to these courses. The church had a great crypt, which was an ideal setting for these evenings. Excellent catering teams were appointed, and gifted leaders who would work through the course with the same group of people for the sake of continuity. Like Alpha, there was a Holy Spirit weekend away at various motels and conference centres, and these proved popular as well.

Mike was a great leader, funny, but with talks full of content, and his own dramatic testimony as he had been a successful lawyer in London as well as struggling with alcoholism. Through these courses, many came to faith but, equally important, Christians got established in their walk with God and their ability to share the gospel. The church began to grow significantly and very soon was probably the biggest Anglican congregation in New Zealand. (It still is, I believe.)

The second, equally important, ingredient was the development of house-groups. This was especially encouraging for Linda and myself as we had been pioneers of the House-church Movement in Britain. For Mike and the team this was never just an 'add-on'; it was integral to the life of the church. Linda and I helped lead a house-group with Murray and Gaye Cruikshank at their lovely home. This then evolved into a cluster of three groups which met for special events. Several of these were particularly memorable, such as booking a cinema for a showing of *Amazing Grace* followed by lunch at an Indian restaurant, or the time we had Rhian Day and her daughter, Mari, from our Bristol church, talking about their work with the prostitutes in Bristol's red-light district.

Such was Mike's faith in this that he closed the church one Sunday every month, and we met in clusters. These were amalgamated groups in a specific area and ours could have up to seventy people meeting. We had some memorable times together and I have never known any establishment church leader take such a bold step. It really said aloud that the House of God was not the building or the institution, but the people. There were always some people who grumbled over this arrangement, but Mike was the kind of leader not easily deterred.

At this point in my story, let me share an observation that I have made since we settled here in 1999. I call it 'God's Joke'. Since we pioneered House-churches, later known as New Church Networks, we felt we were the custodians of fresh understanding of team ministry, the release of all the Ephesians 4 ministries and church-planting, but the joke is on us! I have lived to see many of these old churches become vigorous church-planters, taking historic, defunct buildings in city centres and transforming them! Look at HTB's current record if you don't believe me, and personally, I am thrilled that they are doing such a great job and setting the pace this way. Our London leaders' meetings for Pioneer were often held at Holy Trinity Brompton (of Alpha fame), and Sandy Millar and his team were often with us.

When we realised that the demands of Mike and Bex's family and other factors would inevitably lead to their return to the UK after seven years of fruitful ministry, we became concerned for what the future might look like in terms of direction. At this time, we withdrew to another church, The Edge, situated in converted warehouses close to Eden Park, the hallowed rugby stadium.

At this time, a gifted prophet, Greg Burson, and his wife, Linda, were leading the church. Greg was a very quirky teacher and I enjoyed regular meetings with him over coffee for stimulating conversation. However, it was involvement with the small groups which were the lifeline for us. In talking about these three churches, we see again, so clearly, the important principles that we had helped pioneer during the early days of the House-church Movement in Britain. Some of these we could easily identify:

- Just as the human body is made up of cells that are intrinsic to its life, so it is with the Body of Christ.

- Indisputably, the church in the New Testament was in the house, not chapels and cathedrals. There were large gatherings in open spaces, like the temple courts in early chapters of Acts. How could the thousands that gathered in Acts 2 be confined to the Upper Room? Acts 2:46 shows us quite clearly that they met in the temple courts and from house to house.[110]

- Our language had to change. Hebrews 3:6 says clearly: *We are his house.* I find many church leaders pay lip service to this truth, then use language that contradicts it, for example: 'Welcome to the House of God'! Are they talking about the people or the building?

- We majored on people, not plant. Not difficult when you are an intimate group in the home. We began as five adults in Olveston, but when we grew and joined with other similar groups across the city, the logistics were much more demanding.

- We centred on doing life together, not a weekly religious meeting. (I sometimes ask church leadership groups: 'How much of your time and energy is put into preparing for a weekly church meeting for an hour or two?' This is hardly the gospel of the Kingdom as demonstrated by Jesus.)

---

110. Acts 2:46

- Our emphasis was on our life in these cells, representing the life of the church, it was not a secondary thing to support the main event.

I could go on but, once again, at The Edge, we loved being a part of the vibrant group that met at Bruce and Christine McGrail's house, not far from our home. Meetings were always stimulating. We probably had the best worship leader in New Zealand, Nic Manders, and a remarkable team of musicians. Also, you could always rely on something outside-the-box from Greg's ministry. Sadly, we moved north to Mangawhai after some three years and a commute was out of the question.

For us, two unexpected things converged. We knew our lease on the house was due for review. The original owners, the Melanesia Missions Trust, sold out to an individual who had a ruthless reputation. Land prices in this desirable area of Auckland had escalated beyond belief. Our $5,200 annual lease multiplied more than five times to almost $30,000 per annum – an impossible hit for us! What could we do?

On the home front, an extraordinary thing happened. Our good friends, Lew and Tracey, regularly came to dinner. Lew had been Senior Partner in a medical practice that Linda had previously worked for and had been a close friend since that time. He was looking ahead to retirement, which was still five years away, but they said, 'We've been looking for a potential retirement property and have found something we really like in the coastal village of Mangawhai. However, it's just too soon to act on this.' A couple of weeks later, Lew and Tracey came back to us and said, 'We've bought it!' Then came a second bombshell: 'Would you consider going to live there for the next five years?'

We were stunned, especially as we had very little experience of Mangawhai, which was almost two hours north of Auckland. They explained that we could pay a significantly reduced rent and that they would like to be able to stay with us there from time to time. Linda was quite unsure about this, and we had a lively discussion that ended with an agreement that we should travel with them to view the property.

The house was a spacious, mud-brick property, set on nearly five acres of ground, surrounded by gracious lawns and edged with tropical plants. There was a horse ring and paddocks, plus a retired harness racer, Mr Tan, who belonged to Meg, the previous owner of the house who had now built a residence at the other end of the drive. All of this was set down a secluded drive off King Road, a very desirable location with olive groves and vineyards nearby.

Although still slightly apprehensive of the distance from Auckland, family and our jobs, we felt it was a right move. A big plus was that we could lease out our cottage in Kohi and cover the new lease and rates while we planned a future sale. It was a spectacular property: the master bedroom had a bathroom with a huge glass window that looked on to a private rose garden.

The first Christmas holiday season, we enjoyed a massive treat. (Christmas is the height of summer in New Zealand!) All our family came to stay for a week. We had our daughter

Amanda, Richard and Anna with their five children, and Simon with five more! Bella Jane couldn't come as her friend, who lived in Europe, had shouted her a trip to Paris. It was a busy time, making sure everyone was fed and watered, and supplementing sleeping arrangements with a couple of tents. The children got on well together and the adults had a great time.

Mangawhai is a great destination, with a magnificent estuary and two great surfing beaches at either extremity. In between two distinct communities, Mangawhai Village and Mangawhai Heads, is a great park called the MAZ (Mangawhai Activity Zone) which now has a world-class skateboarding complex and special fitness zone. What we hadn't realised when we arrived was the presence of a dynamic church meeting in the school gymnasium.

Causeway Church is unique for a village community numbering around 3,000, as it has nearly 500 members. Statistically it would be one of the largest churches in the country. We were impressed with their use of special Christian festivals. The Christmas Eve Carol Extravaganza was in three sittings and attracted nearly 1,500 people. The leadership of Colin and Anne Chitty, local farmers, was inspired, and they have developed an excellent worship team of accomplished musicians. Also, Paul and Jan Chambers have made us very welcome. Both PE teachers from our part of the world, they have shared their home, and so many meals and All Black games with us, and Paul always makes us laugh!

We have been part of this church for some six years and particularly liked their emphasis on 'Life Groups'. Here we are, back to our House-church theme. We were soon leading one of these and had nearly two dozen members who made for a very lively group. A big plus for us was that our daughter Amanda decided to leave her high-powered job at Auckland University and come to join us.

For several years, she has been PA to the senior pastors, and concentrated on her writing. During this time, she produced a remarkable novel called *A Better Ending*.[111] Although a novel, it is based on a huge volume of family research and facts which covers three generations of Linda's family through two World Wars. If you have encountered any of Linda's own story you will understand just how miraculous it is that she and her sister Karen have survived.

We have so many friends in Mangawhai, it's hard to go anywhere without bumping into them. Latterly, a remarkable development has taken place that will affect the future for all of us. Amanda had bought a lovely house in Tara Road, just outside the village. For a time, she leased it out to defray costs and lived with us at King Road. When the time came for our friend Lew Randal to retire and move with Tracey into the home they had bought some five years earlier, a great transition took place. Amanda engaged our son Simon, now a builder, to develop a side of her house that had been a garage and create a beautiful flat for us to live in. We were very pleased.

Soon after we moved in, Linda was strolling in the lovely garden and said out loud in a prayerful way, 'The only thing that could change this is if Amanda meets someone.'

---

111. A.J. Lyne, *A Better Ending: It's Never Too Late to Begin a Better Ending* (Independently published, September 2017)

Many years earlier, the prophet, Marcus Arden, had said to her that he felt she would not marry until much later in life. We had held on desperately to this, believing that 'Boaz' would one day arrive. The day after Linda's musings, Linda encountered Amanda as she came in from the village saying, 'I've seen Pete!'

Linda replied, 'You're not going to see him again, are you?'

'Yes, I'm meeting him for coffee tomorrow.'

Linda told me of this development and added, 'I'm sure it will all be over now!'

Not for them, of course, but our cosy arrangement, which was beginning to look very uncertain.

To explain just how incredible this all was, I need to backtrack a little. Once again, the miraculous broke into our lives, especially for our daughter. Pete had been her boyfriend twenty-two years previously and, at that time, Amanda had broken off the relationship. Unaware of each other, they had both come to live in Mangawhai, and Amanda's cottage was just two kilometres away from seven acres of land that he had purchased and was developing. As time had gone on, Pete saw Amanda around the village but didn't disclose his presence. Neither of them had married.

Then, one day, they ran into each other at a local store and Amanda said that two things immediately struck her:

'He's grown a beard, and I like it!'

'He's always been the love of my life!'

Chapter 27

'Head and Shoulders, Knees and Toes!'

During my last four years in New Zealand, I have had both my knees replaced. Now, when I travel overseas, I am always stopped for a search because of my titanium replacements – more of that later. However, I have always had a fascination with hospitals, which began in my youth and continues until now.

Strange as it may seem, I liked going to hospital. For us, living in north-east Bristol, it meant going to Cossham Hospital in Kingswood, which was more like a cottage hospital than the all-powerful Bristol Royal Infirmary. For many years, Bristol University hosted a medical school that equals the best in the country, and this is reflected in the reputation of the BRI. However, I loved Cossham, and was never happier than when I was going there, which was quite a lot!

I was not always the patient. For example, I accompanied my younger brother, Eric, and a neighbour's child when I had fractured both their wrists with one of the tricks I was performing in Page Park at that time. I would lie on my back and bunch my knees on my chest, then the hapless boys would sit on the soles of my feet, and I would catapult them into the air! The results were disastrous, and I had to go with Dad to Cossham with Eric with a Colles fracture, also described as a 'dinner fork deformity', as his wrist was now shaped like a piece of cutlery. I was impressed with the young doctor. He was talking to Eric and, holding his hand in a gentle manner, he suddenly exerted a lot of force and pushed the wrist back into position without anaesthetic. Eric yelled! But it came straight, and I was mightily impressed.

Later, when I was in my early years at grammar school, I was a frequent visitor. Once Dad took us blackberrying and landed us in a wasp nest, and we were all seriously stung. Another time, I was lining up outside a classroom door when Trevor Scantlebury shoved me from behind and I put my hand through a pane of glass. I still have a lump on the side of my finger where a chunk was taken out. Not long after this, we were having a biology lesson in the garden. Unwisely, several of us boys were issued garden forks with long steel prongs. I instituted a great game: I stood my fork upright in the soil and got the boys to throw their forks like darts to see who could come closest. Unfortunately, on the second round I went to retrieve my fork just as my good friend, Fred Ward, threw his! One of the prongs went through the back of my hand, and I still have the scar to prove it.

Dad got me a Saturday job with the local butcher, delivering the Sunday joints. I had this cool, old bike, with a big basket on the front for the packages of meat. One morning, I turned across the main road and was hit by a motorbike coming from behind. Everything was flung across the road, and I landed on my coccyx, the bone at the base of my spine, which took me back to the hospital.

By now, you're thinking that this boy is an accident waiting to happen! You're not wrong. There was an incident when I was sixteen that has permanently damaged me, and it was my own fault. I played soccer for a local team, and on this occasion, I was in goal. Our side was good, and I had nothing to do as we were winning 5-0, and it was very cold. Jumping up and down on the spot I suddenly leapt up into the air and swung on the crossbar. Only one problem! It wasn't bolted down so the bar sprang off and cracked down forcibly on my head. I ran up the field with blood pouring from my head and saying to the ref, 'I'm alright!'

He came across and examined my head and simply said, 'My God!'

So, it was an ambulance and back to Cossham Hospital. They didn't keep me in after several tests and some minor surgery, which involved shaving my hair and inserting a series of stitches back to front. It looked spectacular and eventually turned blue and green. But the main problem was not discovered until much later. The retina of the left eye was detached!

These days, this could probably be re-attached quite successfully, but no one pushed for this, and I concealed my injury for a personal reason. Vanity! I hated the thought of wearing glasses, although I knew my eyesight was impaired. I had to move to the front of the class to see the blackboard. Eventually, my mother took me to the optician, but in those days, there was no thought of sending me to hospital for surgery. Neither was there anything like designer glasses, which are such a fashion statement today. I hated my National Health spectacles and managed to dispose of them not long afterwards. I went on holiday with my friends to the Isle of Wight and, at the end of the week, deliberately left them in a drawer in the hotel bedroom where we had been staying. More than two years later, during a medical in my first year at Loughborough College, my sight impediment was revealed, and the words spoken by our Scottish doctor in his broad dialect have never left me, 'Ye only have one pair of eyes, laddie!'

All through the years, even with glasses, my left eye has been different. Then, about four years ago, living here in New Zealand, I woke one morning to find that I was completely blind in my left eye. There followed several visits to the eye specialists in Auckland, who were concerned that this development shouldn't affect my good eye. Fortunately, it hasn't, but I do have an unusual condition with an unpronounceable name, that cannot be rectified. Fortunately, my right eye is still healthy and my sight good enough for driving.

Another incident occurred in my teens, which was equally serious and involved Cossham Hospital again! I developed a grumbling appendix, and it was considered sufficiently serious to warrant an operation. So, in my last year at grammar school, I was admitted for surgery. Everything went along just fine. I enjoyed being put under anaesthetic and, in fact, still do, and I was making an excellent recovery when a dramatic development took place. Don't be surprised, I seem to attract such things!

A patient was brought in after emergency surgery and put in a bed next to me where I was recovering. He was a gypsy boy and had been in a field climbing a tree when a terrible accident occurred. As he was climbing down the tree, he was lowering a shotgun in front of him, which accidentally went off and shot him right through the stomach! Somehow, he managed to run across a field and jump a five-barred gate where he collapsed and was subsequently taken to hospital. He was in a serious condition and had all sorts of tubes attached to his body, which he kept trying to pull out. Eventually, I stepped in to help the nursing staff who were overstretched and frustrated. I sat by his bed and kept him as still as I could. In the end, I sat there most of the night, and he began his recovery. However, I became very ill myself!

The next minute, all the tubes were being stuck into me. The worst thing was the tube they had to put down my throat. Having enjoyed most of my hospital experiences, this one I didn't enjoy! I had a paralysed gut, and I stayed in hospital for some days while they got to grips with it. I'm glad to say the gypsy boy made a full recovery.

Even though I left Kingswood Grammar School at eighteen and embarked on a three-year course of Teacher-Training in Physical and Religious Education at Loughborough College, I still managed a further visit to my old friends at Cossham Hospital! During an Easter break, I was at home in Bristol and turned out one Saturday for the Grammar Old Boys' side. They were always pleased to have me as I was a good goal kicker. This Saturday I was hit sideways by a vicious tackle on my left knee. I knew something had been torn and I had to limp off the field. Someone drove me to Cossham Hospital and they identified serious cartilage damage and admitted me for an operation. The college authorities weren't very happy with me when I returned to my course, but I engaged in a serious training programme, including a lot of swimming, and quickly recovered. What I didn't realise was that this trauma would affect me in later life – my dodgy knees!

Before I move on to the physical trials I have experienced in the years since we returned from London to New Zealand, that is, in the last twenty years, I must give an account of a very special healing I received soon after we first arrived in the country in 1978. We were based in the Hutt Valley outside of Wellington, from January 1978 until 1980. I was invited to go to a meeting of the Full Gospel Business Men's Fellowship, where my good friend and co-worker Hudson Salisbury's brother-in-law was due to speak. I had scarcely met Jack Lloyd, but soon discovered he had remarkable spiritual gifts. He wasn't the greatest preacher, but when he began to move in words of knowledge, healing and deliverance, he was second to none!

When he finished his message that night, he began to call people for prayer. First, he asked anyone who suffered with migraine to come forward. That was me, I had frequently suffered with migraines that could incapacitate me for days, but I stayed glued to my seat, unwilling to go forward. Next minute, Jack announced my name, 'Peter Lyne – get down here!' All eyes were on me. Jack laid his hands on me and prayed a prayer of faith. Something happened, but it wasn't what I had bargained for. I went home and had one of the worst migraines I have ever had! Next morning, I phoned Jack at his work. He was a carpenter on a building site, and he popped down to pray for me again during his morning tea break.

We all know about the blind man that Jesus prayed for twice, recorded in Mark 8:22-26; well, that was me. I can testify to the glory of God, the wonderful release I have had from those debilitating headaches ever since! I am not against the medical profession. I am so grateful for the gifts God has given to men and women. Luke, who was a doctor, has given us powerful records of healing and deliverance in his gospel and the Acts of the Apostles. It doesn't in any way undermine his professional experience or the help we may need from the medical profession at different times.

During this last twenty years, I have been hospitalised five times. The first was when staying in a friend's house which had recently been built. Apparently, the garage floor did not have a resilient finish and during a storm, when water had leaked under the garage door, I stepped in to take off my wet clothes and slid like an ice skater across the floor, severing a tendon in my upper arm.

Not long after this, we were staying in another friend's house while they were on holiday. Linda cared for their home and, often, their children. It was during a season, as on a number of occasions in our unusual lifestyle, that we were without a home of our own. It was Christmas, the main summer holiday season in New Zealand, and Linda's sister, Karen, had come to stay with us on her first visit to New Zealand. As a Christmas present, she wanted to buy tickets for us to go to the *Cirque du Soleil*, something we were eager to do. We had been in the city at the ticket office during a heavy shower of rain and walking back to where we had parked our car adjacent to Albert Park, I said to Karen and Linda, 'Be careful. The fallen leaves are very wet!'

With that, I turned and my leg slipped from under me and I knew that something was badly torn. A passer-by helped lift me into the back seat of the car and we drove straight to Auckland Hospital. I was immediately admitted as the main tendon above my right knee was severed and required immediate surgery. This was the most depressing New Year's Eve we ever experienced. We had planned so many lovely things for Karen's visit and Linda was excited by the prospect. Now, I had ruined everything. Later in the evening when Linda and Karen were finally going home, I said, 'At least I have a bed by the window and can see the fireworks display from the top of the Sky Tower when the clock strikes twelve.' In the event, I dozed off before it happened and awoke when it was all over!

Linda and Karen didn't fare much better either. They hadn't eaten, so called in to the Diamond take-away to get a *Nasi Goreng*.[112] The owner said, 'Sorry, ladies, we have just cleaned up and are locking the door.' Linda burst into tears, and he took pity on them and provided them with supper. It was the beginning of a very difficult time. Karen's trip was spoiled; Linda was annoyed with me; I rarely had any visitors in the hospital – no chocolates or flowers! People were away on holiday.

How, as Christians, do we explain these incidents, especially as we pray daily for God's protection for ourselves and our loved ones? As the late Robert Schuller of the Crystal Cathedral used to quote: 'Why do bad things happen to good people?'[113] The fact is, there is no simple answer, but we can cling to the promise in Romans 8:

---

112. *Nasi Goreng* – an Indonesian fried rice dish
113. Melvin Tinker, *Why Do Bad Things Happen to Good People?* (Christian Focus; Revised edition, 20 July 2009). R.A. Schuller, *What Happens to Good People When Bad Things Happen* (Orient, 3 October 2011)

*We know that in all things God works for the good of those
who love him, who have been called according to
his purpose.*[114]

Important as this is, we must note that Paul doesn't say that all things are good.

When Karen left, I was still in a wheelchair and a kind friend, who worked with Linda, took us in at a place far out of town. I remember Linda taking me out for a meal on my birthday and I just burst into tears! We were at a fairly low ebb. I have told so many true stories of the miraculous in our lives, but we are not without suffering and, at times, persecution. When Jesus promised the 'hundredfold' to Peter in Mark 10:28-31, it was 'with persecutions' – something that can easily be overlooked when things are going well.

At this acutely difficult time, two miraculous things happened. A friend, now living in America, who had been a part of our church previously, came for a brief visit to New Zealand. He came to see us and encouraged us when I was still in my wheelchair. After taking us for a lovely meal and praying for us, he gave us a gift of $1,000. This really was a *'table in the wilderness'.*[115]

Then, not long after this, we were at St Paul's Church in Symonds Street, one of the oldest Anglican churches in New Zealand. It was right at the start of a team ministry coming from London with Reverend Mike Norris. We gladly

---

114. Romans 8:28 NIV
115. Psalm 78:19 NIV

joined for the next seven years. As we sat in a pew near the front, a couple tapped us on the shoulder. Kerry and Gabriel O'Malley have become some of our closest friends over these years. They had heard we needed a place to live and invited us to a lovely apartment on the side of their home, rent-free and furnished with their impeccable taste. It was close to the waterfront in Kohi, the suburb we had lived in previously. A bonus was that our family was close by. This proved to be the turning of a corner for us and we are so thankful for all that has happened since then.

Notwithstanding, I was to have another unexpected visit to the hospital in that year. I had been asked by our vicar, Mike Norris, to preach at the Sunday morning service in St Paul's, something I was really looking forward to doing. I recall that we were staying with our friends, Hamish and Petra Bagust, and I had popped out early to get coffee and pastries. When I returned to Hamish's house before we left for church, I noticed an unusual bleeding from my rectum. With Linda's help I did my best to staunch the flow and protect it. We proceeded to the church, sat in a front pew, and the leader of the service, Jo Batts, came to speak to me. I still remember her saying, 'It's such an honour for me to introduce you to speak this morning . . .' Jo had lived with us for a year while on her OE in London, but as she spoke, I started to feel very faint! I turned to Linda and said I could feel the bleeding was increasing. The special pad was dislodged, and she realised I needed immediate attention. Again, I was admitted to Auckland Hospital. I had superb care and all manner of tests during a five-day stay, but no clear explanation was found. I remember a surgeon coming to my bed with a team of about six others and his first question was: 'What were you going to preach about on Sunday morning?' So, I gave them a brief synopsis of my message.

Finally, my knees! At least I hope it's final. What you don't realise as a young man, when you press your body to its limits, is that there are often consequences. I had played rugby, soccer, cricket, and did a lot of gymnastics and athletics. Things reached a critical point with my left knee about five years ago. I had an excellent surgeon caring for me and he determined that the left knee needed to be replaced because of the previous damage and now the arthritis that was developing. We had thorough preparation and then the replacement surgery. I was released from hospital after five days, and a serious programme of physiotherapy at the hospital's special unit followed over several weeks.

I made a swift recovery, but during my follow-up visits with Mr Campbell, he recognised a similar problem with my right knee! Every time I saw him, we managed to delay action as I wasn't in severe pain, but then my walking became more impeded, and it was agreed that I should have the necessary surgery. Linda delivered me to the hospital. I went through the same preparation as previously and my trusted surgeon led the operating team. Again, I made a swift recovery; so much so, that the hospital agreed to release me in two-and-a-half days. I was glad to come home.

Sometime on the following day, the leg that had been operated on began to itch. It didn't stop, so we popped over to see our retired doctor friend, Lew, nearby. It was Lew that got me under Andrew Campbell's care in the first place. He took one look at my knee and said, 'You must go back to the hospital immediately.'

Linda drove me back to the A&E in Auckland Hospital, and after several doctors examined me, they called in the surgeon on duty. I can still remember him standing with his hand on his chin looking at my knee. He finally said, 'I don't like what I'm seeing there.'

So, I was admitted back to the ward. Later, they described the infection as a 'sticky nasty' because it could adhere to the new replacement and cause all manner of problems. The next morning, they gave me breakfast on the ward. This was apparently a mistake, as the team arrived and wanted to operate immediately, but the food would complicate things. They said I would now be called at 3pm. It was a Sunday and when 6pm arrived, I thought it would be deferred to the next day, but the orderlies came to wheel me down to the prep room.

Eventually I was transferred to the operating theatre and rolled onto the table ready for the anaesthetic. Suddenly an alarm went off and everything stopped. There was an emergency – someone seriously bleeding! As the surgeon left, he said to one of the doctors, 'Clean up as best you can.'

With this, another doctor came with what looked like a long silver needle, which he proceeded to push into my wound, probably at least fifteen times without anaesthetic. It was absolute agony. I don't think I have ever experienced pain like it. When this cleaning process was over, they rolled me off the table and took me back to the prep room. Now, it was about 9pm Sunday evening. I thought it's unlikely that they will complete this now, but I was wrong. About midnight, they gave me the anaesthetic and did their best to cleanse and restore the wound.

The previous day, when I went back to the hospital with Linda, I thought I would be there for a couple of days. It turned out to be most of July. I was given a PICC[116] line with major antibiotics being delivered above my heart. Later, they only agreed to release me from hospital if they could train Linda to use the PICC line at our house. It was a serious process, three times a day, and Nurse Linda did a marvellous job! I'm not the best of patients, and it was essential that I didn't get re-infected. After several weeks, I was allowed to take my antibiotics orally, but I had to go for blood tests every week at our local surgery, and this continued well into the next year with regular visits to see Mr Campbell.

During my time in the hospital, we had all sorts of opportunities to share our faith. One day, the receptionist came in and asked Linda and me to pray for her. Most of my nurses were from the Philippines, and they were fantastic. I kept my latest book available on the bed-locker: *Ruth: A Parable of the Kingdom*[117] – and there was a lot of interest in this. Something puzzled me so I asked my doctor friend about the nurses from the Philippines, 'Why are there so many from overseas, and are they paid less than New Zealand nationals?'

Lew assured me they had to be paid the official rate, but the answer was simple: 'New Zealand trains countless health professionals, with a great deal of support coming from the government. However, as soon as they qualify, most go overseas, perhaps to Australia, Canada and other

---

116. PICC is a peripherally inserted central catheter.
117. Peter Lyne, *Ruth: A Parable of the Kingdom: A Love Story That Changed the World*, (Malcolm Down Publishing Ltd, January 2016)

countries, where they can earn probably twice as much as they would in New Zealand.'

One thing I must say, I frequently hear criticism these days of the various medical services, both in New Zealand and the UK. I have only received excellent care and attention in the public sector at all times, and am so grateful for the exemplary attitudes I have experienced, especially from nursing staff. Remarkably, all of this has never cost me anything!

This morning during prayer and reflection, I realised I had more to say about my eyes, important as they have been in the overall theme 'Having nothing, yet possessing everything.' I am now totally blind in my left eye as the result of the injury when I was sixteen years old.

When Linda and I moved into the Old Meeting House in Olveston in 1973, an incident happened that had a remarkable outcome. Our ancient kitchen had a cobblestone floor that had been part of the original road through the village. I was horsing around with Linda and other family members by the kitchen sink, flicking a tea towel at arms and legs, when I accidentally knocked my glasses onto the cobbled floor. One lens completely smashed, and I had no spare pair!

An immediate problem presented itself. This happened on a Thursday, and I was due to travel up to Manchester University at the weekend to give two public lectures for the Christian mission there. Also, and this sounds crazy, the first lecture was on Friday night; then I had to take an early train to London on Saturday morning for an important meeting of the *Come Together* core team, convened by my friend, Jean Darnall; then board another train for Manchester in time for my evening lecture. How was I going to manage this without my glasses?

I must backtrack a little. Some weeks before, I crossed the Severn Bridge that is very close to our village of Olveston, not to travel into Wales, but to cross the River Wye at Chepstow and follow the road up the other side of the River Severn towards Lydney. This was on the edge of the lovely Forest of Dean and there was a conference centre there in an old farmhouse. I was the guest speaker for a group of Christian leaders, and a chain of events began which has continued until now, almost fifty years later!

A gentleman approached me after the meeting, whom I had never met before, and introduced himself as David Kear. He said, 'I noticed, while you were speaking, that you are having difficulty with your glasses. You keep having to push them up your nose because they are not fitting correctly.' He then pushed a business card into my hand and said, 'If you need any help in the future, please contact me.' I thanked him and pushed the card into the top pocket of my jacket.

On the occasion of the calamity with my glasses in the kitchen, I suddenly remembered this, and scrambled to find his card in my wardrobe. I immediately called David and described my dilemma. This was his solution: 'How are you travelling to Manchester?'

'On the train,' I replied.

'Good. Then I want you to get off the train at Gloucester Station and follow my directions to the office complex of my supplier, just a short walk from where you disembark. I will arrange for them to provide you with a temporary solution, then when you get home, come and see me as soon as you can.'

I did as David had suggested. His practice was the largest in that region and I made my way to his main consulting rooms in Lydney. I soon discovered that David didn't simply want to prescribe glasses, which he was very accomplished at doing. He wanted to talk to me, and I usually spent more time in his consulting room, discussing important church matters, than having my eyes checked. This then overflowed into various restaurants for lunch and also to his home, to meet his delightful wife, Maureen. He usually gave me two new pairs of glasses with the finest designer frames. Then he drew Linda into the arrangement, and my mother as well, during the last twenty years of her life. What can I say! Those of you who have to visit an optician know that, like dental treatment, it can be very expensive.

When David died a few years back, another good friend, David Adams, stepped into his shoes. It's been a joy to get to know him and also to visit his wife and the church that meets on his property near the practice in Coleford. Just today, as I am writing, I have received confirmation that my current glasses, that had been damaged, are on their way by post from the Forest of Dean to Mangawhai Heads in Northland, New Zealand!

Those of you who know Linda, know she talks to everyone. At our last Sidcup Church Leaders' Conference, I had a prophecy for her that it is as though she is surrounded by a magnetic field. Joel, husband of Mel who manages our Sidcup Office team, took this very seriously and said, 'We must lift Linda up before the Lord.'

Our lot are very active, so after checking she was suitably attired, they hoisted her up in the air, forming a scrum beneath her. It was unforgettable! Well, this magnetism has been evident over the years, especially where our hairdressers, doctors and dentists have been concerned. Of all the hairdressers, none was more important than Richard Bryant and his lovely wife, Marie. I remember when we first chanced upon Richard at his *Shaggers* salon, just off Bristol's city centre. They soon came to dinner with us at Hill House in Olveston, the first of many such occasions. This one I will never forget: over the first course, Richard said, 'I saw a movie last night that really freaked me out! It's called *The Exorcist*. Thank goodness it's not true.'

I jumped in with, 'But it is true.'

Richard's face went as white as a sheet, so I quickly added, 'Well, not that Hollywood version of things. But the gospels describe a number of such encounters in the ministry of Jesus.'

Then we moved on to calmer waters and had the first of many great evenings.

Our doctors have also been our friends, and Linda worked for two of them at Maungakiekie Clinic in Auckland. Paul and Anne Trotman, and, especially, Lew Randal and his partner, Tracey. If you want excitement, watch an All Blacks game with Tracey. You might need ear plugs! To Lew I have been known for some time as 'The English Patient'. Even now he has retired, we always value his advice more than anyone else. Tracey has become a very adventurous cook, and as you will have read in this story, it was in their retirement property at Maungawhai, in the north of New Zealand, that we lived for five years.

When we lived in Olveston, our dentist was Simon O'Shaughnessy. He and his wife, Patti, were part of our community, and our lives have been entwined over the years. Even now, they are living in New Zealand, and it is hard to find a warmer and more generous couple. They came up to see us in our new home above Waipu quite recently for lunch. They turned up with a large box from Farrah, which is the equivalent of a Harrods hamper, complete with two lovely bottles of wine.

None of us is exempt from the struggles of daily life, whether it's with physical health, homes, cars, finances, dealings with banks or whatever, but we've made some wonderful friends along the way. James and Jill Mills hosted us for a week in Valbonne, near Saint-Tropez in the south of France. We will never forget that week. When James met us in Bristol he said, 'Come and speak to our church and we will take you around.' Did they ever! Beautiful villages perched on a fabulous coast. I remember going to the Café de Paris in Monaco. Linda was mortified that she hadn't dressed up for the occasion. There were wonderful dinners at their beautiful estate outside the village. James wrote *The Underground Empire*,[118] an exposure of the influence

---

118. James Mills, *The Underground Empire*: *Where Crime and Governments Embrace* (Sidgwick & Jackson, 27 October 1988)

of drug cartels on political life in the USA, which was made into a television series. Jill had worked closely with Tricia Guild of Designers Guild in London. We were so privileged to have this quality time with them.

For many years now, Robert and Sarah Bond in England have been our special friends. I believe we first met in Salisbury. We had been speaking at a church there and went to their home for lunch. I remember them as being so hospitable, warm and friendly, and I think we hit it off from the start. Over the years Robert has helped us with various vehicles and has developed a great scheme of buying at auction for so many people and church groups. We call Robert, 'Bond of the BBC', as he frequently comments on air on a variety of motoring issues. We often stayed with them at their home and loved the short walk into the city through the extraordinary Cathedral Close. Occasionally we would slip into the cathedral under the tallest spire in Europe, to participate in Evensong. It's important to note that this choral worship has continued every day for over 900 years. On the way home, we would pass a showroom for Lotus cars. Bond of the BBC would call them 'loads of trouble, usually serious'! Robert and Sarah now live in Cornwall at Perranporth, on the coast above Truro. Robert has worked for Cornish MP, Steve Double, also a mutual friend, as speech writer in the House of Commons, and more recently handling the Conservative Party office locally. It's always a privilege to stay at their home so close to the magnificent beach, especially when Robert cooks his legendary rib of beef.

Living in the apartment Kerry and Gabriel O'Malley had provided for us in Kohi proved to be a prelude to something more permanent. Our old friend, Danny Bagust, undertook to set up a special housing trust so that we could look for a suitable home of our own. He contacted supporters, mostly from the UK, who gave gifts to this project. A major gift from old friends, along with other contributions and the promise of a mortgage from our bank, meant that we could look for a modest home, but it would probably have to be out of the city. When a very suitable cottage became available further up Kohi Road where we were living, it was only within our means as it was a leasehold property.

In discussions with our advisors, particularly Danny as chairman of the trust and Graeme Skeates, our lawyer, who has helped us with his services so much over the years, we put in our offer, $200,000, which was accepted. Had this been a normal purchase it would have been at least $500,000. It was a compact, semi-detached cottage in a beautiful bush setting down a tree-lined driveway. Although we were on a very busy main road, it felt like being in the country. The lease for the first ten years was only $5,200 per year, which along with our mortgage, we were able to manage.

As the day of our unconditional purchase of the property approached, a drama unfolded! We had been good customers of the National Bank for twenty-five years, and they had indicated their support for us throughout the process, but our $100,000 mortgage was refused at the last moment. The next morning Linda received a remarkable word from the Lord.

In the morning, LORD, you hear my voice;
in the morning I lay my requests before you
and wait expectantly.[119]

119. Psalm 5:3 NIV

414

Her heart was thumping as she told me, absolutely convinced that everything would be provided. At that moment, the agent handling the sale contacted Linda and asked, 'Is everything OK?'

To which Linda replied, 'Absolutely,' although she knew the reality was that nothing was confirmed at that stage.

She went to a friend's birthday party and an unusual sequence of events occurred that no amount of human manipulation could have orchestrated. She asked the friend whose party it was, if she could have a lift home with her. As they were leaving the restaurant another friend asked if she could have a lift as well. She settled in the back seat and commented to Linda, 'I understand that you're buying a house.'

Linda replied, 'Oh yes, we are hoping to, but we've just had our mortgage for $100,000 turned down at the last minute by our bank.'

Our friend said, 'I've got $100,000 I don't need at present. Would you like to borrow it?'

Linda said, 'That's amazing and very kind of you.' But in her mind, she couldn't imagine taking it in these circumstances.

The next day, Graham contacted his Westpac Bank, who immediately agreed to the mortgage. We signed that afternoon. When we checked on the transfer of our funds from the UK, we discovered it would take another three weeks, long after our completion deadline. Linda thought of the friend who had offered to loan us the money the previous night. She put in the call and was assured the $100,000 would be transferred immediately.

Here's a strange coincidence: the money was transferred from the same branch of the National Bank that had let us down at the last minute. Our home was secured. I went into my bank the next day and withdrew all our remaining funds, about $5,000, and explained to the tellers, all of whom knew us, that I was taking the money across the road to the Westpac Bank who had confirmed our mortgage. They were all gobsmacked as we had been excellent clients for so long!

Over the years I have had some unusual experiences with banks. One of the earliest taught me a great deal. Linda and I had just bought Hill House, the ancient manor house in Olveston. This miraculous story is told in chapter 16, but I must include this incident that happened as soon as we moved in. We had extensive lawns surrounding a lovely, spring-fed lake with a through stream. The owner of Hill House had an excellent sit-on mower, which we needed to maintain the garden. He wanted £500 for it, which I didn't have; so, I went to my bank manager at the Midland in Thornbury to get a temporary loan. His name was Mr Inward – a particularly appropriate name that we have endorsed over the years as 'Inward by name and inward by nature!'

As he asked me numerous questions about my request, he particularly wanted to know where my income came from. I did my best to explain my life of faith and how we were supported by voluntary gifts. This completely floored him. He became increasingly confused and embarrassed and then made a very apologetic statement: 'Peter, if you had a normal job and salary, it would be straightforward.' Then, he used his prime example: 'So, for example, if you had a job down the road at Rolls Royce Engines, our main employer in Bristol, everything would be fine.'

I came away emptyhanded and somewhat humiliated. The next day, an incredible thing happened. Rolls Royce collapsed! It was international news and if the government had not intervened, thousands of employees with their secure incomes would have been out of work.

My good friend Eddie Vince, who had become my property advisor, stepped into the breach. He said, 'You'll never get anywhere with a bank manager like that. I would love to introduce you to my bank manager in Southampton.'

Eddie lived near Richmond Great Park in London, and we were coming from Bristol, but it was worth the drive. It was a branch of Lloyds Bank, that in New Zealand was the National Bank. The manager of this bank couldn't do enough for us. Over all our years travelling to and from New Zealand, he never failed to support and encourage us. We received a personal Christmas Card from him each year.

The same was true in Sidcup during the Nineties until the relational base in banking, as in most industries, was scrapped, and we suddenly found ourselves contacting call-centres in India!

Chapter 28

Special Memories

Since we took our first major trip as a family to New Zealand in November 1977, we have travelled extensively all over the world until now. Only a few months ago, Linda and I visited two new destinations at the end of a two-month trip to the UK: Cyprus, at the eastern end of the Mediterranean, and Israel, specifically Jerusalem. This had not been planned when we left home on our journey but came as a special surprise that we will never forget. Old friends, leading a church in Cyprus, invited us to engage with their community, and added a side trip to Jerusalem – one of Linda's life-long ambitions!

Often our travels have been related to specific ministry opportunities, but not all of them. It seems, looking back, that some very special memories have been woven into all this, for which we are extremely grateful. Here are some of the highlights.

The first extraordinary situation that comes to mind is a visit to Nepal. Usually, we are not travelling as tourists, and so we don't do the usual things that tourists do. But then, we often see and experience things that most tourists don't have the privilege of experiencing. This happened during our time in the Olveston Community. We had met a couple who were doctors with the International Nepal Fellowship mission. They invited us as guest speakers to a week-long conference based in Pokhara with representatives of most of the various missions working in Nepal, including medical missionary staff from the Green Pastures leprosy hospital.

We stayed in the house of our doctor friends and were warned to expect faces at our bedroom window early in the morning. The Nepalese liked to see what we were doing, so when Linda pulled back the curtains in the morning, she was surprised to see several faces pressed against the grimy glass. Welcome to Nepal! The house was basic but full of love, and we quickly adapted to a very different way of life. The first visit to the toilet outside the back door was quite a challenge. You had to stand on two foot-shapes above the hole in the ground while very large ants wandered around your feet and other creatures slid down the walls, none of which led to long contemplations as you sought to aim accurately. Our friend, Barney Coombs, had given us advice for visiting Nepal, 'Don't look down. Look up!'

Slimy mud was everywhere, so you could only wear very basic jandals,[120] but all of this was beneath the most majestic mountains we had ever seen. Linda's great fear before coming to Nepal was that there would be rabid dogs. However, two friendly mongrels attached themselves to us immediately after we arrived and walked with us through the mud to every session of the conference. They even waited outside the funny little café where you could buy a bottled fizzy drink, the safest liquid to consume in Nepal.

The mission here was based around the amazing Shining Hospital, and every day, during the sessions, we could look

---

120. Jandals are called 'flip-flops' in the UK.

out to the dining area, a compressed mud area, where patients and their relatives were preparing lunch on the ground. Most of the meals were a staple of *dal bhat* (rice and lentils). As we walked to the sessions, we would see groups of men sitting and smoking by the side of the road as they played cards, while their womenfolk staggered with enormous burdens, often carrying things like bricks and straw as well as food.

We loved our time in Nepal. There was such a mixed group of missionaries from different countries and denominations. Linda taught them some group dances which she had choreographed with Scripture in Song. These went down very well. We were able to bring encouragement to many people and prayed for them in the midst of all the challenges they were facing. When it came to sacrificial living, it was hard to fault these people. Mike Lavender, a surgeon from Southampton, was doing re-constructive surgery on lepers from a textbook. He proudly displayed one of his first efforts – a man with a reconstructed nose. Mike told us how he had met a high-ranking officer from the famed Gurkha regiment, trained by the British Army, in Pokhara, as he flew in from India one day. The colonel asked him to visit the regiment one afternoon, so Mike followed his directions up one of the tracks they called roads. He arrived at some impressive gates and as he went through them it was as if he was transported to an estate in Surrey with manicured lawns and beautiful flower gardens. The colonel met him on the veranda of a classic building and said, 'Would you like a Pimm's, old boy?'

In complete contrast, we went down to the Shining Hospital for a tour with the matron, as she visited the wards. She took us to the birthing room, and we were surprised by filthy garments and sheets alongside the birthing stool. Matron told us that the formal British nursing programme that they taught could not shake the women from their belief that clean garments and sheets would attract evil spirits to a newborn baby! The conventional toilet was so unspeakably misused that they had to keep it locked up. After tea with matron, we were running late for our next session, so a taxi was called. Linda was up front with the driver, and I was in the back seat. Suddenly, eight of his friends piled in, two in front, actually on top of Linda, and I was crammed against the door with half a dozen in the back seat! The driver let them all out before a police check-point.

On the Sunday morning I was invited to speak at the local church. At that time, if you were baptised as a believer, you could face a year in prison, and if you did the baptising, it could be seven years! I preached what I thought was a good message on Jesus healing the ten lepers. Afterwards, it was pointed out to us that most of the people sat in our row were in fact 'cleansed lepers'.

Before we left Nepal to fly home to England, we went to Kathmandu for two days. A friend had given us money to stay in the famed Yak and Yeti hotel, but we had met a wonderful Australian lady, overseeing a missionary guesthouse in the city, and she very much wanted us to come home with her. We had such a marvellous time together, so we took her to the Yak and Yeti two days running for lunch. It was all very different. Everywhere you walked there were blood sacrifices in the streets, and, again, people wanted to be with us. One man followed

Linda into every shop, so when we decided to escape his attention by getting a taxi back to the house, he desperately tried to get in with us! We didn't get to hike in the Himalayas like our son Richard and his wife Anna did on their honeymoon, but we did fly very close among the colossal peaks in the small plane that took us from the international airport to Pokhara. Nepal will always have a special place in our hearts.

We cannot record our time in Nepal without including the days we spent in India, en route to our international conference. Our purpose was two-fold: we had never visited India, but India had visited us. When I first met Linda, she lived in Derby, close to an area that was increasingly dominated by the culture and cuisine of the East. Temples and mosques were springing up, shops and restaurants had distinctive flavours. Linda, in her Sunday school visitation, was increasingly invited into homes for chapatis and curry, and she was determined, early in our marriage to introduce me to the delights of Indian food. I was not easily persuaded, having shied away from 'foreign food' all my life!

It could be said that the dominant cuisine in Britain is Indian food, though most of the restaurant owners/ operators are in fact from Bangladesh, not India. When we were based in Sidcup through the Nineties, we had at least seven Indian restaurants that were within walking distance of our home. My conversion took about three years from the start of our marriage. Linda lured me into an amazing restaurant in Park Street, Bristol, called the Rajdoot, and it really transformed my prejudices and opened my eyes. Today, if asked what I would like to eat, almost invariably, I would choose Indian!

Anyway, Delhi was a convenient staging post to our final destination in Nepal. Also, an important link had been established by our friends and colleagues, Dave and Rhian Day, who led an international Training School in Bristol for two months every year. Pastor Jay and his wife, Lizzie, lived in Agra, not far from Delhi, and we felt it important to visit them and encourage them in their work.

I must confess, nothing had prepared us for India! Our days there became something of a nightmare, through no fault of Jay and Lizzie's I hasten to add! Our wonderful administrator, Raewyn, had booked us on Kuwait Airlines. It didn't help Linda to discover that they were the most hijacked airline in the world at that time. She was always comforted by having an unfulfilled prophecy with us as we travelled, but the current one mentioned Esther – having *come to the kingdom for such a time as this*,[121] but ending with the words, *if I perish, I perish*! Boarding the plane in London, several rows in front of us were set up with a special tent, and a Holy Man was carried in with much ringing of bells and chanting. Then, a reading from the Koran flashed on our screens, followed by prayers, and we took off! As the journey continued, the toilets had eventually to be locked as it seems many stood to use them and the results were overwhelming. At a brief stop in Kuwait, our women folk were fiercely separated from us and body searched.

When we arrived at the Indira Gandhi International Airport, we didn't understand why so many Indian people were lying on the floor, trying to sleep. Later, we would be

---

121. Esther 4:14-16 ESV

desperate to join them! For starters, it took two hours for our baggage to come through. We had been forewarned to pre-book a taxi and have the vouchers ready, but it didn't help much. Two competing taxi drivers had a fight over our luggage and when we finally got into the car, he had to hold wires together to get it started. On a very busy highway, as we passed a large sign announcing *Delhi Welcomes Careful Drivers*, Linda asked me where our voucher was. The driver immediately slammed on his brakes in the middle of the road as trucks thundered by. Fortunately, we quickly found our voucher, but another surprise awaited. The car was running out of petrol, so the driver drove across to the opposite side of the highway and drove in the wrong direction to a garage, and the hot-wire arrangement kept the engine running as the petrol was pumped!

We were staying the night at a beautiful hotel, as respite from the journey, and as we walked across the foyer, a glamorous young Indian woman in High Street fashion came towards us and said, in impeccable English, 'How was your journey? Oh, don't tell me it was the pits.' We had a wonderful meal with sensational naan bread, and went up to our room. A man in the corridor hovered by our room and asked to take our key, opened the door, then held out his hand for a reward. Everywhere in India, we were confronted by that open hand. During the night, I couldn't sleep, so I peered out through the curtains. Outside was a large dual carriageway with traffic lights. In the middle of the road, where a concrete pavement divided the four lanes at the lights, a whole group of women, carrying babies and with small children, were begging as cars stopped at the lights. This was after midnight! As we travelled in the coming days, Linda had soon emptied her handbag to the point where we had nothing else to give. Even her comb and cosmetics went into desperate hands.

We made it to Agra, famous for the Taj Mahal, and Jay and Lizzie took marvellous care of us. We stayed in a lovely Sikh guesthouse and a chauffeur drove us around in a car with a flag flying on the bonnet. Jay's face fell when I told him, 'We have a problem with our airline tickets.'

In England we had booked all our tickets through a reputable travel agent but try as they did, they couldn't confirm one segment of the journey that took us to another Indian city and a direct flight into Nepal. Eventually, the advice was: 'Just sort it out when you get there.'

Right!

We enjoyed fellowship with Jay and Lizzie and spoke at some meetings for them, but most of our time was spent in airline travel offices! I did try logic, but to no avail. 'Why would you confirm all the segments of our itinerary, except this middle one, which would leave us completely stranded?'

We got a wobble of the head, side to side, and a smile accompanied by, 'We really want to help you.'

'Really?'

After these frustrating days, with great excitement, the travel agent said he had secured the missing segment; then we discovered he had lost the previous segment! By this time, I had lost my cool. I probably didn't understand that we needed to provide bribes. I said to Jay, 'Can you drive us back to Delhi? We must rearrange our flight into Nepal in time to make our conference.'

He was so patient, apologetic and caring. It was quite an arduous journey, but we arrived at the airport and Jay made the arrangement. There was a flight the next morning and Jay got a price that seemed reasonable in the circumstances. When I went to the desk to pay, the fares were immediately doubled and I just couldn't bring myself to argue any more. We left the airport to go to the YMCA for a few hours' sleep; even the car park attendant tried to diddle more money from Jay as we passed his booth. Jay confided in us, 'I'm so ashamed of my own people, and it makes me come to hate them. Please pray for us.'

When we struggled back to the airport after very little sleep, a final indignity awaited us. Linda, not surprisingly, had a headache, but no water. We were in the departure lounge so I went into a tourist shop for a bottle of water. (You can never drink anything from a tap in India.) I produced my money, Indian rupees. The salesgirl said, 'We can't take this. Only American dollars.'

'But this is your money. I changed my currency into rupees!'

As I became more exasperated, she was not budging. However, help was at hand. Two lovely missionary ladies who were sitting nearby witnessed our distress and brought their own bottled water to Linda. Sadly, it was our last impression of India, and I am ashamed to say, we have never been back.

Two other memories of this time remain. We did visit the Taj Mahal and hated that as well! By now, you are thinking, 'What's wrong with these people? This is a wonder of the world and Princess Diana was famously photographed in front of it!' When we joined the crowd pressed inside, in almost total darkness, it felt quite threatening. You are being jostled on every side with people pushing tourist tat in your face. However, that wasn't what impacted us. The notes about the construction claimed that the man who commissioned this monument cut off the hands of the architects, and the thumbs of everyone who worked on the construction. This information left us feeling nauseous!

One of our engagements with the Agra church was to participate in a baptism. This was held in an attractive, colonial-style hotel with a swimming pool. However, there was a problem. The furniture and the surroundings were in a dilapidated state, and the pool looked totally neglected, with an ominous green slime. After the event, I mentioned this to our friend Pastor Jay. 'It's such a shame that these folks don't have the money to maintain this.'

Jay's reply was even more disturbing. 'It's nothing to do with money; it's sheer laziness! They are actually destroying their investment by allowing this deterioration.'

I'm sorry that we have painted such a bleak picture. On our return to Bristol, the travel agent assured me that further enquiries had discovered that our itinerary had been completely booked and paid for. They were shocked by the way we had been treated. We know that India has been rapidly improving with its huge advances in the field of technology. We continue to support, with our

Sidcup church, the amazing work that Dr Kiran Martin and Freddie are doing in the slums of India through ASHA.[122] Towards the end of her medical training, Kiran went into the slums and has devoted much of her life to them ever since. The ASHA Team has managed to get many of these disadvantaged children and young people into education at all levels with extraordinary results. Please help them with your prayers, skills and money where possible.

Another amazing experience for us was among the Aborigines in Central Australia. A special friend, Ron Trudinger, had spent many years among a remote tribe called the Pitjantjatjara. Among his many accomplishments, he had helped translate the New Testament into their native tongue. When his first wife died prematurely, he had returned to the UK and remarried. Later he went back to his first love for these ancient people. When he returned to the tribe, word went out on the local radio that 'the King has come back'. They loved Ron and Sue, and she devoted a great deal of time to negotiating their welfare with the Australian government. We had met up with Ron at a conference in the UK and he had urged us to go out and visit them. Linda had always wanted to visit the Aborigines when we lived in New Zealand, so this was not difficult to plan, especially as we were due at a conference in New Zealand as well. In the end, we encouraged two of our special friends, Richard Burt and John Arundel, to go with us.

We flew into Alice Springs from Sydney. Ron met us with his station wagon and drove us to our first base, the township

---

122. Action for Securing Health for All

of Ernabella (now Pukatja), some five hours' drive away. After the first two hours on a tarred highway, it got more tricky. The mud roads threw up clouds of dust, and cattle, not kangaroos, seemed to wait on the banks at the side of the road ready to charge out as we were passing. The flies were unbelievable! The first minutes in the car, windows down and air-conditioning blasting, we sought to drive them outside. Whenever we stopped for refreshment, the only way you could eat a sandwich or drink tea was to build a fire and hover over it. During the hours of daylight, you had to accept that flies would be all over you.

To go into these Aborigine lands, Ron had to get us special permits and the rules were very strict. Ernabella was the nearest thing to a town that we would see in the next few weeks. Two things immediately struck us. Rubbish was everywhere! Plastic, wastepaper, packaging, all were just thrown down on the ground with no attempt to clear it up. Then the young people! It was so sad to see teenagers with tin cans held up to their faces with string attached to their ears so they could sniff petrol. Alcohol was strictly forbidden in the territories. Like the rubbish, they just couldn't handle it. One day, on a visit to Ayers Rock (Uluru), we pulled into the hotel car park and, as I got out of the car, I was accosted by an Aboriginal woman. She tried thrusting a lot of money into my hands, maybe fifty or a hundred dollars. Ron called out, 'Don't touch it!' Apparently, she wanted me to go into the hotel and purchase alcohol for the family. Ron said I could be arrested for this offence.

The hotel at Ayers Rock was the only public building that we could see. After our time in Ernabella and meeting with the church there, we set out into remote areas. We carried special bedding with us that the Australians call 'swags' as we were now going to be sleeping in dried-up creek beds. It might rain for a few days a year, but often not at all. This came to be a highlight of our experience, but we had to learn the ropes. When we got to our venue for the night, a suitable creek was selected, and fires were built around our camp that had to be maintained at night. The King Brown snake is one of the deadliest reptiles in the world, and they don't like fire. Also, as night fell, the dingoes would circle around our camp. The first night, Linda would not drink anything after 6pm for fear of needing the toilet! She zipped into the swag, wearing ear plugs and swathed with scarves. One night, Ron asked Linda to be responsible for maintaining the fires, so she popped up and down all night, finally collapsing into sleep just before dawn. She couldn't believe it when Ron pronounced, 'Linda, you let the fires go out!'

The sleeping arrangement was more beautiful than anything we could ever have imagined. Waking in the night, the view was spectacular! Thousands of miles of almost absolute nothingness and stillness and the unbelievable view of the heavens literally declaring the glory of God!

The first night I preached in this ancient community was a fast-learning track for me. We came to a platform in the middle of nowhere with a single light bulb overhead. No one was there. Ron confidently said, 'They will come, and what you will see is little campfires being lit and eyes shining in the darkness.' He hadn't mentioned the abundance of wild dogs, or every kind of flying insect that would be crawling over me as I stood under the light bulb. The 'singing blankets' opened proceedings. We called them this because several very large Aboriginal women, mostly with conditions like diabetes, converged on the platform swathed in blankets. There followed several songs, all monotone, with not a musical instrument in sight.

Then it was my turn. Ron was my interpreter and I did my best. I thought, 'I'll keep this really simple,' so I chose the story from the gospels of Peter getting out of the boat and walking on the water. Now I have worked with many interpreters in different parts of the world, but Ron's interpretations got longer and longer. Afterwards he gently explained to me that Aborigines would not be familiar with a body of water like the Sea of Galilee and most of them would never have seen a boat. So much for my cross-cultural communication! But I did get better, and good things came to pass. In this community, the chief's son gave his life to Christ, and we prayed for many people.

Our most memorable experience was a two-day visit to a camel farm. Historically, camels had been released into the wild in Central Australia as they are an excellent form of transport in the desert. We seemed to travel even further out into virgin territory and eventually arrived at the camel farm run by Naninja and Charlie. Naninja would have to be one of the most remarkable women I have ever met. At sixty years of age, she had been one of the key negotiators with the Australian government concerning the re-instatement of tribal lands.

They had a series of houses and buildings erected by the government. We, however, headed down to a nearby creek to set up our swags. Soon, Naninja came to invite us to spend the evening with their community. They had a large fire blazing in a courtyard. Most of them slept out there, as they weren't keen on indoor bedrooms. Food was passed around and we began to sing with them. Then they urged me to preach the gospel.

Naninja told me a story I have repeated again and again around the world. Quite often, groups of tourists were sent in by special planes to visit them for a couple of days. These were high-powered folks from education and industry, believing that they were visiting the most primitive people on earth, and paying thousands of dollars for the privilege. They would provide a full-on experience for the visitors, dressing up and painting themselves, telling their legends. Right at the end, around the same campfire, Naninja would explain that this was not what they believed. She would tell them about God's creation and the glorious gospel of Jesus, the Son of God. Even writing about this after all these years brings tears to my eyes.

The next morning, as we were packing up to leave, Naninja came down to the creek where we had been sleeping, with a special request. She said, 'Peter, we had a delegation of North American and Canadian Indians come here. They put up a totem pole and I feel as if we have been cursed. Would you please break this curse for us?' It was a great privilege for us to pray for them and break this tribal curse. When we returned to Ernabella for the last time, the tribal elders approached us and asked if Linda and I would move there permanently, a request that sadly we were not in a position to fulfil.

It would be remiss of me not to mention in these special memories the Islands of Hawaii. I have recounted elsewhere, how we first came to visit Hawaii through a prophetic word given to us near the end of our first year in New Zealand in 1978. We were travelling back to England but had been asked to visit a missionary family on the Big Island who were in some difficulty. It was a trial of faith for us, as we didn't have sufficient funds to do this, but we managed to fulfil this week before flying on to Vancouver.

In the years that followed, we visited Hawaii on countless occasions for various reasons. For many years, a primary route for us between New Zealand and England was through Honolulu, both with Air New Zealand and Continental Airlines. Our good friends, David and Dale Garratt, were often based there near YWAM's University of the Nations in Kailua-Kona, and provided us with wonderful hospitality. Later, I became involved with one of the Vineyard churches in Hawaii, and my business consultancy with ACX in California also took us there, but, more than anything, it was such a delightful place to stop for a family holiday en route between England and New Zealand. It was much less expensive than most places we have been and has a wonderful climate all year round. I'm sure if you ask my children, our stop-overs in Hawaii would be some of their most memorable experiences. Sadly, the major airlines withdrew their interlinked services in recent years, and we haven't been back for some time. I must confess, it would be my first choice if I had the option.

Let me mention a couple of visits that had some unique features. Linda and I were returning more permanently to England in 1992. We were going ahead of our children who were still completing their studies in New Zealand. Before departure, we made final visits to Wellington, and then

Queenstown. The flight to Wellington's notorious airport was horrendous. Truthfully, our flight should never have taken off as we approached the airport in colossal winds that threw the wings up and down like we have never experienced. Passengers were screaming and mostly on the floor! I don't think we have ever been so frightened on a plane. Spontaneous applause broke out when we landed.

Some days later, we had arranged to meet our oldest friends in New Zealand, Danny and Judi Bagust, in Queenstown to say goodbye. We were travelling back through Wanaka, in quite wintry conditions, when Danny decided to take a shortcut over the Crown Range, a precipitous road that required chains. Danny said he had chains but he failed to put them on. As we climbed higher and higher, on a single track, ploughing through snow and ice, we all became more and more scared. Had we met a vehicle coming the other way, I don't know what would have happened. Judi, Linda and I were all screaming to no avail; Danny couldn't stop, and the drop at the side of the road was precipitous. We made it to the top, but still have palpitations when we think back to it!

However, worse was to come. Within days, we had boarded our Air New Zealand flight to Honolulu on the first leg of our journey home. As the captain addressed us early in the flight telling us we could expect some turbulence, that was not the full story. We landed in Honolulu to discover that they were in a state of emergency! Hurricane Iniki was bearing down on the islands. As soon as we arrived at our favourite hotel, the Moana Surfrider, right on Waikiki Beach, we were instructed to go straight to our room, put all our luggage in the bath and lock the doors, then proceed to the hotel ballroom. When we arrived there, it seemed we had joined hundreds of Japanese, fighting over pillows and blankets to lie on the floor, as a large screen tracked the worst hurricane in Hawaii's history, now moving from Kauai towards Waikiki. We were there all day, trying to sleep on the floor, sustained with sandwiches, when suddenly as the storm was getting closer, a loud crack took out the lights and the screen coverage.

If you know anything about hurricanes, you will understand we were in a perilous position. It's doubtful that our historic hotel could have survived a full-on assault. However, a miracle happened! Suddenly, the hurricane turned north, away from us and headed out into the North Pacific Ocean. We were called to the front desk about 8pm and the hotel graciously upgraded us into a beautiful suite in their tower block looking out over the ocean. Apart from the swimming pool full of sand and some cracked windows, everything returned to normal and we enjoyed a wonderful week together.

A very special memory for us was a visit to the islands with our closest friends in America, John and Carol Gombos. Ever since we first met through our involvement with the Vineyard church in Bakersfield, our lives have been intertwined. Most people who see Carol and Linda together think they are sisters, and John and I love to be together, often sitting together at night, he with his cigars and me sipping a nice cognac as the sun goes down. My life has been ministry focused while John has steered a family business through its highs and lows. Often, he has asked my counsel on specific issues and has engaged me in various projects. I always try to give it my best shot and pray constantly for the extended family and their business, whether we are together or apart.

On this memorable occasion, we were asked to join them in Hawaii for two reasons. Their annual, executive retreat and an important exploration of one of the lesser-known islands. For many years, John has been in the hay business, growing high-yielding grasses such as alfalfa, which are then shipped to special plants, formed into blocks and transported to destinations around the USA and internationally. These grasses are especially for top dairy herds, and racehorses, etc. They are farmed in alternate seasons in the northern hemisphere, and in the southern hemisphere in countries like Chile.

Our visit to Lanai was occasioned by the withdrawal of Dole, the famous pineapple producers from the island. Basically, they withdrew from Hawaii because it is an American state with high labour costs. They could produce their pineapples in countries like the Philippines more cheaply. John wanted to see if the land they had left could be used for the hay business, as it was conveniently placed mid-Pacific for more important markets in the east, like Japan. We were in for a shock!

We flew from Honolulu in a private jet, with a pilot adorned with so many gold chains and rings, he looked like Liberace. Accommodation had been booked in a lovely golf resort above Manele Bay, which is now an exclusive hotel complex. I believe Bill and Melinda Gates married there. Carol and Linda made the most of the spa as John and I went to meet with the chairman of the local authorities. At first, he didn't seem that welcoming, but when he discovered I was a Christian minister and he was a Baptist youth leader, the ice thawed, and we had fruitful discussions. However, viewing the land Dole had left put an end to our enquiries. To put it kindly, it was an ecological disaster. Hideous, plastic irrigation piping was embedded everywhere and had simply been abandoned with no attempt to clear it away! The sheer cost of trying to clear these fields was astronomical, and I'm not sure if anyone was held to account for this.

After a couple of days, we flew on to our favourite island, Kauai. The company held their annual event at the Hyatt Regency, Poipu, over several days. It was a mix of business and pleasure. Partners were invited to the event and enjoyed the magnificent setting with all its facilities. There were special banquets, a golf tournament, and I was asked to give three motivational talks. I remember on the last morning addressing all the couples on the issue of 'Relational Prosperity'. One thing I have noticed in the USA: you don't have to be ashamed of the gospel. We were very warmly received.

I have said that Kauai is our favourite island in the Hawaiian chain, and, of course, many great movies have been made there like *South Pacific* and Elvis's *Blue Hawaii*. Poipu is in the south, and a gateway to the remarkable 'Grand Canyon of the Pacific,' but our favourite spot is at Princeville in the north, looking over the bay to the famous Bali Hai and close to the extraordinary Kaanapali cliffs. One time, Linda and I were staying there, and our waitress told us that the famous band, The Eagles, were doing an impromptu gig in the pub that night, as they owned a beach house nearby. I must confess, I didn't know who they were! My musician friends Noel and Trish Richards never forgave us for this. We didn't go and missed hearing their great repertoire with songs like 'Welcome to the Hotel California'! In fact, John and Carol now live in Santa Barbara and we have had delightful meals in the Goat Tree Coffee Shop, which is in the Hotel California where the song was written.

Over our years of involvement with John and Carol and ACX, we have spent valuable time in the Pacific Northwest near Seattle and south on the Pacific coast in the beautiful Los Angeles suburb of Palos Verdes. One time, we visited Chile and Argentina in the southern hemisphere, with John and Carol. We met the key business leaders and an important YWAM church-planter that they have supported. Both countries made a deep impression on us, and we visited a hot springs area in Chile very similar to Rotorua in New Zealand.

Having been to all these places, and many more, we still see New Zealand as quite unique. The Southern Alps and Fiordland are similar to the west coast of Norway. Everywhere you go, North and South Island, you can have spectacular beaches pretty much to yourself. As you travel further north, a lot is reminiscent of Hawaii, but although the climate is sub-tropical, it's not as consistent as Hawaii or the southern states of America.

We lived for two-and-a-half years on Waiheke Island, just a half-hour commute by ferry to Central Auckland. We rented a lovely home from friends and tried to buy a house there, but it was fortuitous that we didn't put our roots down on the island due to unforeseen circumstances that lay ahead. Frustrated as we were at the time, we know that our heavenly Father has our best interests at heart. My dad's favourite Bible verses were Proverbs 3:5,6:

> *Trust in the LORD with all your heart*
> *and lean not on your own understanding;*
> *in all your ways submit to him,*
> *and he will make your paths straight.*[123]

---

123. NIV

Chapter 29

Amazing Events

This morning, I was reading again the remarkable accounts of Elijah and Elisha in the Old Testament. Initially, Elijah had stopped the rain and assured King Ahab that it wouldn't return except by his word. Sure enough, the land experienced a devasting drought for more than three years. That reminded me of a special incident ...

Linda and I were invited to the wedding of Nicoletta, daughter of our close friends, John and Carol Gombos, in California. As Linda had a hand in getting Nicoletta on the YWAM course in Australia where she met her future husband, we were thrilled to be there. The whole event was to be out at the ranch on Bear Creek Road in the foothills of the Sierra Nevada. We arrived on the Friday for the rehearsal dinner and to help with preparations the next morning.

The San Joaquin valley, bordering the property, had been in drought for three years. On the Friday night, the rehearsal was on the front steps of the ranch, overlooking the gardens and a winding driveway. Afterwards, we dined outside the back porch in a large courtyard where the wedding reception would be held after the ceremony. Everything was arranged to be outside, being California, and there was no way the large number of guests could be inside.

On the morning of the wedding, we received a panic-stricken call at our hotel in Springville, from Carol, saying that thunder clouds were rolling in and could we head over to a big store that had table umbrellas and get as many as we could. When we arrived at the ranch, panic was in the air; the first drops of rain were beginning to fall and everyone on the prep-team was panicking. The table decorations were beautiful but impossible to protect. I got my friend John to join me on the back porch in our favourite spot for fellowship and prayer. I said to him, 'I've only done this a couple of times in my life before, but I feel this is what we must do! Please take my hand.'

With that, I prayed a very specific prayer, agreeing with John to stop the rain in Jesus's name. Within minutes the rain stopped, the prep-team and caterers got to work, and no more rain fell until the last guests had left the reception. It was a proud moment when Nicoletta's grandfather drove her up the winding drive perched on the back of a new Polaris four-wheel drive.

Jesus was there, just as he had been at a wedding crisis in Cana of Galilee.

When this book is published, Linda will be turning seventy-five, but anyone who meets her finds this hard to believe. I must record what happened on her seventieth birthday.

I was in a quandary, looking at our limited income, so much so that I said to her, 'The most I can do is take you out for coffee.'

She doesn't really like coffee, and these days, we rarely go out to dinner. Very soon after I had said this, we received a call from our close friends who live in California, John and Carol Gombos. We hadn't spoken for several months, but Carol said, 'We want you to come over as soon as possible.'

Linda replied, 'Well, that's amazing as it's my seventieth birthday.'

Carol said, 'I know, but also, John has recently lost three close friends, including his father. He especially needs you at this time. Could you come as soon as possible?'

We were able to move swiftly on this and they wired the necessary funds. To cap it all, we flew overnight on Linda's birthday, and as we crossed the dateline, she had a second birthday in California. On arrival at LAX, we were greeted by John and Carol who took us straight to their car. As we settled in, they handed us an envelope that contained nearly $2,000 with instructions to go shopping and do whatever else we wanted.

There followed a whirlwind three weeks, commencing with lunch and dinner at favourite restaurants by way of celebration. Our base was in Bakersfield, close to John's family and business. Soon after our arrival, he drove us up to their Ranch in Bear Creek Road on the edge of the Sierra Nevada. Yes, bears have been known to come onto the property. While there, John took us to a fabulous rodeo, typically American, but very new for us. It was a big, annual event, beginning with worship, prayer and a testimony, followed by an invitation to the Cowhands' Gospel Service the next day. Only in America!

We had such a special three weeks. A highlight of this trip was to visit Santa Barbara, where they were planning to move from Bakersfield. This remarkable, Spanish-influenced community is on the Pacific coast, about two hours north of LA. There are famous residents nearby: Oprah, Ellen DeGeneres and Harry and Meghan. It's a centre for the arts. On a subsequent visit we were taken to a theatre to see a unique presentation of the film *Amadeus*. What made it unique was that the Santa Barbara Philharmonic Orchestra and Chorus provided the soundtrack for the whole film. It was magnificent.

The icing on the cake, as it were, was the celebration of our wedding anniversary at the Ritz-Carlton Bacara, just north of the city, and right on the coast. We were there for two nights, and it was such an extraordinary experience. On the morning of our anniversary, John and I went to see the head chef of the signature restaurant, The Angel Oak. He advised us of the menu for that evening, then took us out to the prime table, on a terrace perched over the Pacific Ocean, that he reserved for us. That night, complimentary drinks flowed as the setting sun dipped over the horizon, and the food was magnificent. I have to say that this whole, unexpected series of celebrations trumped my plans for coffee in Mangawhai!

John and Carol have been such wonderful friends to us and, even now, they have invited us to go up later next year to celebrate my eightieth birthday. Bring it on!

These last three years, many good things have happened for us. When Amanda and Pete married, and her house was sold, we were wonderfully provided for. The newlyweds searched for a new home and made plans that included us in their future.

Pete and Amanda's Wedding (centre)
with Anna, Richard, Peter, Linda, Simon and Bella Jane

In the meantime, mostly dominated by Covid, Mike and Corene gave us a small apartment on the side of their boat shed in the Mangawhai Heads. It was close enough to walk to the village shops and also to walk Henry, a lovely wee dog that we have exercised for an older friend, Barbara, for the last nine years. What generous friends Mike and Corene proved to be. We moved in for a few weeks and were there for nearly two-and-a-half years!

During this time, we developed a small house-group meeting for Bible study, prayer and worship, and we are still leading this with our friend, Maggie Andrews. We had seventeen new members at one time, which has levelled off with some moving away. We still love the church in the house!

At this time, another significant development took place. Just pre-Covid, we had been back in the UK and, at the end of our trip, had a week based in Cyprus with our old friends, Simon and Glenys Hart. Early in my ministry, I met Glenys in the Patchway Youth Centre north of Bristol, so we have known each other for more than fifty years. Recently, a wedding photo was found with us standing outside our Blackhorse Church with our new baby, Amanda, in Linda's arms. Hugh Thompson and I had just married Simon and Glenys in the same building where Linda and I had married the year before! They now live in Cyprus and are leaders in the New Testament Church, Cyprus. We loved being with them and felt a real sense of joining with them after all these years. Through Covid, we became part of their Zoom congregation, along with our neighbour, George Craddock. I have done a lot of ministry and some teaching series, and Linda has led prayer, chosen music and joined me in counsel and prayer with the leaders. Now that Covid is being managed, we are scheduled to be with them on our next UK trip in March/April 2023. George is also part of a prayer group with us in Waipu.

Here's another remarkable story. For some years, travelling to and from the Mangawhai Heads surf beach along Wintle Street, we noticed an amazing home being built, right above the Mangawhai Estuary where it curves out into the ocean. Time without number, I have said to Linda, 'That's the house I love!' It was constructed of black corrugated iron, with huge barn doors and vast windows and decking above the water. The land goes down to Picnic Bay and has its own boat shed and ramp into the water. Just a few weeks ago, orcas were jumping close to the end of the jetty.

Linda had left a number at the vet's so that people could call if they needed help with their animals. One day, she came to collect me in a state of great excitement. The vet had called, and she had been to see a lady who needed help with her Burmese cats. 'You must come at once, Peter! You will never believe where this house is.'

As we turned in to park in front of the house I had so long admired, it was almost too much for me. We have been there regularly ever since. Ian and Lisa have become our good friends, along with their two new kittens, Kobe and Pippi. We recently stayed nearly six weeks, as Ian had an injury en route to a skiing trip in the South Island. Their kindness and appreciation know no bounds, and as I write, we are due to have dinner with them tonight, prior to the funeral of our beloved Queen.

In spite of how beautiful the house in Wintle Street is, we love to be at our new home on the edge of Pete and Amanda's property. They have purchased fifteen acres in the hills above the old Scottish Town of Waipu. They have completed the first stage of a lovely extension for us, also in a superb black corrugated iron finish. I sit outside to meditate and pray as the sun goes down over the Brynderwyn Hills in front of us, with lovely views out to sea across Bream Bay to the Majestic Whangarei Heads. It feels just like the Scottish Highlands.

Although living in Waipu now, we have regularly returned to lead a house-group in Mangawhai that we have helped for more than two years. We have met in two homes alternately, Maggie and John's and Pam's. Pam, or 'Pammy' as we call her, is an amazing woman. She lost her husband just a few years ago, and not long before he died, they both decided to go to the local Baptist church one Sunday, even though they had not been churchgoers for nearly seventy years. This was an extraordinary move and they both came to faith in Jesus and were soon baptised. Although Pam has been a widow now for some time, she's not one to sit and mope. She loves having our group in her home, and it seems many other people are on the receiving end of her hospitality and generosity: she runs craft groups and care groups, feeds the elderly, and greets everyone with a smile and her delicious cakes. Maggie, too, is unique: a gifted teacher, she has shared leadership with me and done a great job. John, her husband, needs constant care but she still loves to help all and sundry. People gravitate to her home and draw on her warmth and wisdom.

We are a blessed family! Amanda and Pete cannot do enough for us. Richard and Anna are in Auckland, Simon and Bella Jane in the South Island near the town of Geraldine. Between them we have ten grandchildren aged from ten to twenty-three. And, of course, as you will know from this story, we have another extended family through Linda's twins in the UK, Tanya and David, and another clutch of grandchildren and great-grandchildren.

I must stop writing, but the story is not yet over! I close with a meditation from the last words of David, which have long been my personal aspiration:

Is not my house right with God?
Has he not made with me an everlasting covenant,
arranged and secured in every part?
Will he not bring to fruition my salvation
and grant me my every desire?[124]

---

124. 2 Samuel 23:5 NIV

Chapter 30

The End is Not the End!

The final writing of this book has coincided with the death of our beloved Queen, Elizabeth II. For the past nine days we have been glued to events on the television leading up to her extraordinary State funeral. We prayed much over this, that it might be a unique testimony to her faith and life of devoted service. We were not disappointed. Imagine, 500 world leaders delaying their visit to the UN Summit in the USA; a global audience numbered in billions; the great words of Scripture ringing out so clearly, in readings, song, prayer and preaching; the name of Jesus lifted high; and the trust of our Queen in God so clearly stated.

One thing was astonishingly evident: the response of the multitudes as the Queen's cortège was passing by from Balmoral to Edinburgh; then in London from Buckingham Palace to Westminster Hall where so many queued for hours just to catch a last glimpse of her closed coffin lying in state. I just received news from my family in England to say that my nephew, Andrew, and his wife, Lisa, slipped into the city and joined the line on Sunday night for nine hours and were among the last to be admitted to see it before the doors were finally shut.

What was evident to us all, was the incredible reverence, awe and prayerfulness of this solemn mass of people at every turn. What must our new Prime Minister have felt to be one of the last to see Her Majesty alive as she welcomed her to lead the Government? It would be only days later that she would stand in the pulpit at Westminster Abbey to read with unfaltering voice the majestic words of John 14 that the Queen had specifically chosen. The Bible given to Elizabeth II at her coronation, with the words that this was the most valuable possession she could have, stayed with her to the end. At moments like these, I am so proud to be a Christian and so thankful that this is simply the prelude to all the marvellous things that God has in store for us!

Only Great Britain can do pageantry, with such faultless precision, to honour a life that has powerfully touched us all. We will probably never see the likes of this again, but we pray that a life so faithfully lived in service to God, this nation and the Commonwealth of Nations, will be like the seed that falls into the ground and bears much fruit.

Linda and I know full well that our testimony may almost pale into insignificance in the light of these extraordinary events, but we are confident that everyone who reads these words of faith can also receive the abundance of grace freely offered through Jesus. Although we really do have nothing, unlike the Queen, yet through his grace, we possess everything.

Waipu, Northland, New Zealand, September 21st, 2022.

Other Publications

Peter Lyne, *First Apostles, Last Apostles* (Sovereign World 1999); commissioned by Gerald Coates and the Pioneer Team. We have copies available.

Peter Lyne, *Baton Change – Releasing the Next Generation* (Sovereign World, 2000 and Regal Books, 2001). To be reprinted in 2023.
   Also published in Buenos Aires for the Spanish-speaking world, and in Indonesian.

Peter Lyne, *Ruth: A Parable of the Kingdom: A Love Story That Changed the World* (Malcolm Down Publishing, January 2016).

A.J. Lyne, *A Better Ending: It's Never Too Late to Begin a Better Ending!* (Independently published, September 2017 and available online). This covers two World Wars and three generations of Linda's family. Available online through Amazon.

Linda Lyne and Peter Goad, *Mawes Paws: A Cornish Bear* – a beautifully illustrated children's book has been published in 2023. Contact lindalyne@mawespaws.com

Highly recommended:

Mary Garnett, *Take your Glory, Lord* (CLC Publications, July 2022), with a foreword by Peter Lyne. The life story of Zulu pastor William Duma of the Umgeni Road Baptist Church, Durban, South Africa. A unique account of the miraculous.

Any queries concerning book availability contact peter@ peterlyne.com